LOVE IN TIME

LOVE IN TIME

An Ethical Inquiry

Fannie Bialek

The University of Chicago Press   Chicago and London

The University of Chicago Press, Chicago 60637
The University of Chicago Press, Ltd., London
© 2025 by The University of Chicago
All rights reserved. No part of this book may be used or reproduced in any manner whatsoever without written permission, except in the case of brief quotations in critical articles and reviews. For more information, contact the University of Chicago Press, 1427 E. 60th St., Chicago, IL 60637.
Published 2025

34 33 32 31 30 29 28 27 26 25   1 2 3 4 5

ISBN-13: 978-0-226-84389-6 (cloth)
ISBN-13: 978-0-226-84391-9 (paper)
ISBN-13: 978-0-226-84390-2 (ebook)
DOI: https://doi.org/10.7208/chicago/9780226843902.001.0001

Library of Congress Cataloging-in-Publication Data

Names: Bialek, Fannie, author.
Title: Love in time : an ethical inquiry / Fannie Bialek.
Description: Chicago : The University of Chicago Press, 2025. | Includes bibliographical references and index.
Identifiers: LCCN 2025001884 | ISBN 9780226843896 (cloth) | ISBN 9780226843919 (paper) | ISBN 9780226843902 (e-book)
Subjects: LCSH: Love. | Interpersonal relations.
Classification: LCC BD436 .B53 2025 | DDC 177/.7—dc23/eng/20250205
LC record available at https://lccn.loc.gov/2025001884

For my parents

Contents

Preface *ix*

1 · Wanting Without Knowing 1
2 · Accounting for Love 34
3 · Christian Agape and the Vulnerability of Worldly Goods 70
4 · Promises and Obligations: On Loving the Dying 113
AFTERWORD · Ethics Without an Ending 151

ACKNOWLEDGMENTS 155
NOTES 161
BIBLIOGRAPHY 179
INDEX 183

Preface

This is a book about beginnings and endings, and what happens in between. Many books—particularly those on love—avoid endings, or arrive at them not as any kind of loss but the creation of an everlasting condition ("ever after," happily or otherwise). Beginnings in stories of love then overtake the narrative, but often only to be recast as the intentions of eternity—accidents of fortune discovered as actually "meant to be." Other works on love try to focus on what happens in between, as in ethical arguments for commitment, constancy, and the steady fulfillment of duties and promises that must have been made out of frame. The end of love in these discussions can be only a kind of error, while beginnings, where they appear at all, seem nearly natural phenomena, no more interesting to ethics than the evolution of an acorn or the mechanics of tides. Actual beginnings and endings are kept out of view, left implicit or mythologized as fate or failure. In their absence, love seems to be extracted from time. It might not be eternal, exactly, but it isn't quite temporal, either. It seems hard to count the days or imagine the hours passing. It's then hard to know how a finite being might be part of the argument or story told. My days are numbered; my hours pass. My loves cannot be everlasting. Of what importance is that to me as a lover? What is love in a life that begins and ends?

One response from many corners of Western philosophy and religious thought is that love intrudes into finite lives plagued by beginnings, endings, and the vulnerability between them as something other to it all: a glimpse of the eternal, a suggestion of the infinite, a promise of transcendence, a relationship with the divine. Love, by these accounts, is not something a finite being can do, know, or feel fully. It addresses me, and teaches me the limitations of my conditions by its difference from them. It also offers me something beyond them, whether in the form of an afterlife, a relationship with something greater than myself, or simply the idea that this isn't all there is. It might inspire me to practice greater constancy and commitment in my own relationships, or to extend commitments beyond them. It might make the infinite something to aspire to—and clear the ground to mourn and condemn worldly relationships for falling short.

But love to a finite being is more than an invitation to grief or condemnation of our conditions, and less than the everlasting, eternal loves romanticized in stories and praised by philosophers and theologians looking to console. Understanding love only to *intrude* on temporal life does not help us understand the experience of love in time. How does it feel to love as a finite being, however imperfectly we may? How does love seem to someone who doesn't know if it will continue or end? How might finitude and the vulnerabilities it determines define love for human beings, instead of defining only our failures within it?

To answer these questions, we need to follow love in time, spending time with it to see what becomes important to lovers, necessary to their experiences, and prominent among their concerns as it proceeds. Love in time, like any temporal experience, is composed of moments of not knowing what will happen next. It is an experience of vulnerability in this way, the lover exposed to an unknown future and waiting to see how it plays out. Lovers must wait to see how their beloveds respond to them, both in initial overtures and at any moment of address. They must wait to learn who their beloveds are, and who they become as time continues. They must wait as well to learn what life spent loving their beloveds will look like, how it will feel, and whether it will continue to seem desirable—and, significantly, whether they will continue to desire it. They might be anxious about whether love will continue, and unsure whether, if it ends, it will seem a waste of precious time. As finite beings, we cannot know how the future will proceed. What we desire, at least in part, is time spent with our beloveds seeing how it goes.

The method of this project is thus to treat love as lovers want to treat their beloveds, spending time together without knowing exactly how that time will proceed. Call it a lover's dialectic: instead of watching the subject determine itself by alienation and sublation toward self-consciousness, we will spend time with the subject—love—and see how it shows itself to be in relation to us, finite beings who love, however imperfectly. The aim is not to find it on its own terms, but to be with it, in its relation to us, over time. Its appearance, like ours, will be shaped by time passing. What we know of it will be contingent on the questions, concerns, pressures, and pleasures that arise in that time. Our knowledge will also never be complete. If love is there tomorrow, there will be more about it to learn.

Where philosophers and theologians seek greater certainty, they often look for definitions of love that might secure our knowledge of it against the vagaries of its experience. Some look for definitions that will make clear what is worth loving and why, so that we might judge our loves against these guides and know whether we're getting them right. Others define love *as* a source of certainty, suggesting that a love worthy of the name will be not only directed at the right person or thing but also without the impermanence of other worldly relations. Uncertainty about whether I love the right person or whether my love will persist can be answered by these projects and overcome by their definitions. Overcoming uncertainty seems to be a crucial aim of their inquiries: lovers' questions should be answered; their anxieties should be quelled.

These are appealing ambitions. But rendering them significant aims of an inquiry into love quickly distorts the ethical thinking in and around love that we need. Turning away from uncertainty distorts our inevitable encounters with it, encouraging us to see what we know now as all there is and to see the vulnerabilities we name now as the whole story of our possible futures. Our choices then seem to become quite clear: if I believe I know what situation I'm in and what situations I'm facing, I can act for the things I desire and against the possibilities I fear. Any uncertainty that creeps in around the edges is a flaw of temporal life to be minimized or overcome. Situations that increase such uncertainty should be minimized or avoided entirely.

Relationships increase uncertainty. They add to one's life more sources of possible actions, feelings, and events; more people one might be accountable to; and generally much more one might need to take into account. They make prediction harder, and they make our vulnerabilities greater. Resistance to uncertainty, then, can make ethical theory broadly averse to ongoing relationships. They appear primarily as arenas of susceptibility and danger, our interactions with others seeming best where they can be negotiated rationally and ended quickly, everyone parting safely and on good terms. If we are trying to minimize uncertainty—even for the admirable effort to protect the goods of our present situation, not least by knowing what they are—the continuation of relationships in which we are always vulnerable seems unwise. But this appearance constrains ethical thinking by making the conditions of temporal, finite life itself unappealing. It also makes the conditions of temporal, finite life worthy of escape. An ethics formed in these ways cannot meet us where we are. It shows us the limitations of our existence but diminishes our ability to think with those limitations toward better understandings of what we need, what we desire, what we fear, and how we should act.

Tracing love in time, by contrast, suggests the importance of its uncertainties to lovers—and the importance of uncertainty to ethics. Eliminating uncertainty in love, for finite beings, requires love to end. But lovers seem to want love to continue—to continue to be with their beloveds, learn about them, discover who they are and who they will become. Whether our beloveds are good for us or we are good for them cannot be answered definitively. Our questions in this vein must be continuously negotiated, as every attempt to know an answer fully will be defied by the possibilities of what happens next.

And lovers, as we'll see, must *desire* uncertainty insofar as they desire a relationship with their beloveds and not only an assertion of their love, without even listening for a reply. Wanting time together is to want that time to be determined, at least in part, by one's beloved. Attempts at greater control thus run against the desires of lovers—sometimes viciously, but also in the name of responsibility, protection, and the preservation of our lives as they are. This is the inclination of an ethics that resists uncertainty and cannot bear the vulnerabilities of temporal life. It is also an inclination of finite beings, attentive to risk and seeking to act responsibly in the face of it.

I think we should be sympathetic to these inclinations where we encounter them in each other, and in ourselves. But we must attend to them well, which requires us to see what aspects of our experience they run against as well as the aspects of our experience they protect and nurture. We must stop looking for a theory of love that will reconcile the lover's desire for uncertainty with the responsibilities of finite beings to know better, mitigate vulnerabilities, and control for risks as best we can. Following love in time, we can see this tension between desire and responsibility not as a failure of theory or practice, but as an animation of life itself.

It is also a tension that animates this book, and we will begin from its consideration in the strange speech of Lysias, Socrates's foil in the *Phaedrus*. Lysias's speech, as Socrates notes, seems reasonable and rational but spectacularly disorganized. It cannot proceed from beginning to end, and it describes an ideal of love that is similarly out of order. But what Lysias suggests amid this mess is a concern for how little lovers can know of whether their loves will go well. I think we should not dismiss this concern too quickly, even if it leads Lysias to particularly undesirable—and ultimately irresponsible—solutions.

Our path from there will follow other efforts to resolve this tension between desire and responsibility, considering a diversity of arguments in Western philosophy and religious thought that each pursue strategies of securing love against the uncertainties of its temporal experience. We will see some of these strategies recur, such as the interest that occupies the first chapter in properly assessing the value of the beloved as a way to ensure our desires are directed responsibly. Where efforts run aground to assess—or even describe—the beloved fully, we will turn to another approach in the definition of our loves as our core sources of values, reasons, and ambitions—the things of which we are certain beyond argument or doubt. The tautologies of Plato's *Euthyphro* will turn us to Harry Frankfurt's argument for love as a source instead of a product of reasons, but then back again to practices of reasoning about love as we encounter doubts and questions about our desires in conversation with others, and ourselves. Vulnerability *to* our desires emerges here alongside the vulnerability *of* our desires, compounding the tension between the lover's want for an uncertain future with their beloved and the fear of it all going wrong. Simultaneously, our vulnerability to definitions of love that seek to answer, fully and finally, questions about whether we're getting love right will emerge alongside the vulnerability *of* such definitions to aspects of our experience of love in time. The continuation of love makes every answer conditional, subject to change as we see more of our beloveds and our relationships to them. A definition of love that promises something more secure will be as vulnerable as we are to whatever the future brings.

The next chapters explore what can be learned from following these vulnerabilities to their extremes. In chapter 3, I will consider an effort to escape them entirely in the promise of the perfect invulnerability of God's love. In modern Protestant considerations of *agape*, principally those of Søren Kierkegaard and Anders Nygren, God's love, agape, is defined in contrast to erotic desire. In this form, it is bestowed by the lover without regard for the value of the beloved and is thus invulnerable to changes in them. This love promises an enviable constancy, but in Nygren's definition of it particularly, it isolates the lover from a relationship with the beloved. Being perfectly invulnerable makes the lover—even the divine lover—assertive of their love but not clearly in relationship with their beloved, never waiting for their beloved to respond, vulnerable to how they will react or reply. Nygren's denial of vulnerability in divine love suggests the importance of vulnerability to lovers. It also suggests the difficulty of being vulnerable in love: even God, knowing how things turn out, must wait to hear how the other responds.

The possibility of responding badly, as well as the pain of waiting for another's reply, sits at the center of the last chapter. We will turn there to a different set of questions about desire, responsibility, and vulnerability, reconfigured by illness as it reconfigures love. In two relationships, each encountered in works of art—one through a series of paintings and the other a fictional couple at the center of a play—the uncertain future desired by lovers becomes increasingly certain, as their beloveds decline toward death. Desire here stands in tension with responsibility not as lovers seek to protect themselves—or not only there—but as lovers struggle with obligations to care for their beloveds, and with others' expectations of what care a lover must provide. Spending time with these lovers, or the works of art in which they are depicted, makes desire seem again insecure, but here as a motivation for care. What we can demand of each other on its foundations seems similarly unsteady, suggesting the limits of love as an ethical ideal and the need for other forms of relation in our fragile, finite lives.

My interlocutors through these discussions are not part of a single existing tradition, except in a broad sense of Western philosophy and religious thought. They are sometimes representative of certain smaller conversations, but I do not offer them specifically in this way. Rather, they constitute a range of approaches to love in time—often through its escape. What they share is some anxiety about how to make love more secure, less vulnerable, and easier to know fully. What I share with them is the sense that love would need to be very different from how we encounter it in time for such anxieties to be overcome. Where we differ, when we do, is over whether that is a worthy ambition—or whether trying to describe love in time might offer more to lives lived within it.

First, a few notes about language. I have spoken about love thus far as if "love" is one thing. Many accounts of love are concerned with defining its multiplicity: different forms of love, defined by different feelings, expectations, behaviors, and surrounding relationships and roles between lover and beloved. In certain contexts, there can be a lot at stake in differentiating the love of parents for children from the love of romantic partners, for instance, or in defining the intimacies of a sexual encounter as something other than the love of a romantic relationship, or otherwise drawing lines around some relationships to hold them apart from others. Differentiating between kinds of love isn't my project here. When I say "love," I mean the broad set of things generally called love, including love between parents and children, family members, romantic partners, friends, and even love for ideas, places, and things. The aspect of love I am interested in—the want for more time with the beloved—is part of each of these relationships in some form. The significant differences among them are important to other questions.[1]

Second, I have used throughout the text the words "lover" and "beloved" to refer to the parties to a loving relationship. These words are not ideal. "Lover," in my experience of the English language, has a tone of licentiousness, or parody. "Beloved" is also more romantically marked, or the language of prayer. It is also not particularly popular; outside of liturgy, it belongs to saccharine greeting cards or hackneyed love poems looking for a rhyme, or, in a very different register, it is hung in the rafters as the title of one of the best novels ever written on the theme (or maybe any other). It is hard to imagine a parent loving a child, a friend loving a friend, or even many romantic couples as a "lover" and "beloved" without stumbling a bit over the terms. I tried others—"lover" and "loved one," "person loving" and "person loved"—but found nothing that wasn't somehow more awkward and unwieldy. I hope the connotations of "lover" and "beloved" will be at worst amusing, and not distracting.

Finally, every example of love reflects social norms of what counts as love; what I am able to see as love; what I am inclined to think is "good" love, "bad" love, or specious as love at all, and so on. I have used a range of examples that generally draw on norms shared by broad swaths of my society as I have experienced it. This practice produces relatively conservative examples. Appealing to your intuitions with them upholds the norms they represent, and thus participates in the forms of exclusion, denigration, discipline, and domination that they enforce. My point in any example is not that it represents the *right* norm to have. My point is usually—as I try to suggest throughout the text—that these are norms and not truths about what love is, determined by social practice and remade in every iteration of their performance, for better or worse.

⊙ 1 ⊙
Wanting Without Knowing

The flirtatious, meandering walk Socrates takes into the countryside with Phaedrus at the beginning of the dialogue bearing the latter's name is worthy of a modern romantic comedy: Socrates, the successful urbanite, is taken beyond the city walls, guided by someone perhaps enamored with him, or with someone else, but certainly with love itself. They tease each other on the walk, coyly dismiss each other's appeals, compliment each other's merits, and self-deprecate in response to the other's compliments. The topic of their conversation is a speech on love by the sophist Lysias. Phaedrus has just heard it but Socrates has not, and he tries to get Phaedrus to recite it for him, suspecting he has a copy hidden under his cloak. When Phaedrus finally agrees, these charming pages come to an abrupt shift in tone with Lysias's first lines, which stage a proposal to a young man to begin a love affair:

> You know about my situation and you have heard that I think that it is of benefit to us if this were to happen.[1]

It is a stunningly unromantic line—and intentionally so, we learn in the next. Lysias writes that this lover is not, in fact, in love. He proposes the affair and expects success with it precisely because of this condition. Erotic relationships, he explains, are best undertaken by people who are not in love. The nonlover is levelheaded and can maintain good judgment about who is worth pursuing and what the limits should be of their pursuit. He won't find himself regretting favors bestowed or money spent in the affair, having maintained "due regard to their own best interests" and doing favors for their beloved only "in proportion to their own resources."[2] And if not in love, love cannot end. It is at the end of love, Lysias tells us, when lovers are struck with loss, grief, and embarrassment about all they did while in love. The nonlover is safe from this fate. His affairs bear no such vulnerability.

The provocation of Lysias's speech is that he begins from the end: he describes love from the perspective of its conclusion, and recommends skipping the parts that come before. He insists that love does end, so we might as well start from there—and it would make no difference anyway to the nonlover. It is lovers who become enthralled by the pleasures of the present moment, who can be tortured by waiting, distracted by memories, or devastated when time with their beloveds comes to an end. The nonlover has no relationship to time in these ways. Why not avoid such vulnerabilities altogether, foreclosing the possibility of an ending by beginning from there?

Socrates is troubled by the speech and by Phaedrus's infatuation with it. Phaedrus is in awe of how *much* Lysias manages to include, asking Socrates if he can imagine "any other Greek would be able to find different things to say about the same subject greater in weight and number" and admiring that "none of the things that can be fitly said on the subject have been left out, so that no one could ever say anything else more fully and of more value."[3] Socrates replies that he thinks he's heard Sappho or Anacreon say some things that might exceed it, though he "can't exactly say offhand."[4] But he is less concerned with whether Lysias has offered a complete account of his subject than with the sense that Lysias hasn't put the things he says in order. Lysias "tries to swim backwards against the current of the *logos*, starting from the end," and seems to have "thrown together" the other parts of the speech in whatever order they "just happened to come into the writers' head."[5] This is a failure of rhetoric that mirrors a failure of love. Harmful lovers, Socrates explains, are similarly inattentive to the passage of time, or in denial of it. They want their beloveds not to change and wish to stunt their growth, keep their faces from aging, and limit the expansion of their minds. They want to pull the beloved out of time, or fix them within it, or otherwise extract them, and themselves, from the temporal order. But as "every speech must be put together like a living creature, with a body of its own," so every beloved must be allowed a body—and life—of their own, and allowed to develop, grow, and change through time.[6] Lysias's decision to start at the end shows him to be untrustworthy as both a lover and a rhetorician: he will not let arguments nor love affairs proceed from their beginnings, and will "swim backwards against the current" as if the strength of his stroke gave him control of the water.

But Lysias has another problem with control. He wants time to flow how he wishes, but he also wants to know how things will turn out. His want to begin at the end of love is a want to know what will happen, and to be able to say in advance whether it will be "of benefit to us" or not. His arguments about love begin and end with claims of completeness of knowledge, the minimization of risk, and the avoidance of regret: "You know about my situation and you have heard that I think that it is of benefit to us if this were to happen." You need to decide whether to take my offer, Lysias is saying, *and you know what you'd be getting.* There is no mystery, no suggestion of possible surprise, nothing vaguely promised with euphemisms nor adumbrated in verse. The indeterminate value or potential harm of further entanglement is cast as a situation that can be fully known, considered, and accepted or declined.

Lysias wants a relationship of knowing instead of wanting. And while there is much to condemn in the way he abandons desire for control, there is an anxiety embedded in his speech that cannot be condemned without making Lysias's mistakes ourselves. Lovers do not know when or how their love might end, what regret they might experience if it does, nor what will seem misguided, disappointing, or even disastrous at that time that seems now like one of so many goods. Lysias may be mistaken to insist that love always and necessarily ends, but he would not have been mistaken to insist on its vulnerability, and the importance of its vulnerability to lovers. Lovers care whether love continues or ends. Lovers also care *how* it continues or ends, and the many undesirable possibilities in its pursuit: to be hurt by our beloveds, to have our love unrequited, to lose a loved one to the ordinary dangers of worldly life, to find ourselves no longer loved by people who loved us before, and so on. We don't know how things will turn out. The want to know might be self-protective, part of a prudent effort to mitigate risks and prepare for potential harm. The want to begin from knowing— to begin from the end—could be an expression of fear as much as an attempt at mastery.

There are contexts in which Lysias's attachment to knowing how things turn out—at the expense, even, of letting them happen—might not be out of place, but love doesn't seem to be one of them. He admits as much by praising the nonlover, thus defining the lover as someone with different aims. I think he defines love quite well by this negation: where his nonlover knows without desire, lovers desire without knowing how things will go. Where Lysias rushes to the ending with no care to see how things proceed, lovers want time with their beloveds without end. But these desires of lovers run up against concerns about whether something is worth their time, would be a waste of time, is too great a risk, or simply too hazy of a prospect. As a lover, I don't want to skip ahead and only see how things turn out, but I also don't want for things to turn out badly. These are the desires Lysias can't seem to put in order, so he skips desire and insists on knowledge instead. (Plato finds him lacking in both.)

Lysias's speech muddles the relationship between desire and knowledge because it credits the fear that can stand between them precisely by pretending to its escape. The challenge isn't to put these terms in order but to put them back in time, to discover that desire and fear can occur simultaneously and the knowledge that could assuage our fears may be endlessly deferred so long as the desire that creates them continues. His speech suggests that to know how things turn out would require love's end. But lovers usually want love not to end, and so seem to desire the uncertainties of its continuation. And this is not some unfortunate reality of temporal life. It is a desire *for* uncertainty, because part of the lover's desire is for the future to proceed in ways they do not determine themselves.

The aim of this chapter, and this book, is to describe love in this way: as a desire for an uncertain future with the beloved, wanting time together without knowing what that time will bring. This desire conflicts with self-protective desires to know as much about the future as possible and prepare accordingly, mitigating vulnerabilities and seeking some measure of control. It also conflicts with certain desires to know at all: efforts to answer questions fully about why we feel the way we do, why we find the world as it seems, and what we are finding in the world and in ourselves. The desire for fullness of knowledge is at odds with the lover's want for the continuation of relationships, in which there is always more to learn. Lovers want to know their beloveds, their love, and themselves without end, instead of answering questions fully and finally about them.

Let me begin with what Lysias wants to know: whether love will seem regrettable after it ends because the formerly beloved will seem unworthy of what the lover has spent on them—money and other resources, as well as attention, affection, and time. This is a question, in part, about the value of the beloved, evaluated by the lover and then reevaluated after love ends. As lovers try to describe their beloveds' value, however, they are defied by all they do not yet know, all that can't be said of what they know already, and by their beloveds themselves, whose uniqueness exceeds description. They may want more time with their beloveds, in part, because there is no end to what they can learn. In his refusal of this endless desire for knowledge and the unknowing it implies, Lysias points toward some of what lovers fear but fails to describe what lovers want. His mistake is not only that he pursues his arguments and affairs out of order, but that by not proceeding from their beginnings, he fails to discover that they may not have full and final ends.

DESIRING KNOWLEDGE

Lysias wants to know whether love will be worth his time. He frames the concern in terms of the value of the beloved: the affair will be worth his and his potential beloved's time because they are each valuable to the other. He promises that his value will not be squandered in the distractions of passion nor go missing altogether as love changes his interests, ambitions, or character. He cannot, of course, guarantee that his valuable qualities will not be lost to other forces, but he is trying to make the point that he is someone of value whom his potential beloved should want because of it. And Lysias insists he would propose the relationship only to a young man who has valuable qualities himself. Time spent together will be worthwhile because each can say, with confidence, that they are "someone worthy of your affection."[7] Most significantly for Lysias, neither will seem a regrettable beloved after the relationship ends because the evaluation has been made apart from love, without any interference from desire.

Is the value of the beloved what lovers desire? Will love be worth one's time so long as the beloved is sufficiently valuable? Is love then dependent on the beloved's value such that we must be wary of how it could change, or the possibility that we have misjudged it? Lysias's speech alludes to many fears—some profound, and some less so—about unwanted changes in our beloveds, ourselves, and our loves. He rightly suggests the multiplicity of vulnerabilities the lover faces, including to both changes in the beloved and changes in how the lover perceives them. But he responds to these concerns with what amounts to a statement of technical specifications and a contract that seems only a few lines short of a money-back guarantee. He insists on knowing, tallying, and securing the value of everyone involved before a relationship can begin. Lysias treats both lover and beloved as goods for purchase, reduced to a set of valuable features that the vendor promises will perform consistently. He turns concerns about the vulnerability of these goods and the lover's evaluation of them into reasons to evaluate the beloved as a commodity: something whose value is determined by comparison to other goods at market, ready to be exchanged. Is this what lovers desire? Or is such evaluation as repugnant to lovers as a love that begins from the end?

The Value of the Beloved

The beloved seems, maybe without exception, valuable to the lover. We don't tend to call it love if you say, "I love her, but I don't value her at all," nor do we seem eager to call something love, at least without further explanation, if you say, "I love him, but I can't tell you anything particularly valuable about him." Describing the beloved's value seems important to love and to the lover. But accounts of love defined by value can produce strange and often uncomfortable results, particularly when value is defined in terms of qualities and characteristics shared by others. If my love is a response to the value of my beloved in these terms—I love him because he's handsome, smart, funny, warm, and so on—why don't I love just anyone with those same qualities, or love others more if they possess those qualities to greater degrees? If I have many funny friends and I love them "because they're funny," do I love each one in proportion to their relative good humor? If I meet a new, even funnier person, shouldn't I trade in my other friends for them on these grounds?

"Trading in" and "trading up" seem anathema to what we mean

when we say we love someone, suggesting one of the ways the value of the beloved may be a strange measure in love overall.[8] If we press the issue, we can generate even more inconsistencies: we love people, for instance, knowing that they aren't the best versions of what we value in them, and love people through many changes in their valuable qualities that seem not to change our love for them at all. I love my funny friends in full awareness that they aren't the funniest people alive, or even the funniest people I know. This is not because I sought such a friendship only to be disappointed and now faced with the possibility of trading them in, which I don't do, but because I didn't seek them out on those terms, and I didn't come to love them with that in mind. Similarly, we often continue to love through tremendous changes in the qualities of our beloveds without even stopping to ask whether the decline or loss of those qualities should cause us to reconsider our love for them. The possibility of change may be a specter to lovers concerned with whether love will continue or end, but the endurance of love through significant change is not uncommon.

Accounting for love as a response to the value of the beloved seems to stumble over many of our experiences of love in these and other ways. In response, some have argued that the equation should be reversed: I don't love someone because of their value; my beloved is valuable to me because I love them.[9] On this view, it is *because* a parent loves their child, for example, that their child's qualities at different ages are valuable to them. When the child matures and no longer possesses whatever qualities were valued at an earlier stage, the parent loves whomever they become instead, valuing the qualities they come to possess and perhaps no longer even remembering many qualities once prized and praised. The parents of adult children (who aren't yet yearning for grandchildren) might be relatively uninterested in the kinds of curiosity that they couldn't stop talking about when their kids were young, or their being good sleepers or good eaters, or, for that matter, *cute*. If my funny friends from childhood go on to pursue quite unfunny careers, have tragic experiences that can't provoke even gallows humor, or our time together is simply no longer spent in laughter, I would likely, on reflection, say that what changed (if anything) is how much I value humor in my friends, not how much I value them. I love them and so I value them. If they change, I value the people they have become. I don't value them less because they no longer accord with my original evaluation—and were that to be the case, I would be more likely to say that my love for them had declined or ended, but not because they had failed to earn it. Love is not earned at all, on this view, and needs no persistence of qualities and characteristics to sustain it.

We might think of this view—that love renders the beloved valuable to the lover instead of responding to their value—as describing precisely the experience of love Lysias wants to escape. To say that love renders valuable might be descriptively appealing for cases like the friend or parent, to account for the persistence of love through change, but it seems to set us up well for regret and offers no guide for enduring or avoiding it. If the people I love are valuable to me because I love them, their value to me will change if I stop loving them. They may still seem worthy of my having loved them, at least for the time I did, or they may not. After my love for them has ended, it might be hard to imagine what I saw in them or to recreate how I could have cared so much about someone who seems no longer so great. I might muster a kind of gentleness toward my prior self, remembering the version of myself who loved this person with sympathy or even a bit of nostalgic affection. Or I may not, and be plagued by the kinds of regrets Lysias wants to avoid. His ambition to be in relationships only with people worthy of his time and affection as judged from somewhere securely outside any desire for them does seem more appealing by these lights. It can be painful to consider days and years spent with people we no longer love, or even like.

The wisdom of this anxiety about worthiness might be most apparent when considered more broadly than in the immediate cycle of love and regret that Lysias describes. It is not just that I don't want my passions to wane and find they were directed at someone I now find unworthy. I also have a larger concern for the way I spend my time. We are finite creatures with limited time and thus some reasonable concern not to spend it badly. The desire to determine the beloved's value without being clouded by my desire for them might be one way of seeking some reassurance that I'm spending my time well.

The difficulty is when I want love to continue, never affording me the outsider's view of my beloveds that might be reassuring, *and* I want to know whether I'm spending my time well by spending it with them. That desire for knowledge seeks a foreclosure of vulnerability, but that vulnerability is part of what the lover desires in wanting love to continue. When the lover experiences these desires simultaneously—as I think we often do—they push against each other and pull the lover apart. The mistake available is to ignore their conflict: to imagine that my interest in securing my future by foreclosing its vulnerabilities is part of what it means to be a good lover, or to recast my love as something dependent on knowing the other with some kind of satisfaction, certain that I know what time with them will bring.

To say that these desires conflict is not to say that the continuation of love is proof of the value of the beloved, nor that the value of the beloved, properly discerned, should guarantee the continuation of love. This factual question of whether love is motivated by value or value is bestowed by love either can't be answered because there are no sufficient criteria by which to judge it; resolves to a triviality because we may not be able to do other than spend our lives loving the people we love; or must be answered according to a larger understanding of how it is best to spend one's life, in which case we needn't wonder about our loves so much as reason through their resemblance to that view. Discussions of love in Western thought often begin and end with versions of this question. I will discuss different approaches to it in the next chapter, but here I want to consider the conflict between the desires themselves: the desire for time with the beloved, without end, and the desire for knowledge of whether we're spending our time well by spending it with them.

The conflict between these desires sets two crucial aspects of love into relief: lovers want time with their beloveds without knowing what it will bring, and the beloved is particular to the lover, not interchangeable with others like them or reducible to some set of valuable qualities known and named. Both aspects of love point to what the lover doesn't know, but desires. They also point to the lover's desire not to know such that there is nothing more to learn. This relationship to unknowing sets love apart from many other parts of life, where we seem more often to want to know in a way that satisfies the questions we've asked.

Understanding the conflict between these desires hinges on how we understand the value of the beloved and its importance to lovers. However, focusing on the conflict between desires recasts this more traditional controversy over whether the beloved's value is the reason for love or love is why they are valuable to the lover. That question asks what criteria of evaluation matter to the lover: those determined outside of their desire for the beloved, or those determined by it. I want to ask what we seek in evaluating the beloved at all. Are we trying to know something with certainty or at least a measure of confidence, and if so, for what purpose? To reassure ourselves that we're not wasting our time? Or are we trying to describe our beloveds, expressing our love for them in terms of how and what we see in them? Are we trying to boast of their great value, describe them to themselves, or perhaps share something of ourselves in sharing what we value in them? I think there are more reasons we talk about the value of the beloved than arguments about love and value sometimes credit. Distinguishing among them allows us to see which of those reasons belong to us as lovers and which belong to us in other roles.

Market Values

In an excellent essay on the role of value in love, Susan Wolf argues for the "unexciting" thesis that the value of our beloveds is at least relevant to the question of whom we should love. Concern for worthiness connects us to the world, she argues. It expresses our want not to live "in a fantasy" in which our desires determine what is valuable for us wholly disconnected from anything else around us. Determining the worthiness of our beloveds may be "complex and pocketed with indeterminacies," she writes, but "total skepticism about value seems to me unwarranted."[10] We must have some connection between our will and the world, some way of asking whether we are directing ourselves in the right ways, and some way of understanding our own questions about whether our loves are worthy of us, or whether we could "do better" in some meaningful way. Wolf describes the sense of worthiness she's interested in as only a "minimal condition," however, "almost always satisfied without even thinking about it."[11] Views that produce a stronger condition are likely monstrous: they would require differentiations among people that we are unlikely to accept, and shouldn't even if we were.

But worthiness is also worth talking about, she writes, for another reason altogether:

In a world in which people's tastes and passions are increasingly determined by market forces that do not have the good of their subjects or of the world at heart, the possibility that people will increasingly come to care about what is not worth caring about may be a growing danger.[12]

We may not need to interrogate whether each of our loves is precisely as valuable as it should be to be worthy of us, but if we are constantly encouraged by market forces to care about some things and not others, we may need to be more skeptical of what and whom we find ourselves caring about. Minimal conditions may not be met, as our sense of what is worth loving is shaped and reshaped by senses of worth that have nothing to do with us as lovers at all.

Wolf does not explore the point further, but I raise it here to consider one of the more concerning—and illuminating—possibilities for what the project of evaluating the beloved might seek. Talking about value is to speak in the language of markets. We may try to specify that we understand a person's value very differently from economic senses, but many of the terms are the same, and the connotations linger. Market valuation may even seem to be a good model for thinking about the value of the beloved, if it describes a version of value set by desire. But market forces are not simple reflections of consumer desire, and as Wolf suggests, they do not have the good of consumers in mind. They shape consumer desire sometimes more than reflecting it, and often directly against people's assessments of the good where those assessments interfere with what sellers can offer most profitably. If value is the reason for love, we need criteria by which to evaluate potential beloveds. Markets are ready to meet that need, teaching us what we should value in accordance with what is profitable and possible to sell.

Markets also shape *how* we desire. They render desire a competitive project of choosing the best thing to buy, where "best" is defined in part—though only in part—by the aggregated desires of other buyers. For the consumer, this sense of desire is made personal with the promise that what is being sold *is* what you desire or need. And desire is constructed as choice among available options. *Choosing* becomes the essential project of consumer life. The consumer's desires are shaped in some tension with their resources, so the project of the consumer becomes another version of a conflict between desire and prudent concern not to waste resources on something unworthy. The consumer's project is to buy, and to *choose* what to buy. Abstinence from choosing at all—the prudence of saving money, repairing instead of replacing goods, or making do with what you have already—is cast as a kind of relic of the Depression era or a memory of the early months of the COVID-19 pandemic when global supply chains were disrupted and so many consumer products were no longer within reach.[13] By market logics, finding something out of reach is my failure as a consumer to put myself in a position to buy it. Nothing is ever fully out of reach for everyone; our lives as consumers are defined by our choices among options and our ability to have as many options as possible.

Byung-Chul Han argues that this "society of the consumer" has had a profound effect on our ability to value or desire anything outside of the project of being good shoppers on these terms.[14] In his view, the effect emerges from consumer society's need to assimilate everything to a possible purchase, such that everything is interchangeable and nothing is wholly other to anything else. Consumer society "endeavors to eliminate atopic otherness in favor of consumable—heterotopic—differences."[15] Markets work best when things are differentiable but not other: commensurate, comparable, and available for coherent choices between and among different options. Thus we separate things constantly in consumer society into categories of better and worse, greater value and lesser. We erect fences and walls to separate the rich from the poor, Han writes, but these are not "thresholds or transitions to the other."[16] They designate achievement among assimilable possibilities. Markets require interchangeability, so the subject created in consumer society encounters only difference among possibilities, not alterity.

The assimilation of everything to an interchangeable option shapes our lives in a significant way: because nothing is wholly other to ourselves, we define ourselves by what we can achieve in our universe of possibilities. Han calls the subject of consumer society the "achievement subject" for this reason.[17] As achievement subjects, we seek to be productive and successful, to perform well, and to accomplish our goals, projects, and initiatives. We strive for the next accomplishment in a society "wholly dominated by the modal verb *can*" rather than "*should*." Han writes that the subject governed by "should" belongs to a "disciplinary society" like that described by Foucault, "which issues prohibitions."[18] We might imagine the subject governed by "should" in a moral or religious realm as well, the "should" of duty, divine command, or divine example. The achievement subject, by contrast, "no longer understands him- or herself as a subjugated subject"—subjugated to the power determining what they "should" do—"but as a project in the process of realizing itself."[19] If there is a hint here of a kind of mastery, it is of a weak form, because the achievement subject is able to master only possibilities within the realm of the achievable—or, more precisely, everything is achievable in consumer society, so no achievement is mastery over something greater than a goal within reach. "Everything is possible," as Han describes it, but this is not a form of freedom.[20] The promise of possibility is a dramatic contraction of existence. If nothing is beyond us as achievement subjects, nothing is truly other to ourselves, and so "the world appears only as adumbrations of the . . . self." We have no boundaries of self, and so "no alterity."[21]

It is a kind of alterity in the otherness of an unknown future that Lysias seems to want to escape when he wants to know before love begins whether the beloved will still seem worthy of his love after their relationship has ended. The challenge is that he cannot escape the alterity of the future without escaping the alterity of the beloved themselves: he can't know who the beloved is and who they will be to him without skipping to the end of their time together. This is the alterity we also escape as achievement subjects—or that we cannot encounter at all. As we seek to be successful in love as a project like any other, we imagine the beloved and our future with them to be knowable in the way the specifications of a product or aims of a project can be known. The beloved is not other to us, unknown and at least partly unknowable. The beloved, for the achievement subject, is another thing to learn about, evaluate, and decide whether to acquire. We pride ourselves as consumers in making informed decisions and assimilating any surprises quickly into our knowledge of the options we can choose among. Love, for the consumer, is thus a project of trying to know what we would be getting if we were to love someone, not of desiring them themselves.

As consumers, we know that we might be surprised by the products we buy: some last longer than we expect and others wear out more quickly than we thought they would, some are less useful than we anticipated and others we find ourselves using and enjoying much more than we imagined. We do not, however, tend to *desire* such surprise. We want accurate and representative descriptions of the qualities and characteristics of the products we buy, even some testing according to standards set beyond ourselves, and maybe a guarantee of value or at least insurance against declining worth (or a generous return policy). We want to know what we're choosing so that we can make the best choice. The ways of knowing we pursue as consumers presume that the world is knowable, in part because we have limited ways of using knowledge as consumers, and thus of thinking about what knowledge we could want. Consumers use knowledge to choose among options, so we need to know only enough to choose well, with the criteria comfortably provided by the market itself. We don't need to wonder what lies beyond that knowledge—or to wonder at all. We seek only the possible, the achievable, the purchasable. As consumers, we don't even imagine that anything else exists.

Han argues that we cannot talk about the value of the beloved in consumer society without eliminating love altogether by rendering it a project to achieve. Our assessments of value or worth will always imply comparison and interchangeability, and our job, as consumer-lovers, can only ever be to find the best among options, not to respond to someone particularly, loving them perhaps without knowing why. Such unknowing would be a failure of the consumer subject, or at least a kind of carelessness, akin to taking a job without assessing whether it will suit you, or buying something without looking into whether it actually has the features required to meet your needs. We would be bad shoppers, in these cases, and may suffer from our failures. And our suffering should encourage us, by consumer logics, only to seek ever more complete knowledge of our options, a bigger and better selection, and a more conservative choice from it, in terms of the chance we think we're taking on our selection turning out as we think it will. A vague sense of that chance that things might not turn out as we expect is as close as the consumer gets to a sense of otherness, and every encounter with it is framed as a lesson that we should try to get further away from ever encountering it again.

This might seem a bleak picture of our lives in consumer society and the prospect for love within them. But as with Lysias's rather bleak account of love, I think the consumer subject's confinement in constant choice among knowable options suggests an anxiety we shouldn't dismiss too quickly—and one represented in some versions of interest in the value of the beloved as a cause or result of love. Like lovers, the consumer doesn't know how things will go: whether their choices will be successful or unfortunate, whether they will achieve what they aim to do or fail in ways that they didn't anticipate, and so on. Markets ratchet up the stakes of these possibilities by creating arenas of scarcity, enhancing the possibility of failure as a consumer while also not allowing for anything to be completely out of reach, so failure becomes always the consumer's fault. The desire to make a good choice in these conditions seems again self-protective, a kind of prudence born of fear.

The difference between the consumer's encounter with this fear and the lover's is that consumer society makes the foreclosure of vulnerabilities seem possible. Indeed, it's premised on that foreclosure: we choose among options that promise to seal up vulnerabilities and fill needs and gaps in ways that will make life complete, or at least allow us to have achieved something completely. We're then offered another product to close another gap tomorrow, and the next day, and the next, with the implication that every lack can be filled and every vulnerability eliminated because each is the shape of a product, and we just need to choose the right one. We can buy ourselves out of anything we might be afraid of with the right preparatory purchases. The problem, as it appears to the consumer, is not that I don't know how things will proceed. The problem is that I might not have made the right choice when it was available—and I could have known better, since nothing, even that knowledge, is fully out of reach.

The consumer can't quite share Lysias's anxiety about the future because they can't quite imagine the kind of radical unknowing he is attempting to avoid. Both Lysias and the consumer, however, are shaped by versions of the anxiety that they will fail to make the right choices in the present as judged by a future self who knows how those choices turn out. Both then turn their versions of this concern into invitations to redescribe what they can know about the present as the only thing that matters, now or ever. Lysias insists that dispassionate evaluation of the potential beloved will be the only evaluation that matters because it will be the same before and after love ends. The consumer-lover imagines the future only in terms of the set of possibilities that will be available at that time: it is not unknown; it simply isn't available yet. What matters is to choose well among the options they know about now, in relation to the needs and wants they know now. Some needs and wants might be set in the future—I will want shelter on a camping trip, so I buy a tent today—but the anxiety is not about what will happen, but whether I will have prepared well enough for the many possibilities I know could occur.

Information and Narration

One result of both Lysias's and the consumer's resistance to the unknown is that they each end up with a lot of information on their hands. Lysias has a great quantity of things to say, as Phaedrus admires, but he can't figure out how to put anything in order, moving to every new thought with the transition "again" or "and then" (καὶ μὲν δή)— Plato's small joke, it seems, that the speech is somehow both repetitive and offers too many different thoughts, without pulling them together into a coherent narrative.[22] The consumer has an even bigger problem, because the consumer's project of choosing requires the accumulation of information about an increasingly vast set of possibilities. The consumer seeks both the best among options and the most options from which to choose. We can be bad shoppers not only by not knowing everything we can about what we choose, but also by not seeking more possibilities from which to make our choice.

Having more choices, however, encourages us to think even more strictly in terms of comparison and thus of the qualities by which our options can be compared. A mutually reinforcing cycle forms between the quantity of things about which we need to know and the reduction of those things into comparable qualities and characteristics. Having more choices encourages us to think about how we value our options according to classificatory criteria, and to desire in ways that are rationally responsive to those criteria. "Increasing choice," as in the appearance of endless faces and descriptions on a dating app, "entails the rationalization of desire," Han writes with reference to the work of sociologist Eva Illouz.[23] We struggle with "data storage," and we learn to interact with the world through classifications that support it. In Han's description, what we know in these conditions becomes information without a story—it sits on a shelf or in a catalog, metaphorically, not as something that has happened or existed that we can place in a coherent story of the past. We turn the past into a "museum," as we try to organize what we know to be readily available for viewing. It is not held as "memory," part of a story that existed prior to us and that points to a future beyond us.²⁴ "No narrative tension animates it. As such, it falls apart into mere information."²⁵

Our descriptions of other people, which might form the beginning of our evaluations of them, are sometimes rendered in this way: I hear someone is funny, beautiful, or kind, but as a fact without a story. Their attributes are merely present, knowable and usable for projects, but not part of an ongoing relationship with them. We store facts about people, extracted from time, and make choices on the basis of that knowledge. This is who we are as subjects of consumer society: people who can only understand each other, and ourselves, in comparative judgments among possibilities. We are well poised in this condition to evaluate the beloved, but only as part of our projects of picking the best among options—as a good shopper instead of a lover at all.

I think it is precisely in our enumerations of valuable qualities and characteristics, however, that we experience the sense that something is wrong about imagining love to be a project of this kind. Mere information, known and named by classifications used for comparison, doesn't describe people particularly well. We don't live as collections of attributes; we live in time, as part of stories with a past, present, and future. When we extract facts from those stories, I think we notice the loss of information even if we aren't quite sure what is missing. If I say that I had dinner with someone and you ask what they were like, saying simply that they were "handsome, funny, and a bit quiet" is clearly not the whole story. How did I come to these assessments? In what sense were they quiet? What made them funny? And, perhaps most important, do I want to see them again? My evaluation represents a larger story, and we know that—even as consumers—because we know it is an evaluation of things that *happened*, the way a person behaved or seemed, not of something that exists statically, somehow outside of time.

I share Han's concern that we are increasingly shaped by consumer society into unloving subjects, but I don't think that we are as so fully bound by it as he suggests. We encounter cracks in the smooth surface of possibility, not only fences and walls. We discover some things to be wholly out of reach in ways that make us question the assimilation of everything to the possible. We think we know what we're getting as we make a choice and then discover something we didn't know was possible at all. The achievement subject can't account for the experience of the failures and discoveries they can't *choose*. These experiences intrude on our lives of possibility. We are confounded by their alterity as they break into our experience by remaining somehow always beyond our grasp.

I think we notice these intrusions of alterity in many places, including the failure to describe the people we love. Language itself falls apart, not into "mere information" but confusions of tense: he *was* quiet, or he *is* quiet? He *was* funny or he *is*, and so he likely will be again? We discover questions we can't answer about our experience, both as it happened—and what we should learn from what happened—and as it points to an indeterminate future. We enumerate qualities and characteristics and discover we can't provide the information we would need for evaluation without at least implying the existence of the kinds of stories that muddle comparison and defy efficient "data storage." Something seems to be missing from every description, though we're not sure exactly what is being left out.

We've now moved a few steps away from anxieties about what we don't know—about the future, our beloveds, or the other options for love we might be missing—and into a frustration with the effort to articulate what we do know. But why should we be frustrated? We encounter the reductive effects of language constantly without experiencing them as barriers to evaluation or impediments to good judgment, let alone as radical alterity. The insufficiencies of description in many contexts don't suggest loss or lack so much as efficiency and even understanding. We can say less about some things because we know more, both about the thing itself and about what information is needed for whatever purpose we're describing it. When we buy a pair of shoes, we want to know about specific features of them, and maybe something about others' experiences with similar pairs. We do not, on the whole, want to know the number of the shipping container they traveled on, or why the truck driver who delivered them to the store decided to become a truck driver. The implication that there are longer stories to tell isn't always a problem.

Linguistic reduction is frustrating in our descriptions of people, however, when it matters that they are *themselves*, and not just one iteration of a type or a bearer of some set of qualities. This seems to be one of the problems we encounter when we try to discuss the value of the beloved. The problem with saying that I love my friends "because they're funny" comes well before any thought of trading them in for funnier friends. The statement seems wrong because their humor isn't the whole story—not of why I love them, but more significantly, not of *them*. Someone couldn't even pick them out of a crowd on that description, except maybe at some extremes. To describe them as *them*, I need to say a lot more. And lovers seem to want to keep talking, in many cases: we narrate and enumerate, sometimes at great length, the things about our beloveds that we love and the things that simply make them themselves. We can't escape the reductive effects of descriptive language entirely, but we don't restrict ourselves to classificatory descriptors chosen for comparison and efficient information processing. We tell stories of our beloveds, eager to describe them particularly, wanting to narrate them as *themselves*.

Particularity is something that both Lysias and the consumer-lover ignore completely. They each need to treat the beloved as interchangeable to protect themselves from decisions where interest in a particular person interferes with the selection of who would be best. This is part of why neither really seems to love, but *only* to evaluate. They think dispassionate evaluation will protect them from bad choices and bad outcomes because they'll know what they're getting. But they reduce their worlds considerably in this pursuit, to the knowable and, even better, the known.

Their lack of interest in particularity also affords a different perspective on the problems Socrates raises about getting things in order. Both Lysias and the consumer-lover want to evaluate first and then decide whether to love on the basis of their evaluation. But as we'll see in the next section, even in Plato's account of a love more strictly responsive to the value of the beloved, that's not what the lover seeks. Love is not something I decide to do after having evaluated someone as worthy. Knowledge and desire go in the other order: I want to know the beloved's value because I desire it, because I desire *them*.

THE PARTICULARITY OF THE BELOVED

The particularity of the beloved matters to lovers. This is why so many ways of talking about the value of the beloved seem so strange, as we use a language of comparison that can say many things about the people we love but cannot identify them as themselves. The lover's interest in particularity defines their relationship to knowing the beloved overall: you will still be you tomorrow, so I will still be learning who you are. Everything I learn, every new description I can offer, every new experience I have of you points to the insufficiency of what I know because it points to a future of who you are that I cannot know yet. Lovers are not uninterested in knowledge of their beloveds. They are defied in their desire for it by the particularity of the beloved and the alterity of who they will be in time.

To talk about the value of the beloved without rendering them imparticular, the lover must abandon the project of articulating knowledge of them that pretends to be complete. It is the effort to complete the thought, to have nothing left to say, that distorts the beloved into an interchangeable item for purchase. What can we say that trains us away from knowledge of this kind? Will evaluative language always encourage us to finish our descriptions—and see unfinished descriptions as failures of knowledge, even of love? Or are there ways of talking about the beloved that express the insufficiency of what we say?

Desire and Description

Let us consider the project of evaluation in another context. Works of art can be liked or disliked, even loved, and as in love, we are often eager to talk about why we love them. They encourage the kinds of descriptions we offer of our beloveds: we say we like them because of things about them, because they're interesting, beautiful, graceful, bold, and so on. Do we like them, then, for the attributes we name? Are we trying to justify our liking them when we elaborate their fine qualities and characteristics? Do our descriptions imply comparisons to other pieces, and does the implication of comparison suggest a willingness for exchange? When talking about art, we are talking about something we generally take to be significantly particular. But we are also talking about something that can be evaluated in comparison to other, similar things: valued as unique, yet priced for sale at market.

In *Only a Promise of Happiness*, Alexander Nehamas argues that the categories we use when we talk about art cannot account for why we find the art beautiful, if we do, or worth looking at, as might be analogous to being "worth loving."²⁶ Even when we are reviewing art, and intentionally trying to offer some kind of verdict on the piece, the verdict comes not in the description of the qualities of the piece that sound like the basis of our reasoning but in the ascription of whether the piece is worth spending time with. I can talk for hours about what I see in a painting I love, but it would be very strange for me to say at the end of the conversation "thus I think it's good" without also saying, or at least implying, *that I think you should go see it*. All the evaluative categories I use to describe the piece, all the reasons I can give you for why I think it's good, all the things I can say I've gotten from it or from time spent with it—it all amounts to a prescription for you to spend time with it in turn, if I'm prescribing anything, as a reviewer often is. And if I'm not in that role, my discussion at least displays the same point for my case: *I* want to spend time with it, which is why I'm turning our time together into time spent thinking and talking about the work.

This is an argument about the relationship between desire and description. But philosophy has long tried to disassociate the two, Nehamas argues, particularly in inquiries into the beautiful. What began as an inquiry into beauty in ancient philosophy, he writes, was transformed in the Enlightenment into a discussion of "aesthetic value" because of a mistrust of the passion and desire beauty inspires. Nehamas casts Kant as a primary perpetrator of this shift, as Kant redescribes beauty as something found only in art or nature, and only where their contemplation "produces 'a satisfaction without any interest.'" It is not complicated by passion or want; "it is a pleasure bereft of desire."²⁷ Beauty, for Kant, is *present*, set in a museum or park, available for the achievement of satisfaction on a single visit. Where Han gave us the image of information stored as if in a museum, Nehamas's Kant gives us art actually hung on museum walls. It is not part of ongoing desire and discovery, interest, narration, and interpretation. Freed of desire, Kant's aesthetic is freed also of story, memory, and future. There is nothing in it we haven't yet obtained.

Beauty that provokes desire, that interests me in *more*, that makes me *want* without satisfaction, thus became unimportant to philosophy, and to other parts of (highbrow) Western culture as well. But this shift ignored what inspires curiosity about beauty in the first place, Nehamas argues. We become interested in beauty because it inspires *love*. We want to know more because we desire more. Nehamas cites this understanding of beauty to Plato, for whom "the only reaction appropriate to beauty is *eros*—love, the desire to possess it."[28] Far from a dispassionate philosophy of the aesthetic, Plato's philosophy of beauty begins from love. We see a beautiful person and we want to know more, seeking understanding of what it is we find ourselves desiring:

> But since the reaction appropriate to beauty is love, a more philosophical man would now want to understand what makes the human body in general beautiful and inspires him to love it and what in turn accounts for the beauty of that, and would go on asking until he reached a full and final answer.[29]

This "more philosophical man" presents a different aim of inquiry into the value of the beloved than the fear-fueled efforts of Lysias or the consumer's projects within a wholly achievable world. He isn't interested in the value of his beloved in order to compare them to others and make sure he chose well. He isn't insecure in his love at all. His questions begin from love and seek to understand it, instead of seeking reassurance that he's loving the right thing.

But he still seems to be at least as strange a lover as Lysias, or, like Lysias, not a lover at all. He sees someone beautiful and desires them, and then immediately seeks something other than them in the *knowledge* of beauty—and not their beauty, but beauty "in general." He finds the promise of inquiry in the generalization of their qualities, not in knowing them better, learning who they are, and discovering more about them than he may have known to desire in the first place. He seems thus to represent another way that talking about the beloved's value seems contrary to love itself, or at least runs counter to the desires of lovers. He puts desire and knowledge in the right order, but he seems to move from desire to knowledge of the wrong thing. Or perhaps he is simply a most strictly "philosophical man": he desires *only* wisdom, and so his desire for this person must be turned into a desire for something he can come to know as such.

For all his apparent confidence in desire, we seem to have arrived again at a kind of insecurity in the rush to escape a situation of unknowing. It is a less personal insecurity than Lysias's or the consumer's, as the philosophical man seems unconcerned with what happens to himself in his endeavor to know what he desires and how to account for it. He is concerned instead with what one can know, and wants to turn what he desires into something knowable. He pursues truth, not safety, but it seems to require a similar kind of escape from unknowing. And it is an escape, once again, of the beloved themselves: that particular beloved, the person he saw and found himself desiring, who stands before him and seems to threaten the possibility of knowledge itself.

Perhaps we should expect nothing less from philosophers, as Adriana Cavarero might suggest. Philosophy may begin from desire, but the project of philosophy, she argues, is to reduce every uniqueness into judgments and classifications, qualities and characteristics, universals that "rescue the particular from its finitude":

> Taken as a concept, uniqueness corresponds with the extreme form of the particular—or better, to the absolute "one"; or, rather, to a form of the particular that is *free* of any universality that tries to redeem it, or erase the miracle of finitude. Because this, from Plato onwards, has been precisely the mission that philosophy, seduced by the universal, originally decided to take upon itself: to redeem, to save, to rescue the particular from its finitude, and uniqueness from its scandal. This task of redemption, however, logically transformed into an act of erasure. As Hegel admits—and as Arendt does not fail to point out—"philosophical contemplation has no other intention than to abolish the accidental." *To save by suppressing* is of course an ancient law that philosophers call dialectic.[30]

Cavarero writes to rescue the accidental, the finite, the unique from these ambitions of a "seduced" philosophy, and lays the problem of imparticular description at the feet of philosophers, not lovers, in this way. Philosophers are the ones who seek to capture narratives and turn them into definitions and judgments, evaluated in terms of their applicability beyond a particular case. But lovers describe endlessly, their stories of their beloveds not reductive so long as they are never meant to conclude. The fact that we must speak in terms that represent value judgments, including the comparative language that suggests interchangeability, is a limitation of language that the lover seeks to narrate past and through. And lovers can, Cavarero suggests, when we narrate our loves to each other. It's when the philosophers get involved that evaluative language becomes reductive and destructive, misused for definitions and arguments about something other than what we want, as lovers, to describe.

Cavarero locates the desire for narration at the heart of love itself. We want to be told who we are by the people we love, and we love people who tell us stories we recognize and love about ourselves. The intimacy of love demands as much, as we try to show ourselves to the people we love in order to be known by them. And the "joy of love" lies in being thus exposed to the other and hearing our exposure described in ways we recognize and desire. "Love is indeed often characterized by a spontaneous narrative reciprocity," she writes. "On the stage of love, the questions 'who am I?' and 'who are you?' form the beat of body language and the language of storytelling, which maintain a secret rhythm."[31]

These are questions about "who" we are as unique beings, not about our qualities in comparison to others or "what" we are in generalizable terms. Cavarero is drawing here on Hannah Arendt's distinction between "who" and "what" a person is. "What" I am is what I am to others, as I appear before them in society. It is described in terms defined beyond just my case, universal descriptors that designate us into classes and types: man, woman, old, young, beautiful, industrious, diligent, kind, and so on. "Who" I am is an irreducibly unique individual, myself and not another, as I appear to others who are attending to me as such. "Who" I am is exposed to the other and radically vulnerable in that exposure, as we appear before them without recourse to a universal "what." I am dependent on the way the other responds to me: they could do harm, exploiting my vulnerability with violence or a lack of response. I am also dependent on their narration of what they see: they can make me into a person I may not want to be, or tell me who I am in ways that make me want only to be as they say they see me. The latter is one way we fall in love, Cavarero suggests: by discovering that someone sees us in ways we desire to be seen, and narrates our stories and selves as we desire to be described. As we narrate each other to each other, we experience love as the failure of description and evaluation for public comparison. Love is "where the judgment on the *what* of the loved-one becomes powerless before the appearance of *who the beloved is*."[32]

It might be little wonder that the philosopher, the consumer, and Lysias all want to escape this experience into the knowable and the known. Cavarero is describing an extreme vulnerability in the reciprocal exposure of two people in love, each defied by the other's particularity and thus denied the relative security of reductive but socially meaningful descriptors and evaluative claims that place the other into broader classes and types. While Cavarero focuses on the experience of reciprocal exposure and narration between two people in love with each other, the vulnerabilities at stake might be even more clear if we return to the perspective of one lover only, who desires the other without knowing how they will respond. This is the situation our various would-be lovers have faced thus far and tried to disassemble into something more secure: finding themselves powerless before someone who appears to them as radically, irreducibly unique; desiring them; and knowing they can't know fully what they desire, or why, or how time desiring them will go.

This could be a wholly terrifying experience, especially if our habits of concern tend toward trying to know what to expect in order to mitigate vulnerability and minimize surprise. It is an experience of desire in which what we desire is what we cannot know or name, and we desire it *as such*. We do not want our beloveds to appear to us as only "what" they are, as they appear to others. We want them to appear to us as themselves. What we say about them, then, must not seek a kind of knowing that would reduce them to "what" they are. When we say we love them because they're beautiful, this must not be a full and final answer, or even the beginning of one. So what are we trying to say?

"Evaluation Settles Nothing"

There is a genre in discussions of art—to return to the analogy—that looks as if it's aiming at something full and final indeed. "A verdict, positive or negative, is exactly what we expect, and what we get" from a review, whether it is provided as a complex articulation of a work's aesthetic value or as a number of stars in a newspaper's arts and entertainment section.[33] But this apparent purpose is "deceiving," Nehamas argues. Reviews actually seem to be aimed at encouraging others to go spend time with the art themselves. The reviewer offers their ideas about the work, but with the implication that "only looking for yourself will move you one way or the other."[34] The verdict is not "the end of the matter." It encourages further engagement, and suggests there's more to experience, to learn, and to say. Where a review is understood as the end of the matter, it is a rejection of the arts themselves. "The passion for ranking, the fervor for verdicts," Nehamas writes, "has deformed our attitude toward the arts, and our lives, [as] simply another manifestation of selfishness"—or self-achievement, in Han's language, where rankings represent the completion of projects of viewing and evaluation.[35] A review for the sake of the art and not the ego or accomplishment of its author should be an invitation beyond evaluations to time spent with the work itself.

We don't talk about art for the sake of giving a verdict just as we don't go to meet a new friend of a friend for the sake of being able to say at the end of the meeting "I liked her" or "I didn't like her." Elaborated in his later work *On Friendship*, Nehamas makes this connection in *Only a Promise of Happiness* in this way:

> Reviewers have a very ordinary counterpart in the rest of life: friends who want me to get acquainted with someone they believe I will appreciate. Nothing they tell me about such a person can be very specific or very informative; their terms are bound to be generic: they'll tell me you are attractive, intelligent, interesting, unusual, kind, sensitive, sophisticated, generous to your friends, from an exotic background, and so on. If I agree to meet you on such grounds, I will be taking a chance, and I will go to our meeting *hoping* to do so but not *in order to* enjoy it and certainly not in order to *decide* whether it is worth enjoying. Of course, I will *want* to enjoy it, but that won't be my goal, which is only to get to know someone who may add to my life. If everything turns out as all of us had hoped and, once we've met, I find you and your company enjoyable, then, far from resting on that "verdict," I shall want to get to know you better. The "verdict" is not at all the end of the matter: it expresses my sense that you have more to offer me— that we have more to offer each other—and my desire to make you, to some extent or another, a part of my life so that I can find out what it is. Instead of signifying the end of our interaction, the "verdict" indicates that far from thinking it's over, I want it to continue.... Evaluation settles nothing. It is a commitment to the future.[36]

And so it seems with love. Our evaluation of our beloveds settles nothing, and not because it is insufficient as an expression of what we value in our beloveds, though it likely is that as well. It settles nothing because the lover isn't trying to settle: settling the issue, deciding whether a person is worthy of love, is not the point. To love is to determine that there's more to the story. It is a commitment, as Nehamas says, to the future. This is what Nehamas calls "the promise of happiness": I find the work of art beautiful or the new friend wonderful in that I find myself committed to spending more time with them, which is to say that I find in them the *promise* of happiness in time spent together. But we would replicate the problems we've identified in value-based discussions of love or beauty if the "promise of happiness" is understood to be a contractual kind of promise that we expect to be fulfilled in determinate terms, or one whose probability of fulfillment can be calculated and evaluated as such. If I meet the new friend and say that time together is promising because she promises to teach me Spanish, which I've always wanted to learn, we wouldn't call that "friendship" so much as "finding a Spanish teacher." Similarly, if I say that I want to read the work of Italo Calvino because he promises to be a great source of thought experiments, we wouldn't say that I was falling in love with Calvino's work, we would say that I found a good source of thought experiments. Time with them promises something specific and specifiable, and it might be worth spending it together. But this isn't love. It's *a* promise, of a knowable, specifiable thing.

What Nehamas is describing must be an *indeterminate* promise, lest it turn into a description of predicted value or, effectively, a verdict deferred. What is promised is "happiness," from the root "hap-", implying the indeterminacy of luck and chance. Hence the promise, though maybe happy now, may turn out badly, as with all indeterminate futures. Our time together could be unfulfilling, the second coffee not as good as the first. Or the second coffee could be wonderful, and the third, and the fourth, and we could be lifelong friends, but you could come to change my life throughout that friendship in ways that are hurtful or harmful or simply unpleasant. Perhaps you have a terrible brother-in-law you often convince me to let stay on my couch, or perhaps you regularly put me in the uncomfortable position of having to say "no" to such a request. Perhaps you entice me through our friendship to do something I find unethical that I never would have had reason—or even the thought—to do without my relationship to you. When I suffer from that act, by my own conscience or through its harmful consequences, it seems appropriate to say that you have made my life demonstrably worse. And perhaps the life I would have led if I had simply met someone else would have been much better, but I'll never know—though I may have some vague sense of unfulfillment later on, as I see others who seem to have more, to be more, *because* of their friends.

These possibilities are part of why Nehamas holds that the promise of happiness is *only* a promise, not a guarantee. But here he might fall into a trap he otherwise avoids of assessing something by a standard like the "verdict" or the "full and final answer." The promise of happiness is a promise, we might think, that should be judged by its fulfillment: by whether happiness is in fact realized or achieved. If this is the meaning of the "promise of happiness," however, it amounts to a prediction of what the verdict will be. What I want is for the review to be good, in the artistic equivalent, not to spend time with the painting or even see the show. The promise of happiness must be less determinate than that—a feeling, rather, that this relationship seems promising and *I don't know what exactly is being promised*. "Happiness" is a shorthand where the grammar of promise requires determination, but the experience Nehamas describes must be explicitly indeterminate, and significantly so. Thus it might be more precise to say that happiness belongs to the feeling of promise now—a happiness of promise—not that what is being promised is happiness in the future, lest we confuse the indeterminate happiness of an unknown future with the sort of determinate happiness we might think about in an age of depression screenings and "happiness quotients." What the lover feels, what the viewer of a beautiful piece of art feels, is happiness in the promise of the future, an enjoyment of and delight in its unknown possibilities. Or, more precisely, what they feel is *desire* for an unknown future. They might not experience that desire exactly as delight or pleasant feeling, as I'll suggest in a moment, but they want a future with this person or piece, and in that sense at least, they find the future together promising.

This is not a critique so much as a clarification of Nehamas's argument, and one oriented toward a slightly different set of concerns than Nehamas's own. He is interested in the description of what we find beautiful, and the desire for knowledge about the things and people we desire. He is not the philosophical man searching for a full and final answer, but he is pursuing *understanding*, the want for which, he attests, emerges from the experience of finding something beautiful: "To find something beautiful," Nehamas tells us, "is inseparable from the need to understand what makes it so, the features that make it stand out in my world."³⁷ It is to pursue an understanding of what it is, and what it is *particularly*: an interpretation of its distinguishing features, its remarkable qualities, its individual attributes, something like a story of its uniqueness that doesn't erase but describes, learns, and seeks to know. Where for Cavarero, particularity makes us want to narrate our beloved endlessly, for Nehamas, particularity inspires a pursuit of knowledge, understanding, and interpretation, "to try to see in things what is distinctly their own."³⁸ We seek to know why they stand out to us, and whether it's something in them or in us that makes them so outstanding. Where the pursuit of this knowledge tends toward philosophical generalities, it abandons the beloved in pursuit of knowledge of something else. The lover desires knowledge, but finds always in its pursuit the irreducible particularity of the beloved.

The lover's confrontation with particularity makes it difficult to answer the kinds of questions about their value that might reassure us, or others, of their worthiness. "Every explanation is so disappointingly thin," Nehamas writes of the effort to say why he loves his friends, because "they all contain an implicit 'And so on,' an open end or ellipsis that reveals that the friendship is still alive." What is left out is not only the full and final description of the friend. What is left out is "that commitment to the future—the hope for a better life that remains unknown for now."³⁹ We can't say whether or why the beloved is worthy of our time because we can't say what that time will bring. We can't make a prudent choice about them, *knowing what we're choosing*. At some point, the sentences must trail off. We can only say, then, that we know we desire a future with them—not that we know what that future will be.

Nehamas approaches these questions of knowledge and description at some distance from questions of whether we're *right* to pursue this person or thing and not another. These could be Plato's questions, with whom Nehamas is in close conversation throughout his work, but he explicitly distances himself from the connections Plato draws between desire, beauty, love, and the good. "Unlike Plato," Nehamas writes, "I don't believe that the pursuit of beauty leads necessarily to virtue."⁴⁰ Ethical questions of the right and the good cannot be answered by inquiries into beauty, he argues, nor can they be answered with inquiries into what we enjoy—and love—about our friends. In his account of friendship, he turns away from Aristotle's friendship of virtue as well and argues for something closer to a love of the people you find yourself loving, not motivated or sustained by your identification of their virtues. Friendship, for Nehamas, shapes our lives, but it does not define what is right, good, or virtuous "in the abstract," nor our responsibilities to others, or ourselves.[41]

I appreciate that Nehamas holds considerations of love and beauty at a distance from ethical questions of the right and the good. Many accounts of love too quickly hold them together, assuming love will provide answers to (all of, many of) our questions about how we should live, or that the pursuit of beauty, to be worth pursuing at all, must have some ethical or political worth. Love and beauty won't answer all of our questions, nor should their worth be determined by whether they do. And as I'll discuss in later chapters, there may be at least as much danger in assuming they will guide us in our responsibilities to each other as there is in turning away from accounting for love and beauty in ethical terms. Hence the importance, to bring us back to the point, of emphasizing that we find the future promising, instead of focusing on whether the promise of happiness will be fulfilled. The latter encourages us to ask whether it's still worth pursuing what seems promising now even if that promise doesn't come to fruition: a question of whether the risk of a bad outcome is worth whatever good we see in the project at this point. This is the kind of thinking that too often characterizes conversations about vulnerability in ethics and politics, and the kind of thinking Lysias wants to pursue instead of love at all. The vision of uncertainty as always undesirable encourages us to find that our responsibilities lie in the protection and conservation of what goods we have now, instead of in the pursuit of other things that may put those goods at risk.

What we seek in love is time together, wanting more time with this person without knowing what that time will bring. The sentence could continue "... because we think that time together will be happy"—well spent, bringing further happiness, and so on—but the sentence need not continue at all. We may want more time with our beloveds without having more to say for our desire—though we may have plenty more to say about the people we love.

Wanting Time Together

The want to spend more time with the people we love may take the form of wanting to be in their presence for as much time as we can be together. That is surely one version of the desire, and a version that seems to be part of many accounts of many different kinds of love. People want to see and be with friends, family, and romantic lovers; we imagine a future with them, desiring our time together to continue indefinitely and indeterminately. We may not be able to say why we want more time together or what we think it will bring, or we might talk endlessly about all we imagine of the future, all the promise we see in time spent with them. We say these things to our beloveds and to others. We plan and dream, we rearrange our lives, we "make time" we don't have, and "find time" we can't make.

But I want to suggest that the idea of love as an experience of desiring an uncertain future applies as well to some relationships we often call "love" that don't seem to involve a wish for such close contact over time. We often love people we may not want to be around all the time, or even whom we don't wish to be around very much at all. We may love family members, for instance, whom we may not wish to see very often—maybe their political views are daunting to engage, they are regularly judgmental in ways we find hurtful, or their presence reminds us of a painful past. Some might argue that these are different forms of love than the kind of desirous loves I've been discussing, and the idea that we want time together simply doesn't apply. But I think we do want a future in these relationships too, even if we don't want to spend all of it at close quarters, and that this is a meaningful form of wanting time together as well. We want to continue to be in relationship with them, in some way or another, or at least we do not desire to have that relationship end. So long as there is some desire for a future together, some feeling that a future together is desirable, love continues on the terms I've described. The "time together" the lover desires is not a specific kind of time or amount of time, "quality time" or visitation. It is an indeterminate future. We may desire an indeterminate future with some people and also know we don't want certain versions of that future—spending every minute in each other's company, for instance, or even so many minutes overall.

The want for time with our beloveds may compete with other desires, such as a want for the pursuit of the beloved's own good. Parents may want their children to grow up and have lives of their own, for example, while knowing their vocations and relationships will occupy them in ways that mean they spend much less time with their parents. They desire time with their child and desire their child to live as they want and to live well. One desire need not negate the other, though each cannot be wholly pursued at the same time. Similarly, friends may want their friends to find romantic partners, have children they adore, and, of course, have other friends, if these are the things their friends want for themselves. If my friends want these things, I want them for them. These things will take them away from time spent with me, which might sometimes be disappointing—or it might not. I want them to be happy in the ways they wish to be. Wanting time together isn't all there is to love. And wanting a future with someone is not to want every moment of that future together.

Sometimes our desire for time together has to make way, in practice, for a need not to be in contact at all. We may love people we know are harmful to us and we may need to separate ourselves from them, to remain apart for a time or even never spend time together again. The want to spend time with our beloveds in these cases might have to cede, in practice, to our acknowledgment of our need not to. This doesn't mean we don't desire time together; it means we see that we shouldn't pursue that desire because its dangers are too likely, and our vulnerability to them is too great. But we may also find time with this person no longer promising, feeling pretty certain that time together will be bad, harmful, or dangerous in some way. We often find ourselves, rightfully, thinking about the future in terms of our vulnerability to bad outcomes. That might be appropriate, even imperative, when our desire for time together is overwhelmed by the realization that we don't see much chance it could bring anything other than harm and grief. We may desire to find time together promising as we once did, wishing we could love them without reserve, but find we can't, our love damaged by the anticipation of what time together will bring. In some cases, love persists, neither fading nor rediscovering a less equivocal promise in the future. In other cases, the wounds of anticipation prove fatal and love fades, as all visions of a promising future together darken, then disappear.

Love also fades in much less difficult circumstances: we find ourselves no longer loving, sometimes without anything to suggest how that happened at all. Part of the descriptive power of thinking about love in this way is that it can account for love's end without any change in the value of the beloved or the lover's assessment of them. Love ends when we no longer desire a future together. I may think my beloved is just as great as when I first fell in love with them, and maybe even better than I knew then. I may have learned much more about them in the time we spent together, value our shared history, and think even more highly of them now than I could have imagined before. But I find myself no longer wanting time together, and so my love has ended. I may wish my love had not ended because of all I see in them to admire, or all I can imagine would be the advantage of continuing to love them. I may be quite sure my life with them would be great in many ways, but I no longer desire that future. I may even fear the future spent otherwise than with them, finding it hard to fathom what it could be. But if I no longer desire a future with them, my love has ended. I may have nothing more to say about it than that.

The want to know how things turn out—out of fear of how they could—distorts the desires of lovers by demanding full and final answers about an experience that teaches us, constantly, how much more there is to learn. Ethical imperatives to know better, to prepare for the future, and to mitigate vulnerabilities as best we can thus run against the desires of lovers, both defied by the particularity of the beloved. If it matters that I love this person and not another, I can't secure myself against changes in them and differences between how I know them now and who they will become in time. Lovers desire their beloveds without knowing exactly what they're desiring.

We also desire, sometimes, without knowing exactly why. We might imagine "why" is a good question for our more philosophical man, or for a philosopher, at least, seeking reasons for what they feel and see. But their projects, too, can falter at the uncertainties of love in time, and especially the uncertainties that matter to lovers. Lovers care whether love continues or ends, as we've seen. They also have little control over when and how either might happen. Let's turn now to how that shapes accounts of love, both philosophical accounts and lovers' own.

◉ 2 ◉
Accounting for Love

Anne Carson begins her first book, on love, with a recounting of Kafka's story of a philosopher struggling to fulfill his desires. The story is about children spinning tops. Carson tells us that it is about "a philosopher who spends his spare time around children so he can grab their tops in spin."[1] "To catch a top still spinning," she continues, "makes him happy for a moment in his belief 'that the understanding of any detail, that of a spinning top for instance, was sufficient for the understanding of all things.'" He seems to believe that catching a top would allow or constitute some form of understanding, some knowledge grasped and held. He is, of course, disappointed. Catching a top in spin is not a way to hold a spinning top; it is a way to hold a top that was just spinning until you grabbed it. It is also a way to ruin a child's game.

Kafka's philosopher seems bad at observing, inquiring, and desiring. He doesn't play the right role in the scene from any view, and he doesn't play what roles he takes on very well. He seems strange for spending his time lingering around children, waiting for them to play with tops. He ruins their game. He ruins it for the desire of something that cannot be obtained by his actions, or perhaps by any others. And he does it all on the premise that grasping a spinning top would be to hold a mere "detail," but that he—more than others—understands the significance of details for the understanding of all things. That last part seems to be his contribution to the story as a philosopher: the ability to turn the understanding of a detail into the understanding of all things. This is a strange idea in itself, and one we might imagine to be the primary strangeness of the story if not for the more glaring absurdity of a philosopher running after tops, or the even stranger moments of his excitement as "top-spinning preparations begin among the children." Carson tells us that this is a story "about the delight we take in metaphor":

> A meaning spins, remaining upright on an axis of normalcy aligned with the conventions of connotation and denotation, and yet, to spin is not normal, and to dissemble normal uprightness by means of this fantastic motion is impertinent.[2]

It is, for Carson, a story about the relation between what is normal and what is not, and the way we seek understanding through the impertinence of rendering things less stable than they might have seemed before—or in these lines, the inverse, finding the desire to understand in the impertinence of unstable things. It is also a story about loving well and loving badly: about self-defeating desires, like the philosopher's to grasp the spinning top, and necessarily unrequited desires, like the "lover's aim" to run after the beloved, "to be running breathlessly, but not yet arrived," which is "itself delightful." It is in this way a story about love and time, and the mistakes of inquiry and understanding between them. It is about the hope in preparations for watching something one wants to understand, and the "nausea" at ruining it as one tries to grasp it fully.[3] It is about not knowing what role you play at each moment in the preparation, duration, or end, or of not knowing what moment you occupy in the story at all. It is a story about a philosopher causing a premature end to a delightful scene, and a man who can't tell what to do with a beginning except to cause an ending.

Finding oneself in love can seem, at times, closer to being a top in spin than the philosopher wanting to catch it. Love can be a kind of "fantastic motion," motivating actions, emotions, and behaviors we otherwise couldn't or wouldn't get off the ground, while simultaneously seeming more stable and even normal than anything else in view. We do things because of love without any other way to justify our actions, and we love people without being able to explain why our lives, sometimes suddenly, revolve around them. The desire to understand love might come from delight in its impertinent stability or a need to make sense of its experience where it makes the world seem to spin. We have, after all, questions about our lives that it seems right and responsible to want to answer: whether we're living as we should, doing the best we can with what we have, and spending our time and energy on the right people and things. Where love absorbs and directs our lives, it seems reasonable to want to understand it better, even grasp it fully, to answer these and other concerns.

Many philosophical accounts of love seek a definition of the term by which we could convince each other, and ourselves, whether we're getting love right: whether we're loving the right people and things, and whether we're loving them well. Others argue for the impossibility of such a project, taking love as a key example of how ethical arguments aimed at "reasons or proofs" for how we should live are viciously circular and thus doomed to incoherence.[4] To determine whom and how one should love, the argument goes, requires a determination of what is worth loving, but the criteria for what is worth loving are determined by what we love. The definition turns back on itself, and the philosopher finds himself going in circles. A definition that could tell us whether we're getting love "right" on some secure, rational foundation remains, on this view, always out of reach.

If this is right, I think the failure is revealing—and consonant with many experiences of love. It suggests a significant lack of rational control over how one's love is directed, and when or whether it begins or ends. If I cannot find a rational basis for love without some recourse to my existing desires, I am vulnerable to what and whom I find myself desiring. I may find myself loving someone with whom I otherwise think I shouldn't be involved, or find myself unable to muster even minimal affection for someone to whom I think I should be devoted. I may chase after definitions of whom I should love precisely because I find myself loving or not loving in these ways, and hope to convince myself to love correctly—or convince myself I already am. But like the philosopher going in circles to define what is worth loving, my efforts to secure a definition of whom I should or shouldn't love run up against the limits of reason to change how I feel. I cannot convince myself to love or stop loving what I don't already as I can be convinced in an argument to believe other than I had before. My problem, then, is not to find a definition of love to resolve such an argument, to reason my way to a convincingly secure, rational answer, but to account for my loves, to myself and others, and consider concerns about them from there. The failure to define love from rational foundations only goes so far—there are other accounts of love to give beyond such circularities.

This is a book about the kinds of accounts we can give when we stop trying to define love from secure, rational foundations or toward security by other means and consider instead the way we experience love in time, extending indeterminately into an unknown future. Love can seem to defy the vulnerabilities of finitude and connect us to something more stable, continuous, and perfect—even infinite—than the limitations of a finite world usually afford. And where it seems more precarious, it is easy to imagine our task is to establish it more securely: to define it by reason, duty, commitment, or otherwise against the possibility of change. But such efforts mistake the significance of love's indeterminacy to lovers, as we saw in the previous chapter. They will also fail, and fail to describe many aspects of love in the process, as I'll consider here.

My focus in this chapter is on how attempts to define love can falter at our vulnerability to our own desires and suggest as they do certain contours of the experience of love neglected by many attempts at definition: the limits of rational control over our loves; the challenges of finding ourselves loving against the expectations of our communities, loved ones, and even ourselves; and the desire to account for our loves even without such motivations to do so, as we try to understand ourselves better and share who we are with others, including the people we love. Set apart from the philosopher's chase after definitions, efforts to understand our loves better, describe them well, and reason about them can be practices of accounting for what we experience in love. As such they are significantly *social* practices, defining and defined by social norms. They are negotiated in relationships, where participants encounter both the possibilities and limits of what they can account for. These practices are often strained, but not by the demands of rational foundations and universal definitions. They are strained as relationships are strained: by what we owe people, including ourselves; how well we understand and agree with others about what is due; and how well we are able to provide it. But they are also joyful, as relationships are joyful: not as a delight in knowledge grasped and held but in sharing how we feel running after our beloveds and discovering that others looking on may approve of the chase, and even take joy themselves in seeing us pursue it.

NEEDING REASONS

An account of love—by which I mean, for the moment, the broadest sense of an effort to describe what it is to love and be loved, what it could be, or what it should be—could aim to answer many questions, or none. "None" is an impertinent aim, as Carson might say, but it may also be the right one if we are warned by the philosopher in Kafka's story not to overdetermine our inquiries before they begin. "Suppression of impertinence," after all, "is not the lover's aim," Carson tells us. "Nor can I believe this philosopher really runs after understanding. Rather, he has become a philosopher (that is, one whose profession is to delight in understanding) in order to furnish himself with pretexts for running after tops."[5] This is a gentle reading, even a lovely one, as it casts the philosopher in a sweeter light and obscures the rest of the scene—except with the suggestion of "pretext." A pretext implies an audience, and perhaps an audience skeptical of what the pretext seeks to justify or excuse. And here we encounter the aim of many accounts of love, which are concerned in different ways with what can be justified or excused, and what reasons can be provided to do so. But do we need reasons—or even a pretext—to justify our loves? In what circumstances, in response to what questions, posed by whom?

One of the most common reasons given for love is the value of the beloved, as we've considered at some length in the previous chapter. For the ancient Greeks, erotic love was defined as the appropriate response to the value of the beloved, something we should feel when we encounter people and things of great value and should not when we encounter people and things without significant goods. Such a definition of love is helpful for a range of questions and concerns: we can assess whether loving this person and not another will be worth our time and energy, if value is the reason for love in this way. We might worry, like Lysias, whether we'll regret loving them when our view of them is no longer colored by desire, but our understanding of the risk of regret is clearly defined in terms of their value.

There are also circumstances in which the things we choose to run after in love seem worthy of our pursuit, but their pursuit conflicts with the pursuit of other things, takes us to places we don't want to go, or leads us away from places we want to be. Love takes time and energy. It absorbs us with its demands as well as its delights. It keeps us from other things that could do the same. Sometimes the demands and delights of our loves conflict with each other. Perhaps that takes the simple form of a conflict in time: two friends I want to be with at the same moment; multiple children in need of the attention of the same parent; or infatuations with two new acquaintances, each of whom I would like to get to know better, over many hours, which cannot be spent with them both. Perhaps it takes the form of a conflict of aspirations: different dreams of who to become, how to live, or what to devote myself to that cannot be pursued simultaneously as each is wholly encompassing of my life or personality. It might take the form of a conflict of commitment, as when I want to have a relationship of special priority to one person and to another, but the terms of the relationship I want can't allow its pursuit with more than one. This is far from an exhaustive list.

Some of these conflicts might be described in terms of the classical understanding of tragedy, a conflict among goods in which a person must choose—and act—against some insofar as they pursue any. Many philosophers have thought these situations worth running after, or watching, at least, to understand the challenges posed by our finite and resultingly messy lives, constrained by time and space and frustrated by overlapping needs and desires. Others have found the mess repulsive, its supposed intractability a sign of insufficient reasoning and a weak understanding of the moral order. Martha Nussbaum cites the rejection of tragedy to the very "beginning of moral philosophy," when "Socrates tells Euthyphro (himself enmeshed, we might think, in just such a dilemma) that stories depicting the collisions of competing claims of right are repugnant to reason."[6] With a clearer understanding of the right, the good, and the logical relations between them, the argument goes, the intractable conflicts of tragedy could be resolved. Apparently competing claims could be put in order, and the choice against one for another could be seen as correct and thus a "guilt-free course."[7] A person might be sad that they had to act against one good for another, but they would not be blameworthy for it. Their sadness should fade, or at least not interfere with a reasoned judgment of the right course of action.

The kinds of conflicts among loves I have mentioned seem relatively susceptible to the criticism that a more mature and rational understanding would allow their resolution. Surely a decent philosopher should be able to figure out which of two friends to spend time with and be able to justify the decline or omission of one invitation on some reasonable grounds. And surely a decently mature person, philosopher or not, should be able to recognize their sadness at missing the one friend for the other as something far from tragic, at least in the stronger sense of a situation in which you have been constrained by circumstance to act *unethically* against one good for the sake of another. This view might amount to the response that these aren't tragedies at all, because the demand of each desire is not the kind of good that is really so bad to have to choose against.

I could add details to the example that might make it more compelling as a tragic case, such as being *needed* by each friend in some way: maybe one has lost a loved one in recent days, and the other their livelihood, and each is in need of consolation, care, and company. Maybe I am uniquely positioned in each of their lives to provide these things, by their own reports. To spend time with one would be to leave the other alone and without aid, which in their situations could be a form of harm, or at least an exacerbation of it.

Critics of tragedy from Socrates onward might respond that the situation is still not intractable, it is just in need of a better account of love: what is worth loving, what loves are more important than others, what love entails and requires, and what entailments and requirements are more important than others, in turn. Some might respond that what is needed is a better account of love among other things: love's relation to obligation, duty, or desert, or the ordering of loves in relation to other demands on our time and effort. This second approach is likely what makes the revised version of the example more compelling: instead of being a conflict between desires to be with friends, it becomes a conflict between needs and the care they demand in response. A common account of love places such demands in the realm of obligation or duty and outside the realm of desirous love, either by describing two different forms of love or by describing one as love and the other as something else: infatuation, desire, or selfishness, on the one side, as opposed to a "true" love of caring attention; or moral duty, obligation, or self-giving, on the other, as opposed to a desirous love, worthy, perhaps, of the unqualified name but not of moral priority. The latter set of relations—duty, obligation, and self-giving—are often ordered as more important, with further criteria pursued to determine which duties and obligations are more important than others, which needs are more urgent or more worthy of care, and which opportunities to provide for a person in need should be pursued over others.

This might be what we want from an account of love: a framework for determining what to pursue when what appear to be loves appear to conflict, that could show us a guilt-free course of action by helping us put our loves in order and put love in its place in a larger order of things. Our interest in such a framework could come from the experience of conflicts among loves or its anticipation. Or it might come from a belief in the existence of a correct order of loves beyond one's experience. We might be interested in this sense in the nature of love on the idea that to grasp its nature would be to know the answers to questions of what is worthy of love and to what degrees, and what love is worth in an order of other relations. We might also be interested in valuable things, and offer an account of love as a description of our recognition of their value. Both of these approaches might follow in the tradition of Kafka's philosopher running after tops, or more flatteringly, of Socrates asking about the nature of piety to inquire into Euthyphro's tangled explanation of his actions. They do not seek an understanding of what is normal and what is not, or a description of situations in love that make the world seem to spin. They seek an understanding of love or the value of the beloved—or one in terms of the other—that might be used to resolve situations of conflict, offering an answer and not merely a pretext to questions of what we should love and how, what is worth loving, and what loves are more worthy than others.

It may not be surprising, then, that discussions of love in Anglo-American philosophy over the last few decades have often resembled a version of the Euthyphro problem.[8] Socrates's famous dilemma, posed to the dense and self-righteous Euthyphro and met with confusion and an abrupt escape, is arranged as a question of the direction of the defining relation between its two terms. "Just consider," Socrates says, "is that which is holy loved by the gods because it is holy, or is it holy because it is loved by the gods?"[9] The "love-related version of the dilemma goes something like this," as Massimo Piggliucci summarized it in Anglo-American philosophy: "is what we love of value to us because we love it, or do we love it because it has value?"[10] In place of the gods and the holy, *lovers* and the *value of the beloved* comprise the terms of this dilemma, with similar questions of relation. Is value the reason for love, or the result of it? Is love an appraisal of value, or is the value of the beloved bestowed by the lover?[11]

A Euthyphro Problem, One Way or Another

The original terms of the Euthyphro dilemma—*the holy* and *the gods*—are picked out by Socrates from Euthyphro's fumbling through different explanations for why he is sure that he is pursuing the right course in bringing charges against his father. The case is a sad one. A day laborer, unnamed, was working on their family's land when he got into a disagreement with an enslaved worker, also unnamed, and killed him. Euthyphro's father bound the laborer and threw him into a ditch while awaiting word from a religious adviser in Athens about what to do. The laborer died from exposure, hunger, and thirst before word was received. Euthyphro sees Socrates outside the courthouse as he is on his way to prosecute his father for the murder of the laborer, despite other family members' objections that "it is unholy for a son to prosecute his father for murder," especially when the victim was not another relative. Their concerns represent the prevailing understandings of piety and holiness at the time, but Euthyphro insists to Socrates that this only "shows how little they know what the divine law is in regards to holiness and unholiness."[12]

Socrates asks an interesting question in response: "Do you think your knowledge about divine laws and holiness and unholiness is so exact that, when the facts are as you say, you are not afraid of doing something unholy yourself in prosecuting your father for murder?" In response to a complex situation in which two lives have been lost, Euthyphro's father's life may now be at stake, and Euthyphro's relations to his family are crucially at stake as well, Socrates asks after the *exactness* of Euthyphro's knowledge. And he wants this knowledge in the form of exact *definitions*, not knowledge, say, of what to do in this case, or how to discuss it further with his concerned relatives. Euthyphro responds with pomposity and almost comical self-distinction: "I should be of no use, Socrates, and Euthyphro would be in no way different from other men, if I did not have exact knowledge about all such things."[13]

His role in the dialogue as an arrogant braggart is secure, though any articulation of this "exact knowledge" is much less so.

Euthyphro continues to try to articulate his knowledge and Socrates continues to find holes in his reasoning at every turn—or to turn him around in the conversation so much that every line of reasoning becomes the outline of one. The conversation circles the definition of holiness, the standards for which are determined by Socrates through his objections to Euthyphro's claims. One standard made apparent is the insistence on definition itself: that to have knowledge of holiness, as Euthyphro insists he has, is to have knowledge of the *definition* of holiness, of what holiness *is*. Euthyphro first tries to define holiness by pointing to his actions that day and explaining them a bit further, but Socrates objects that a definition must be general, and not made up of examples. Euthyphro then tries to explain holiness and unholiness in terms of what the gods love. Socrates rejects these attempts in a few ways, including the prospect that the gods disagree, which would render some things both holy and unholy if they were loved by some gods and hated by others.[14]

We are shown in this discussion that for Socrates, at least—or at least here—definitions are best when they can reduce our messy problems into measurable things, specifically things that can be weighed and measured against each other to get an answer about which there cannot be disagreement. "Let us look at it in this way," Socrates says to Euthyphro. "If you and I were to disagree about number, for instance, which of two numbers were greater, would the disagreement about these matters make us enemies and make us angry with each other, or should we not quickly settle it by resorting to arithmetic?"[15] "Of course we should," Euthyphro replies, and Socrates continues with other examples, suggesting that what can be counted or measured allows us to settle our differences "without becoming enemies." Other ideas, like "right and wrong, and noble and disgraceful, and good and bad," however, are "the questions about which you and I and other people become enemies... because we differ about them and cannot reach any satisfactory agreement."[16] Holiness and unholiness are the sorts of ideas about which you and I can disagree, as can the gods, and thus a definition dependent on their agreement is too unstable to be a ready resolution to much of anything. If only there was a measurable standard, Socrates implies—a way of counting or weighing, adding things up and comparing totals, to resolve something as difficult as Euthyphro's conflict with his family and community about how to respond to the laborer's death.

Euthyphro next adapts his definition with a provision of divine agreement, but Socrates objects again, arguing that identifying what is loved is to identify something that has happened to it, not to identify what it *is*. He makes the analogy to something "carried," "led," or "seen," which is not defined by these descriptions.[17] Being "carried" is what is happening to the carried thing, not a definition of it; likewise with "led," "seen," or "loved." It might help to pick out which of some set of things you are discussing, but it does not define the thing indicated. If the holy is "what the gods love," Socrates insists, we still do not know what it *is*. We might know *why* it is holy in the sense of how it *became* holy, but we are not closer, by Socrates's standards, to a definition of the thing itself. Thus the famous dilemma of whether "that which is holy [is] loved by the gods because it is holy, or [whether it is] holy because it is loved by the gods" doesn't lead to the right kind of definition. Its apparent symmetry is actually a circle, and a vicious one, Socrates suggests. "So, if you please, do not hide it from me," Socrates says to Euthyphro after these many rounds of attempts at definition, "but begin over again and tell me what holiness is, no matter whether it is loved by the gods or anything else happens to it."[18] Euthyphro responds wearily: "But Socrates, I do not know how to say what I mean. For whatever statement we advance, somehow or other it moves about and won't stay where we put it."

What could it mean to treat love in this way, to look for a definition that stays where we put it? Is this what philosophers are looking for when conversations about love come to resemble a Euthyphro dilemma? Or are they looking for stories of becoming and happening: of how things come to be loved, or how love comes to occur? As Socrates suggests, accounts of becoming and happening may not give us the knowledge we need to resolve complicated cases, to know how to reach satisfactory agreement and not "become enemies" over conflicting claims. But the knowledge he seeks might not help us much either. Socrates moves quickly from the immediate problems of the story to definitions of holiness and unholiness, perhaps because of Euthyphro's insistence on his knowledge of them or maybe for reasons of his own. He doesn't approach the tragedy at the heart of the case after its initial introduction, nor the question of what, in fact, Euthyphro should do. The dialogue does not seek to resolve these questions; it seeks a definition of holiness that might be applied to other cases, notably Socrates's own. And it reveals, in so many revolutions, the difficulty of defining what something *is* without succumbing to circularities.

One difference between the Euthyphro dilemma and its "love-related version" in recent Anglo-American philosophy is that the latter tends to take up its topic with an eye toward more practical questions. Socrates could have done the same, and perhaps spared Euthyphro from some of his own foolishness. But as Harry Frankfurt describes of ancient Greek philosophers more generally, their inquiries "began in wonder" without such practical aims.[19] "They were eager to overcome their ignorance," he writes, "but that was not because they thought they needed the information."[20] They seek instead "to dispel their initial surprise that things are as they are, by developing a reasoned understanding of why it would be unnatural—or even impossible—for things to be any other way." In these terms, Euthyphro is doing something, in testifying against his father, that surprises Socrates. It is surprising because it goes against what Socrates expects of a son. He begins his inquiry toward the resolution of his surprise, so that it might become clear that the way things are is only to be expected.

But what Euthyphro is doing is not just surprising. It is, according to the understanding of those around him, wrong. Socrates's surprise registers as much, as does Euthyphro's testimony to his other family members' disapproval. These are people to whom Euthyphro is accountable, or so we might imagine. But he insists on his accountability only to the truth, in the form of a definition of holiness, or justice, or piety (the terms, as well as their definitions, don't stay where he puts them). To look for a true definition of holiness might be enough for Euthyphro, then, and enough for Socrates, but it isn't clear what it offers to the family at home, concerned for their loved one who may yet be tried and executed for murder—not to mention the families of the murdered. And perhaps that's just as well, Socrates seems to be saying, both in his direction of the dialogue and later in the *Apology*. Truth should triumph over social convention, and the feelings of a murderer's loved ones shouldn't be a reason to exempt him from prosecution. But what would Euthyphro's knowledge of the truth, were he to succeed in articulating it, mean to Euthyphro's family? Does he ever intend to explain his "exact knowledge" to them, and does it matter if he can convince them he's right? Would his efforts to explain himself to Socrates be aided, even, by considering their concerns? The dialogue's tangle in definitions ignores the relationships in which Euthyphro must explain himself, and the kinds of reasons he needs to justify his actions within them. Instead, he goes to great pains to assert his knowledge to the one character in the story who has no clear claim on him to ask, except as a favor to help in his own case. The relationships in which Euthyphro must account for his actions are all out of view, and it is hard to imagine how what we witness could help in those conversations.

The "love-related version" of the dilemma should not ignore such relationships, and might be better framed by attending to them than by seeking definitions that "stay where you put them." The value of the beloved is a particularly beguiling term for such definitions, a compelling pretense for loves we want to convince others, and ourselves, we are right to pursue. It is a currency of conversations in which we are called to account for our loves or in which we seek to do so. But it often fails as a convincing reason for love, as I'll suggest in the next section, both because it is hard to measure and because we so often love people we cannot prove to others are so great. They are great to us, and that might be enough—though it would hardly satisfy Socrates.

Finding Ourselves Loving

An account of love as a response to the value of the beloved seems to offer something very useful for a range of questions we might ask or be asked in trying to love well and resolve conflicts among the ways our loves direct us. If love is based on something we assess, we might simply reassess when love is called into question. If I love you because of your valuable qualities and characteristics—your good humor, intelligence, and physical beauty, say—then if I am asked about my love, I can refer to these qualities, reassess them, and resolve the matter one way or the other. I could even confirm my assessments with a friend, who might assure me that you still have all of those qualities, and maybe even have them in greater quantity, or better, more mature versions of them than when my love began. I might then assess them in relation to other things, and assure myself I still love the best thing the most, and otherwise love proportionately to how much I value each of my beloveds. These assessments are much messier, of course, than a weighing or measuring of mass or distance, as our extraordinary vocabularies for describing each other's merits and mediocrities suggest. They are also things about which reasonable people can disagree, which could become a problem. Still, a definition of love as a response to value seems to offer a concrete path to someone questioning their loves or being questioned about them.

But love doesn't seem to work this way at all, as we've seen. We sometimes love people we assess, initially and continuously, not to be particularly great in many important ways. We love people who seem strange to love given other things we value. We discover that people we love are not who we thought they were, or that they've changed in ways we find disappointing or disconcerting, and yet our loves endure. Many of these loves seem worthy of the name—and worthy, where called into question, of affirmation—but wouldn't stand to tests of reassessment. Testing might instead inspire further doubt: doubt in our assessments of our beloveds, our assessments of people generally, and our capacity for assessment at all, including the simple and arresting questions of whether we really know what we're looking for, and whether we'd know it when we see it.

Moments of doubt about whether we love the right people or things reveal an incoherence in the question they pose, or that provoked them. We lack the possibility of an answer not because it's hard to measure or name the value of our beloveds—though it may be—but because it's hard to know what point we'd be making if we could. If I tell you that I'm going to break things off with the person I've been dating as I no longer love him and you say, "but he's so kind!" are you trying to persuade me that I *should* love him because of this? What can you say if I tell you that it doesn't matter, or confide that while I may want it to matter, and even previously thought it did, I nonetheless find myself no longer in love? I might join you in some regret that a relationship with such a kind man didn't work out, but it won't compel me to love him if, in fact, I don't. You can tell me plenty of other great things about him and I might agree with your assessments but still find myself unmoved. I might admire him more than ever, but still not love him. I might want to love him because of how much I admire him, and still find these many reasons move me not at all—or only to greater regret about how in fact I do feel.

I may want reasons for love to answer questions and doubts about it, but it isn't clear what I can do with reasons like the value of my beloved to change how I feel. Love seems beyond the force of reasons, to some extent, and perhaps beyond rational control altogether. For Harry Frankfurt, this is because we are not compelled by reasons to love at all, but compelled by love to do other things, including valuing the things that make our beloveds themselves. He inverts what he calls the "common view" of love in this way, which he defines as an account in which we imagine the value of the beloved to be the reason for love: the reason our loves begin, what "captivates us and turns us into lovers," and also the reason our loves continue, and the reason that they should. "We begin loving the things that we love because we are struck by their value," we think, "and we continue to love them for the sake of their value."[21] We believe our love is dependent on this value, too: that "if we did not find the beloved valuable, we would not love it." Hence the promise of reassurance by reassessment, on this "common view" of love, for a reasoned conclusion that we do in fact love whom we should. But the search for reasons will be disappointing. We will find little to persuade us, if plenty to say. And we confuse ourselves with the ambition in ways that sow dissatisfaction and doubt precisely at moments we most need "clarity and confidence" in what and whom we love.

The value of the beloved is not a compelling reason for love to resolve very many questions and concerns, Frankfurt argues, because it only expresses what the lover values, not what the lover *should* value according to standards beyond themselves. I think this still allows it to be a useful part of practices of accounting for love, as I'll discuss further in a moment. But for Frankfurt, it is a vicious circularity that suggests a broad incoherence to most projects of accounting for love. The circularity is similar to the one Euthyphro encounters in his attempt to define holiness: the beloved is valuable to the lover because the lover loves them. They *became* valuable to the lover because of their love, but we don't know whether they *are* valuable by a standard beyond this story of becoming and happening. Frankfurt argues against the "common view" of love in this way as an iteration of his critique of common methods of moral inquiry into the question of how we should live. That question, he writes, is "both ultimate and preliminary," but this description already suggests the circularity of the inquiry by which he will condemn it.[22] Let us consider the question directly before turning to how it defines his account of love, and mine.

Most people seem to have at least some answers to the question of how we should live ready to hand. There are things we think are right or wrong, worthwhile or wastes of time, generally of interest or generally uninteresting. We think we should live in some accord with these ideas and define what we should do at different turns on their basis. But we may also have the modest sense that these views are personally preferential, the things *I* like or want to do and not a systematic answer to the question of how one should live most generally. I might defer to Socrates, then, in the search for a universal or categorical answer, a definition that goes beyond what seems right or good in just my case. Or I might find others' answers disappointing along these lines: an expression of what *they* think one should do, which might be good for them, but isn't the answer for me. I don't want them to impose their preferences on me with a veneer of philosophical generality. I may begin a systemic inquiry into the question precisely because I don't want others' answers imposed on me as my own.

Suppose, for example, that you think the way we should live is by trying to be as healthy as possible. I ask you for reasons to support your claim, skeptical that while you may care a lot about your health, I shouldn't have to care about mine. You might reply that trying to be healthy allows you to minimize pain and extend your life as long as possible. But perhaps I'm not so worried about pain or the extension of life, or at least not nearly as worried about these things as I am about something else: caring for my family, say, or pursuing pleasures that in fact might be very costly to my health. What can you say then? At best—or so Frankfurt would argue—you can appeal to the things I've said I care about, trying to show me that if I care about my family, for instance, I should care about being around for them as long as possible, and thus should care about my health. That might convince me that health is among the things I should care about *because* I care about my family, but you haven't dislodged my care for my family as an ultimate concern in my life. That care, in this example, specifies at least part of my answer for how I should live: in devotion to my family, with other specifications of how I should live following from that. But this is an answer to how *I* should live, based on what *I* care about, revealed by my objections to how you think you should live. I lack reasons for my answer as you did for yours. "The trouble here is a rather obvious sort of circularity," Frankfurt writes. "In order for a person to be able even to conceive and to initiate an inquiry into how to live, he must already have settled upon the judgments at which the inquiry aims."[23]

What we need is not an answer to the question of how we should live, Frankfurt argues, but an answer to "the *factual* question of what [a person] actually *does* care about":

> The pan-rationalist fantasy of demonstrating—from the ground up— how we have most reason to live is incoherent and must be abandoned. It is not the factual question about caring that misses the point, but the normative one. If we are to resolve our difficulties and hesitations in settling upon a way to live, what we need most fundamentally is not reasons or proofs. It is clarity and confidence.[24]

Clarity and confidence in what we care about is not simply the best we can do in the absence of an "exhaustively rational warrant" for how we should live, in Frankfurt's view.[25] His argument responds to the incoherence of the normative inquiry as he identifies it, but it aims to describe nothing less than the structure of the will. The things we care about, in Frankfurt's definition, direct our lives: we are "devoted" to them, "invested" in them, dedicated to their well-being or successful pursuit because we find our wills oriented toward them in this way, and thus we will do the things that care for them requires.[26]

Love, for Frankfurt, is a species of care, so his argument for the importance of what we care about is also his account of love.[27] We cannot ask whom we should love as we cannot ask how we should live, expecting to find an "exhaustively rational warrant" for an answer. We would find ourselves entangled in the same circularities we encounter in the larger ethical question, grasping at our own answers as the criteria for assessing any. Thus we do not love because we have reason to do so, and we cannot provide reasons for love that can justify it "from the ground up." But unlike our moral inquiries into the question of how we should live, we seem much less worried about the lack of reasons for our loves—or so Frankfurt argues from the example of the love of parents for their children. We do not take parents to be irrational because they cannot justify their love for their children, and to challenge a parent to justify their love would seem very strange. The answer "because they're my child" seems like reason enough—and any further questions, which would likely be unanswerable by the parent, would suggest not the parent's unreasonableness but the inquirer's. Parental love thus displays the problem with value-responsive accounts of love particularly well, in Frankfurt's view. Children are valuable to their parents, but that value is not the reason their parents love them nor a condition on which that love is dependent.

Parental love is often described as "unconditional," steady through changes in the child and persistent beyond much more than we might think we could tolerate in other relationships. But where in other loves we might name value, however mistakenly, as the reason for love, with parental love it seems strange to tell a story of coming to love a child because of their value, or of persisting in love because of their extraordinary merit or worth. "I can declare with unequivocal confidence," Frankfurt writes, "that I do not love my children because I am aware of some value that inheres in them independent of my love for them. The fact is that I loved them even before they were born—before I had any especially relevant information about their personal characteristics or their particular merits and virtues."[28] He did know, of course, that they were *his children*, which we might imagine to be especially relevant indeed. They are particular people, particular to him, instead of some people in a line of interchangeable candidates for love waiting to be assessed. Frankfurt emphasizes the lack of assessment here more than their particularity, or the relationship to him by which he can identify them "even before they are born"—issues we'll return to shortly. But his emphasis seems aimed at reinforcing his argument against reasons for love, defined by value or otherwise: we do not love people because of their value, as we do not love on the basis of reasons at all. Our beloveds make things valuable to us, including, perhaps most significantly, themselves.

Loving situates us in a world of reasons, but our loves are not themselves rationally warranted, in Frankfurt's view. We do not love because we have reason to love; our loves create reasons to do other things. Indeed, they may create reasons to do things that are profoundly inconvenient, dangerous, or otherwise unappealing, but we find ourselves doing them because of what we care about. "The capacity to rule does not belong uniquely to reason," Frankfurt writes. "There are ruling passions as well."²⁹ Our experience of this "rule" by what we care about is what Frankfurt calls "volitional necessity," the constraint of the will to do or not do, even where we might see every reason to do otherwise. To act against someone we love, for example, may be simply impossible for us to will ourselves to do. This is not because we can't see a way to accomplish the relevant task or reasons why we should, in a given circumstance, but because we cannot will ourselves to do so.³⁰ Similarly, the needs of someone we love may direct us to do something we otherwise could not will ourselves to do, such as acting against a law or principle we thought we could never violate. I find myself able to act in this way—I find myself *having* to—for someone I love because in fact I care about the principle less than the person. My love for the person gives me reasons to act against the principle, Frankfurt would say. But these are reasons particular to me, not "exhaustively rational warrants" that apply also to others. I may instead see significant rational warrant *not* to act against the law or principle and still find myself unable to do otherwise because of my love for the person.

Consider Abraham hearing God's call to sacrifice his son Isaac—a very different example of parental love than Frankfurt's testimony to his own.³¹ It is a terrifying story. Isaac doesn't die, but the horror of Abraham's willingness to sacrifice him suggests how vulnerability can inflict something akin to wounds even when left unrealized in its worst form. It is also a story of unknowing, filled with silence: Abraham says nothing in response to God's command. Abraham and Isaac depart without word to Sarah. Isaac makes the journey seemingly unaware of his father's intentions. Abraham binds him on the altar without any exchange between them. The silence between father and son is broken only once in the journey by Isaac's single question to Abraham: "Here are the firestone and the wood, but where is the sheep for the burnt offering?"³² It isn't clear if this is an oblique expression of fear or simply confusion about where they will get the sheep; Abraham's response, that God will "see to the sheep," is followed only by the description that they keep walking.³³

God intervenes just as Abraham is about to bring the blade to Isaac's neck, sparing his son after an ultimate test of faith.³⁴ But part of what many find fascinating, inspiring, and deeply troubling in the story is how Abraham could bring himself to raise his hand in the first place, to pick up the blade, to take Isaac up Mount Moriah, or even to set out on the journey with any intent to heed God's call. For many, Abraham's actions might be simply impossible, their love of their child overwhelming their will even to follow the instruction of God. To some readers, then, what makes Abraham an exemplar of faith is that his relationship to God overrides even the necessities of his love for his son.[35] To others, this makes him a monster, a failure as both a father and a creation of God.

Whether you find Abraham's actions exemplary or horrendous, they do not seem to be the product of *reasons*. He does not reason his way to compliance with God's command. The silence among Abraham, Isaac, and Sarah amplifies the lack of reasoning; there isn't even conversation. I'm not sure what could be said, but I find it more haunting to carry on without saying anything. Instead, the story seems to be about what Abraham cares about, and what he's able to will himself to do because of what he cares about. He doesn't *decide* on his overriding care but finds it revealed by his actions: a love of God that directs him to act, even against another great love.[36]

In my discussion thus far, I have sometimes used the somewhat strange construction "to find oneself loving." In various examples, I have "found myself" loving one person or another, or not loving someone I have plenty of reasons to love. Abraham "finds himself" following God's command, in this sense, relieved only by God's own interruption of the act. We don't know if this surprises Abraham or horrifies him, or if he would have been more surprised or more horrified to find he couldn't follow God's command, but whatever his response, he discovers something in the test. This sense of discovery is one important implication of understanding what we care about to impose an unreasoned necessity. I can discover my feelings as a kind of fact, which might help me understand myself better, or at least describe myself better, even if I cannot understand why I am as I find myself to be. I also think it describes many experiences of love very well. I find myself loving or not loving, sometimes contrary to how I might like to find I feel. I love people it would be much easier not to love, and I stop loving people I wish I could continue to love. Relationships sometimes end with regret. They also continue at great cost to lovers who might well choose otherwise were love their choice to make. But I cannot decide to love someone or stop loving them as I decide to hire or fire someone for a job, and I cannot be compelled to love someone as I can be compelled to believe it is raining by evidence of precipitation. I find myself loving, sometimes to my great surprise—and inconvenience, disadvantage, disappointment, and worse.

Reasoning About Love

If I cannot find reasons for love that would justify it "from the ground up," that tell me whom I should love without any appeal to what and whom I already do, I am vulnerable to my own desires. I may find myself loving someone who is harmful to me or to other people I love. I may find myself with loves that conflict with each other in other ways, as in the examples with which I began. I am also vulnerable to my loves changing without my permission, including beginning at times I didn't intend and ending when I might have liked them to continue. Without exhaustive reasons love *should* begin, continue, end, or be directed toward some person and not another, I am subject, to a significant extent, to how I find myself loving. I am also vulnerable to a problem more tightly entangled with the circularities we've just considered. If I value my beloveds because I love them, how can I tell if I love people who are worthy of my love? What if my loves are badly directed, toward things of little value by any standard other than their value to me? Our time and energy are spent in love, our lives shaped in certain ways and not others. Finitude makes love risky, in a very particular way: we want to use our limited time well, or at least we don't want to use it poorly. Hence I may want to ask whether I love worthy people and things—I still want to know, as I find myself loving, whether I've gotten it right.

We might imagine that the question of worthiness is a question we simply can't ask in light of the circularities of definitions by value we've just considered. Worthiness is an essentially normative question of precisely the kind Frankfurt rejects, asking whether I *should* love this person or thing, given their value, when, for Frankfurt, all I can actually discern is whether I *do*. I may still have a difficult project of discernment, however, as I may not care about the things I think or thought I cared about. We are not always insightful about our desires or transparent to ourselves. Our wills also change, and we do not always realize that they have, particularly if there are reasons we might want to resist the realization. It may be hard for me to see that I've stopped loving someone I've organized my life around loving, for example, in part because I may not want my love to have ended or the disruption it will cause to my life. I may begin to ask questions about whether they are worthy of my love in the hope of finding some convincing evidence that my love should continue. But such evidence cannot change the orientation of my will, Frankfurt would argue. To resolve my unease, I must come to accept how in fact I do feel.

In response to doubts about how we should live or whom we should love, we must identify what and whom we care about and also, Frankfurt argues, identify *with* our loves and cares. He calls such identification "wholeheartedness": when we identify with our cares and endorse them, thinking—as a "second-order care"—that they are the right things to care about.[37] This is surely a pleasant experience, to find ourselves caring about something and wholeheartedly feeling that we should. We might find ourselves, in such circumstances, feeling we are precisely where we should be, doing exactly what we should do. But we do not always identify with our cares so wholeheartedly: we suffer often, and significantly, from self-alienation and other divisions within ourselves. These might come in the form of finding ourselves only half-hearted in caring about something, not quite mustering the sense that we care about it enough to direct ourselves effectively. We might also find that we care about something to significant effect, but we want not to care about it. These are different forms of consternation than the conflicts among loves and cares we considered earlier, in which the demands of something we care about cannot be pursued because of the demands of something else we care about. Here, the conflict is within ourselves. I find myself loving someone I think I shouldn't love, for instance, or I want to love someone and find my love fading, despite very much wishing it would continue. In each case, I have a second-order care—"I want [or want not] to love them"—that is at odds with the first-order care I find myself having. It can be difficult, in these conditions, to pursue anything at all, let alone with "clarity and confidence."

We might turn to the relationships *among* our loves and cares in these circumstances. Our cares give us reasons to do or not do other things, including valuing them as what we should or shouldn't care about, in the circular sense of "should." They give us reasons to value or not value our other cares, as well. And thus we can use our other cares to give us reasons to resist something we find ourselves caring about, to continue caring about someone we find ourselves pulling away from, and otherwise to reason *about* our loves. Suppose I love someone who routinely hurts me, physically or emotionally. I also love myself, which makes me want not to be hurt. My love for myself gives me reasons to stop loving the person who hurts me. These reasons cannot compel me to stop loving or caring, as our loves and cares cannot be compelled by reason. I may find myself still loving my hurtful beloved even after recognizing that my love for myself gives me reasons to stop loving them. I may never stop loving them, and may find that love painful for the rest of my life because I am also directed not to love them by my care for myself. Many have experienced such pain, and I think it is a credit to Frankfurt's account that it can describe that experience clearly—as arational and not irrational, beyond the limits of reason's control instead of a failure of the lover to understand the evident reasons to stop loving.

But there are still things I can do for myself as my love continues. I can remove myself from situations where I would see my hurtful beloved, and they would have a chance to hurt me further. I can cut off communication, and enlist others to help me prevent contact. I can try to focus my mind on the ways they have hurt me, and do, and try not to let myself linger on loving feelings I have for them when they emerge. Some of these measures help me protect myself from further harm regardless of whether I still love the hurtful person, furthering my care for myself over and against my care for them. Some aim to chip away at my love for them, in the hope that by immersing myself in a world in which love for them seems bad, I might, eventually, find myself no longer loving them at all.

I would not be compelled by reason to arrive at this outcome, but I might be able to leverage other loves and cares against my love for this hurtful beloved such that I can protect myself from its worst effects and occupy myself in ways that might help to redirect my will. It might not work. But we can see in this example one way we might reason *about* our loves, despite not having reasons "from the ground up" for or against them. And we could describe the process in terms of value and worth: I can assess the worthiness of my beloveds in response to concerns about my loves not by looking for their inherent value, in qualities and characteristics that might be assessed and admired apart from who they are to me, but by looking for their value to me as people I care about, and *given the other things I care about* as well. I can assess whether this love, by the standards I derive from all of the things I care about, is worthy of my time, attention, and the effect it has and may have on my life. I can leverage my cares against each other in this way to try to resolve my doubts and concerns, not with reference to a sense of value and worthiness generally, but value and worthiness defined by what I care about.

Susan Wolf describes this kind of reasoning about love through the standards of my other loves as an "agape of possibility," drawing on Frankfurt's description in an early paper of "what makes it more suitable for a person to make one object rather than another important to himself." Frankfurt writes,

> It seems that it must be the fact that it is *possible* for him to care about the one and not about the other, or to care about the one in a way which is more important to him than the way in which it is possible for him to care about the other. When a person makes something important to himself, accordingly, the situation resembles an instance of divine *agape* at least in a certain respect. The person does not care about the object because its worthiness commands that he do so. On the other hand, the worthiness of the activity of caring commands that he choose an object which he will be able to care about.[38]

Wolf suggests that Frankfurt opens himself to a very simple objection here, which was never fully addressed as his work on love and care progressed. By advocating only "that we care about what we can," with no recourse to the worthiness of the object defined beyond the individual, he has nothing to say to a person who cares about very bad things indeed. "If our make-up and circumstances are such that we will be more rewarded by caring about helping people rather than hurting them, then we should cultivate our sympathies," Wolf writes. "If, however, we would be more fulfilled by taking up the call of sadism, nothing in Frankfurt's remarks seems to discourage it."[39] But this can't be right, even if we agree that evaluations of worthiness may not effectively sway our wills in many circumstances. We must be able to ask about the worthiness of our beloveds, beyond their value as defined strictly by our own loves and cares, relative only to ourselves. This simply isn't enough for "coherence" with the world, Wolf argues.[40] If our loves are seen as utterly worthless by everyone else, or if our sense of their worthiness challenges credulity in other ways, we will experience them, to some extent, as incoherent. For Frankfurt, the question of worthiness defined by standards beyond one's own loves and cares is incoherent, because we will always have to turn inward for our standards of evaluation anyway. But Wolf is proposing another incoherence in the relation between a person's loves and the world around them, suggesting the "unexciting" thesis that worthiness matters in at least some minimal way. "We want our lives to have some positive relation to things or people or ideas that are valuable independently of us," she writes. Worthiness in this sense may be "a condition that is almost always satisfied without even thinking about it," but we do care about our loves and cares according *with* standards beyond ourselves, even if we don't come to care and love according *to* them.[41]

One might reply in Frankfurt's defense that Wolf is simply naming (or failing to name directly) some set of standards that she and many others may care about for what is worth loving and what isn't: a care of *hers* that directs *her* to assess her loves according to the standards of what she already cares about in the form of these standards of worthiness. But this response ignores the crucial suggestion of her argument that the question of whether we care about the right things cannot be a purely internal, volitional matter. We may sometimes experience our wills as frustratingly resistant to the world beyond ourselves, but we do live in the world, and endless friction between the commands of our loves and their reception and effect in the world is likely unsustainable. It will wear on the possibility of wholeheartedness—our relationship to ourselves—and our relationships with others. It may wear on our epistemic confidence as well, if we find ourselves consistently directed in ways that put us out of step with others' judgments.

The limits of reason to control our loves thus create multiple forms of vulnerability to my own desires. I am vulnerable to confusion about my loves, and forms of misrecognition that make me ineffective or dissatisfied with my pursuit of them. I am also vulnerable to changes in my loves, and feelings of self-alienation where I don't identify with them. And I am vulnerable to whether my loves are directed in ways that make it hard to live in the world. These might be challenges I suffer inescapably, but also challenges I want to take on with the intention of some resolution: a change in my loves, or a change to what in the world as I experience it makes them difficult. My efforts might fail, suggesting one more vulnerability to my own desires: the risk of embattlement, with myself and others, or disappointment, or even some more final defeat—the plot, perhaps, of many classical tragedies.

These vulnerabilities demand and define a measure of humility about how much our reasoning about love can affect our experience of it. We might have many good reasons to love or not love, and philosophers ready to supply more, and still find ourselves loving or not loving against them—or against the reasons of those around us, in ways that make our lives more difficult than they otherwise might be. They also suggest a different realm of concern in the effect of our loves on other people: what and whom we find ourselves loving may make the lives of *others* more difficult, too. We may owe people reasons, or explanations, at least, for how our loves affect them, even if we cannot provide a rational warrant for our loves "from the ground up," or any reasons to justify our loves at all. Abraham was not the only person who might have been surprised, and horrified, to find himself loving God to the point of willingness to sacrifice his son. Isaac and Sarah must have had their own reactions, not least if they were to have asked for an explanation and found Abraham with nothing to say.

REASONING WITH OTHERS

It might be the loves that direct us in difficult or surprising ways for which we feel we need reasons the most—or, like Socrates's surprise at Euthyphro, the loves that are judged by those around us to be wrong. "Wrong" is not a word used very often for loves, but people do call loves "wrong" in cases that violate taboos, for example, such as sexual or romantic desires for close family members or children.[42] Like the judgment that Euthyphro is wrong to testify against one's father, the judgment that someone's love is wrong constitutes and expresses social norms. Some might think it *only* expresses social norms, believing that there are no universal truths about what and whom we should love. Many may disagree, particularly where a larger order of truths about the proper objects of love and the proper love for them is part of what they care about. To many Christians, for example, it would be wrong to love a person more than God, not as a matter of social norms but as a matter of the truth revealed by God in the Bible and the life of Jesus

Christ. To find oneself loving otherwise may be a surprise, but more significantly, it would be a sin, in need of forgiveness and correction. And for many Christians, it would be a sin for anyone to love wrongly in this way, not only for people who share their love of God. Part of what they believe is that one *should* love God, even if one doesn't already, or doesn't already care about doing so.

I think the circularities we've just considered are still useful for someone with such beliefs. What they suggest primarily is not that there is no truth of the matter about what or whom one should love but that we won't be able to ground any version of it in reasons that go "all the way down." Thus we won't be able to convince others, or ourselves, of what or whom we should love without some appeal to the things we already do. That doesn't mean there *isn't* a universal answer, but that we won't be able to find and define it as such in a way that could convince any rational person regardless of what they already care about.[43] My own view is that there isn't a universal answer, but I think the circularity should be meaningful—maybe even more meaningful—to those who think there is. It describes a limit of reason important to anyone who wishes to persuade others, or themselves, to love other than as they do.

Reasoning *about* love, however, still seems possible within the limit defined—and crucial, where we find ourselves loving or not loving in ways we doubt, condemn, or otherwise worry about. This is the crux of the matter: we can doubt, condemn, and worry about loves we find ourselves having even if we don't have an exhaustively rational warrant for what and whom we should love instead. A love can seem wrong because we would like to be other than the person who loves in that way. My society, community, and loved ones may have views of whom and how I should love as well. Their judgment calls my loves into question because I care about them, or care about things their judgment affects. They may not have an exhaustively rational warrant with which to question my loves as I don't have an exhaustively rational warrant with which to justify my loves to them in turn. But there are people I care about—and people who can affect people I care about—whose concerns about my loves will shake my "clarity and confidence" in ways that I need to think about, and *reason* about, however limited reason may be to change how I feel.

Frankfurt talks very little about reasoning with others, about love or anything else. In his writings, one worries whether one *has* reasons for what one thinks or does or wants to do, but he doesn't show people exchanging reasons, what those conversations might look like, or how they might matter to the lover. Rationally warranting is an interior project, in his descriptions, or at least it isn't something that seems to require or involve anyone else. I doubt this is because he's not interested in how we talk to each other at all, but it might be, at least in part, because he thinks that most of the reasons we could give or demand about matters of the will are, as such, mistaken. By Frankfurt's lights, we do not have reasons to give to justify ourselves in our loves and cares "all the way down." When we talk about our loves in the language of reasons, then, we trade on common misconceptions that there is something to say—even something we must say—to be entitled to love the people we do.

He leans on examples in which giving and asking for reasons seems out of place: the question of whether to care about one's own survival, and the love of parents for their children. These are matters, he tells us, that we tend to be "decisively and robustly confident in caring about," and not at all uncertain that we should.[44] And "we do not suppose that the sturdy confidence that typically characterizes our attitudes regarding them actually depends—nor do we suppose that it should depend—upon a conviction that the confidence can be vindicated by rationally compelling arguments."[45] "Normal people," he writes, do not question parents about their loves for their children in this way, as we've discussed, nor do parents often question themselves about whether they should love their own, as he suggests from his own experience. We might have questions, for ourselves and each other, about how we should *act* on our love for our children, but we do not press parents for reasons for their love before believing them to be entitled to it. We might find it strange to begin the conversation at all: "Why do you love your children?" seems like a question everywhere out of place, at least insofar as it suggests you could fail to warrant your love by failing to provide sufficient reasons.

This is probably right, as far as it goes. But I don't think it goes particularly far. For one thing, it seems important—if slightly to the side of Frankfurt's point—that there are situations in which we do interrogate parents, sometimes quite harshly, about their love for their children: we interrogate them when we suspect that they may *not*. Parents are sometimes accused by co-parents, other family members, members of their community, and even their children themselves of *not* loving, or not loving as much as the questioner thinks they should. These interrogations fall into the realm of questioning *whether* they love their children instead of questioning whether they should, the factual question and not the normative one, as Frankfurt argues we should be interested in.[46] But they imply a normative claim in their address of the parent in the first place, particularly within the relationship in which the question may be asked. To ask "Do you love me?" or "Do you love our child?" may be to say "You should love me—why don't you?" or "You should love our child—why does it seem like you don't?"[47] The factual question wouldn't come up without the normative concern, and what is at stake in the question is not just the fact of the matter.

The idea that we do not ask parents to prove on the basis of reasons that they should love their children looks a bit narrower by these lights, particularly if we follow the scene a few steps further. Suppose a parent finds they don't have much to say in response. They may even find, on reflection, that they don't love their children, or at least not as much as others expect them to. Frankfurt would say that this is not because they lack reasons to do so, or even because they lack the desire to do so, as a second-order care, but because they find themselves not loving as they and others might wish they did. They may achieve a measure of clarity about their loves and cares in this realization, but it seems unlikely that they would achieve confidence, or wholeheartedness, in them—or to do so may be profoundly troubling. "You're right, I don't love my children" may be difficult to imagine a parent saying, and not because it couldn't be true, nor because it could never be rationally warranted. It's hard to imagine because in the society to which both I and Frankfurt belong, people tend to think parents should love their children. One might be able to accept, following Frankfurt, that one could not persuade them to love their children if they do not. But people seem to have views on whether they should, and may try to reason with them about the matter as best they could. The example suggests that we do not press loving parents for reasons because we approve of their love already, not because we think there are no reasons to give.

We may rarely interrogate parental love in these ways, but other loves seem far less unquestionable. People do ask each other for reasons to justify loves that they are having trouble accepting. They may have specific objections to certain loves and want to ask lovers to defend themselves against them. These objections may be personal and particular ("how could you love *him*, after what he did?") or primarily defined by and made in reference to social norms ("how could someone like you love someone like her?"). Both kinds of objection reflect and enact social norms, as well as the cares, concerns, views, and prejudices of the person voicing them, which have also been shaped by social norms (including in resistance to them, in some cases). Any discussion along these lines necessarily reflects socially contingent norms of how the discussants think loving relationships should be. You and I might not share these norms; Frankfurt and I might disagree as well. The project of asking and reasoning about love, however, is not made impossible or uninteresting by these disagreements. It is made significant, and even necessary.

Suppose a teenager announces to her parents that she is in love with one of her teachers, someone decades her senior who has been rumored to have had harmful relationships with other students. She reports that they have been in a relationship for a few months; they love each other, and now they plan to marry. Within the society to which I belong, it would be far more appropriate to ask questions in this case than in the examples of parental love Frankfurt discusses. It would not seem out of place, even, for her parents to ask precisely the question of whether she *should* love this person. The normative question, in fact, seems more crucially at stake than the factual one: she may well love this person as a matter of the current configuration of her will, but her parents seem entitled to ask her to show them that she *should*, or at least to defend herself against the reasons they might see for why she shouldn't. They also seem entitled to ask whether and why she should pursue the commands of that love in ways that alter her life. They could accept that she does love this person, but require that she show why she should let that love direct her life in ways that are more effectively under her control.

These discussions would be complex, and they may not go very far to change our protagonist's love for her beloved. She may not be persuaded that she *shouldn't* love him, either. But she might be persuaded that she shouldn't marry him, or that she otherwise shouldn't pursue the things her love encourages her to do. What would persuade her, were she persuaded in this way, would probably be an appeal to other things she cares about leveraged against this love, as we discussed in the last section. Among the loves and cares she might find competing with this love could be her love for her parents. If she loves them, their concerns or disapproval would direct her, too. They do not need to persuade her by rational warrant that she should not love him, then, but by their concerns and desires *as people she cares about*. Given the circularities we've considered in defining love and care, it must be the case that we care what the people we care about think about us. If we value things they value because they value them, we also condemn the things they condemn because they condemn them—or at least, we will be inclined to consider whether we should also be against them. If the people we love condemn *us*, we will be faced with some division of our will, if not a full-blown crisis of confidence in what we care about.

There's a version of this point that describes a contest strictly among our loves and cares: our loved ones' challenges to our other loves do not have the status of *reasons* so much as competing pulls on our volition. But the way our cares direct our lives is not so wholly disconnected from reasoning in this way, as I've suggested. We reason about the best ways to pursue our loves and cares, or how to understand what would be in the best interests of what and whom we care about. We think and argue about what it means to care about someone or something. We experiment with different actions and interpretations of ourselves; we question what our want to do something or not do something might reveal of us, and to us. The answers are not obvious, and they may require more than our discernment of the orientation of the will as if it were a compass and we needed only to know the direction we are facing. Given the complex interactions of the things we find ourselves caring about, the will is at least more like a sextant: triangulating among multiple loves and cares and their demands, locating us at different orientations to them, and different distances from them, as we try to determine where we are and where we are going.

The conceptual content of the reasons given by the teenage lover's parents in the example above is also not arbitrary to the way their daughter will be swayed. They need to be good reasons, or at least, we can imagine the damage bad reasons might do to the parents' efforts and their relationship with their daughter overall. If their questions reflect prejudices their daughter doesn't share, for example, she may find herself more alienated from them and the concerns they have for her, however well meant they may be on the part of the parents. If their questions show that they understand what she cares about, however, and that they've thought about what her cares require and entail, she may be more likely to be swayed—both by their evident care for her and the rational warrant they provide against pursuing her love. Any project of reasoning may not work to persuade someone to stop loving—they may be constrained, out of the reach of any reasons, by the will—but lovers are not fully outside the reach of reasons altogether. We may be outside some "pan-rationalist fantasy" of universal definition, or even a more moderate rationalism that seeks reasons beyond just our case. But this should encourage us to consider how reasons work within our relationships, instead of suggesting a much broader rejection of reasons for love.

Justification and Entitlement

The examples we've just considered of parental love and parental questioning exemplify the distinction between an "exhaustively rational warrant" and rational *entitlement* to claims. Frankfurt's "pan-rationalists"—if I might personify the position for just a moment—require compelling reasons to be provided for love to be considered reasonable. Frankfurt uses the example of parental love against them to say that the active provision of reasons is not generally required in the case of love, and thus love is not something that is or can be rationally entitled. It is an orientation of the will, not a rational commitment. But this argument makes a significant assumption—or assertion—about the requirements for entitlement. It seems to assume that being rationally entitled to love someone means that one has actively provided "an exhaustively rational warrant" for loving them. Why would something as strong as that be the only form of providing reasons, and the only way to be rationally entitled? The example could be interpreted instead to suggest that there are forms of rational entitlement that do not require the active provision of reasons, but rather consider someone entitled to love by default, perhaps only until reasons *against* that love can be provided. Frankfurt doesn't distinguish between being entitled to a belief—or love, I want to suggest—and being able to justify that belief or love with the provision of reasons. But these ideas are meaningfully distinct.

The relevant distinction is one used in discussions of religious reasons in public life. Richard Rorty famously described religion as a "conversation-stopper" in political discourse because, in his view, the introduction of religious premises renders certain positions in the conversation invulnerable to critique, or even the request for justification.[48] It is also in "bad taste," he writes, bringing a part of a person's "private life" into a public conversation.[49] In response, Jeffrey Stout has argued that religious claims brought into public conversation would be better interpreted as part of a class of "faith-claims" that express "a cognitive commitment without claiming entitlement to that commitment."[50]

> If I make a faith-claim, I am authorizing others to attribute the commitment to me and perhaps giving them a better understanding of why I have undertaken certain other cognitive or practical commitments. I am also making the claim available to others as a premise they might wish to employ in their reasoning. But I am not accepting the responsibility of demonstrating my entitlement to it. If pressed for such a demonstration, I might say simply that it is a matter of faith. In other words, "Don't ask me for reasons. I don't have any."[51]

Religious claims, Stout argues, do not always take this form, and not all claims that take this form are religious. "Everyone holds some beliefs on nonreligious topics without claiming to know that they are true," and we tend not to treat people as unreasonable for having them.[52] When they are offered in conversation, the person making the claim may be asked to justify it with the provision of reasons, and they may be unable to do so in such a way that we no longer take them to be entitled to hold that belief. But they also may not be challenged at all, or their failure to provide reasons may not change our sense of their entitlement to their belief, though it might lead us to understand it as a faith-claim instead of a justifiable one, if we hadn't understood it that way already. Rational entitlement need not depend on the provision of reasons justifying a claim. And there are many situations where we may not even ask, perhaps because it would be in "bad taste," or simply because we may not have further questions. People do not, on the whole, seem to be in the business of Frankfurt's pan-rationalists, actively looking to justify everything "from the ground up." Some claims do not warrant this kind of interrogation, and we may not see ourselves as always entitled to engage in it.

Claims to love seem to work similarly. Love is not a belief of the kind Rorty and Stout are discussing, but we do describe it to others in the form of claims expressing "cognitive or practical commitments": "I love this person," or "I am doing this thing because I love this person." When we offer these claims to others, we may offer them knowingly as faith-claims, something about which I know I have no reasons to give. We may say these things in conversation not because they let us *win* an argument with something that cannot be challenged further, a conversation-stopper that seeks a kind of victorious invulnerability, as Rorty implies is part of some religious interjections into public discourse. Rather, we may offer them to convey something about ourselves, why we believe, do, or are something that we cannot explain any other way.[53] A claim of love need not be a way to stop the conversation, to invalidate some set of reasons you've given me or resist further discussion. It might be a way to give you the best reasons I have. And our relationship may strengthen in this exchange even as our exchange of reasons has stalled. I have shared something of myself with you, so that you understand why I am behaving the way I am. I have also admitted that I do not have any way to convince or justify to you that I am entitled on the basis of reasons to my claims—an admission that may encourage us to keep talking, if toward different ends than a fully reasoned justification.

When we are seeking to reach a common understanding or agreement on a political question, a certain amount of acceptance of faith-claims is probably necessary for the continuation of the political process itself. Stout argues that this is what Rorty should mean by "conversation": a "discursive exchange [kept] going at those very points where 'normal' discourse—that is, discourse on the basis of commonly accepted standards—cannot straightforwardly adjudicate between competing claims."[54] We need to be able to talk through things that cannot be warranted "from the ground up," and we cannot do that if we reject people's faith-claims on principle. Those claims are part of how we show each other who we are.

Rorty himself has a name for what we are revealing in these moments: a person's "final vocabulary."

> All human beings carry about a set of words which they employ to justify their actions, their beliefs, and their lives. These are the words in which we formulate praise of our friends and contempt for our enemies, our long-term projects, our deepest self-doubts and our highest hopes. They are the words in which we tell, sometimes prospectively and sometimes retrospectively, the story of our lives.[55]

These are the words for the things we care about. Rorty is describing a linguistic version of the loves and cares that order our lives, the things that set the standards of what matters to us, what has value for us, what we will do, and what we have reason to do. They are the words for which we can provide no further explanation, because they provide the terms by which we evaluate and explain. They form a "final" vocabulary, Rorty writes, "in the sense that if doubt is cast on the worth of these words, their user has no noncircular argumentative recourse. Those words are as far as he can go with language; beyond them there is only helpless passivity or a resort to force."[56] As with the things we care about, we cannot argue for their worth. Our arguments will return to the language we are being challenged to justify otherwise, and we will not be able to appeal to any terms beyond our final vocabulary. The attempt to justify or explain our loves succumbs to a similar circularity, as we've seen. What we care about is the volitional vocabulary that spurs our actions, interests, and aims. They are the orientations of the will—of the heart—in which we find ourselves loving our friends and rejecting our enemies, pursuing our long-term projects, and discovering our deepest doubts, in self-division, and our highest hopes, in the aspirations they determine for our lives.

"Conversation," Stout writes, "is a good name for what is needed at those points where people employing different final vocabularies reach a momentary impasse."[57] Conversation of this kind is part of what happens when we ask each other for reasons for love. The fact that we will reach a point where we have no reasons to give does not mean we can't keep talking, nor that the conversation isn't worth having. It must acknowledge the limitations of reason to justify what and whom we find ourselves loving, and not castigate lovers by default where they are unable to provide convincing reasons for their loves. It must also have an appropriate occasion, and be engaged by appropriate people, as with political conversations of the kind Rorty and Stout are discussing. Who and what counts as appropriate is always in flux, but I do not as a rule owe reasons for my political views to anyone who asks for them. I owe reasons to my neighbors, to the people I am in political relationship with, and to people affected by my political relationships. Similarly, I do not owe reasons for my loves to anyone who decides to ask. Some questions, from some people, *are* in bad taste—or worse, are forms of aggression or threat disguised as opportunities to justify myself. But people I am in relationship with, whom I care about and who care about me, might ask about my loves and cares such that I owe them a reply. The parent whose child asks whether they love them owes the child a reply, regardless of whether they can provide reasons for or about the way they find themselves loving or not loving. The teenager of the earlier example whose parents want to know about her love for her teacher, given the norms of their community, may owe her parents a reply—reasons, or at least conversation, even if they may not be able to change each other's hearts or minds. I owe my friends a reply were they to express concern about a hurtful beloved, a new friend who seems to make me unhappy, or a new passion for which I have neglected much else I used to care about. I owe myself a reply, too, where I notice such things and find myself concerned. I may not be able to provide more than to say "I love them," but I owe them—and myself—as much. Circularities are not always vicious. And sometimes silence, to avoid a failure to justify ourselves, is a greater vice.

⊙ 3 ⊙

Christian Agape and the Vulnerability of Worldly Goods

The emphasis of my account thus far has been on the uncertainty we experience in love as we want a future with our beloveds that we cannot know or account for completely. Understanding love in this way draws attention to the many other uncertainties and vulnerabilities we encounter in and around it. Desires waver without our permission. We are vulnerable to our desires, vulnerable in the relationships they may or may not establish as we wish, and vulnerable to others' reception of our desires and relationships. These forms of vulnerability, however, may seem at odds with the feeling of many loving relationships, in which we sometimes find ourselves feeling most secure, most at home, and most certain about the future. (There's a reason "we finish each other's sentences" is a description of love.) Love can seem a refuge from relationships in which we feel insecure or disregarded, unsure of ourselves or others, or both. Feelings of comfort, security, and safety can be part of what it means to find the future together promising, to desire it without knowing exactly how it will be determined.

In response to such feelings of security, it might be churlish to insist on the technical uncertainty of the experience itself. It might be dangerous, too, as insistence on uncertainty can fuel violence where it suggests an overriding need to secure one's conditions against any possible threats. And it can diminish life where it doesn't destroy it, encouraging distance, distrust, and the avoidance of intimacy, making one's future overall—with anyone—seem more terrifying than promising in every sense. Life cannot be lived well in these conditions.

In describing the uncertainty of love, I don't want to insist on *feeling* uncertain, insecure, or vulnerable. Indeed, my interest in love as an experience of uncertainty comes in part from the observation that its uncertainty is often far from the lover's mind. But there are better and worse ways to think about what it means to find oneself feeling certain, safe, or secure in love, if one does. One is to marvel at the "impertinence" of the feeling, as Anne Carson might say: to be delighted and fascinated by its fantastic stability in contrast to the vulnerability we know defines our finite lives. Another is to assert the irrelevance of vulnerability given such a feeling of constancy, taking love to override vulnerability as an antidote to or consolation for it, or as wholly indifferent to the vulnerability of goods on which other relationships depend. One might then imagine such love to be worthy of emulation in other relations in which vulnerability seems inescapable, and inescapably troubling. The feeling of security in love might be transformed into a model for the rest of our lives, showing what we must do to live without having to confront the threatening limitations of finitude so frequently.

In Christian thought, God's love for human beings is sometimes construed as the ultimate force of constant, ever-flowing love, washing abundantly over the vulnerable, finite worldly goods on which other loves depend. Undeterred by the frailty and failures of God's human beloveds, in such descriptions, God's love exceeds any constancy we might think we know in human relationships and sets the vulnerability of our worldly loves into relief. It thus seems a potent example for human beings to emulate. But what kind of example does this understanding of divine love present? What is love without the vulnerability and uncertainty we know in other relations?

For Kierkegaard, God's love exemplifies the security human love lacks, illuminating the vulnerability of our lives and loves with new light. The love we find ourselves having for other people, the "instinctive and inclinational love" we feel for friends and lovers, can change to hate or jealousy, weaken to fondness or mere familiarity, or bottom out into the devastation of indifference. It will surprise no one familiar with Kierkegaard that he is attentive to these possibilities. A great theorist of anxiety, he reminds the readers of *Works of Love* that even the happiest lovers are insecure, their worry most evident in ready oaths to love "forever," swearing "fidelity" and promising to remain "true."[1] But these oaths are also unsecured, sworn on "love itself" instead of something higher. "Precisely this is the beautiful, touching, enigmatic, poetic misunderstanding," he writes.[2] Love seems grand enough in its happy moments to bond lovers forever, but it is not in fact great enough to secure the bond. Its "luster" impresses lovers and poets adorn it further, describing it in "riddles" that obscure its insecurity by praising how well it will endure, how readily it will pass the tests of the years. But "testing is always related to possibility; it is always possible that what is being tested would not stand the test."[3] Where lovers and poets praise love's passing, they admit how readily it might pass in other senses. To praise the endurance of love is to disclose its vulnerability; to swear it will endure "a most beguiling jest."[4]

Part of what makes these oaths so foolish, to Kierkegaard, is that they mistake the basis of the love itself. Friends and lovers are not attached by their promises but by what they see in the other, the beauty and goodness of their beloveds. They are drawn to the "perfection of the object," loving "the beloved, the friend, the admired one, the rare, the extraordinary person" for their inherent value, often measured in comparison to others, as we've seen in earlier chapters. To swear on "love itself" cannot secure such a love because it cannot secure the qualities that make the beloved valuable, or how well these qualities compare beyond them. Thus even "the perfection of the object is not the perfection of the love," which will remain dependent on the object and never be free of the possibility of its diminishment.[5]

Dependence on the value of the beloved, this "something else" beyond love itself, sets erotic love and friendship in stark contrast to the Christian love of neighbor. While these forms of love are "defined by the object," the Christian's love of neighbor, in Kierkegaard's description, is "defined by love."[6] It is not motivated by the value of the beloved and may not even regard it for more than practical purposes. It is motivated and sustained by the love of God, through God's command to love the neighbor. The possibility of change in its object doesn't threaten it, since it is not defined, caused, motivated, or sustained by the value of its object. Poetic promises in these terms are irrelevant; nothing in the world is needed to secure it. It is independent in this way of the vagaries of worldly goods, intruding into our vulnerable, uncertain lives with a constancy unknown in other relations. It may be precisely the invulnerable, unchangeable love the anxious lovers of earlier chapters desired: a love that won't diminish with age or accident, and isn't dependent on the steadiness of human will or whim.

But Christian love, agape, as both the commanded love of neighbor and the love of God, is often described as intruding into worldly life not with constancy but with *excess*. Given to the undeserving and undesirable, it tramples ordinary rules and expectations of relation with excessive attention, care, and regard. It exceeds what we merit or inspire in others. It is given to people who have nothing much to recommend them, loving gratuitously beyond what our attractions stir. It forgives, loving even those who harm us or threaten to do harm. It interrupts justice with mercy. It disrupts ordinary relations by giving more than we are otherwise inclined, more than the good of others seems to demand, and more than worldly goods may be able to inspire at all. This excessive nature of Christian love challenges ordinary friendships, familial relations, and romantic loves by challenging their motivation in vulnerable, finite, worldly goods, as Kierkegaard suggests, and our discrimination among potential beloveds on their basis. It also disrupts political life in its loyalties and enmities, and wherever it is governed by the calculations of justice, the meting out of precisely what people are due.

I want to suggest that these two ways of narrating agape's intrusion into worldly life are significantly connected: that the excesses of Christian love, by some descriptions, also promise a form of security from worldly vulnerability, and that difficulties with these promises—or at least their articulation and interpretation by human beings—can show us why vulnerability matters to lovers. My focus will be on a strand of twentieth-century Protestant ethics following Kierkegaard and Anders Nygren to develop accounts of agape by its contrast to other forms of love. In these arguments, the constancy of Christian love, "defined by love" and not dependent on anything outside of it, disrupts the vulnerability of finite existence as it exceeds what we merit or deserve. It intrudes on a world in which our relations seem determined by value and thus we fear the decline or destruction of what is valued in us. Agape is not described as a consolation to these fears nor a salve to the pains of finitude, but its gratuitous extension bridges chasms in our finite lives by offering an ultimate bridge between the finite and the infinite. Understood in this way, it offers a substantial response to worldly vulnerability: *God loves*, and God's love will not fade as we fade and falter. Christians who love likewise, in accordance with God's command, will do in the world a welcome imitation of God's steady embrace.

By this description, however, agape does not respond so well to the experiences of temporal life: the uncertainty, as a vulnerable being, of not knowing what happens next, not knowing what will endure, and how, or what will end, and in what ways. These authors have often left relatively obscure the way their arguments position agape to address the vulnerability of worldly goods and temporal, finite lives made uncertain by it. I want to recover these themes, and ask whether the promise of constancy and security from worldly vulnerability is coherent, or as unsteady as Kierkegaard's poet's vows.

The question hinges on the understanding of divine love as the model for Christians' love of neighbor. Where divine love is described as constant and invulnerable because of its independence from worldly goods, it is easily misconstrued as a model for worldly relations, leaving the ethics that follow inconsiderate of their own risks. Where Christian ethics is interested in love's disruptive potential and the needs of finite creatures to whom the constancy of divine love extends, it must contend with the uncertainty of worldly existence as something that matters to lovers and beloveds—and to those who feel themselves without love in this world at all.

To see the problem more clearly, I want to look closely at Anders Nygren's influential but often criticized account of agape as strictly the love of God, bestowed on undeserving human beings without any cause or motivation. The extremity of Nygren's work and the problems it creates suggest that divine constancy is easily misconstrued as a model for worldly relations not because it is an unreachable goal for human beings, though it may be that as well. Rather, divine constancy—or in Nygren's theology, divine perfection—undoes the vulnerability fundamental to love. Perfecting love in the sense of making it invulnerable and independent of any vulnerability of the lover, the beloved, and each to each other, misses the point. Relationships require some measure of being affected by the other, or at least vulnerable to the possibility of effect. They begin, in a finite world, without knowing how the other will respond, how you will be received or noticed, and how your beloved will change your life and determine your future. This unknowing is the temporal experience of a vulnerability to the other that lovers desire. It is vulnerability to the other that makes love a relationship and not only an assertion of the lover. In our temporal lives, vulnerability and uncertainty are knit closely together. But even a being who knows how things turn out cannot escape their own vulnerability to the beloved without threatening the sense in which they have a relationship with them at all.

God is differently affected by these vulnerabilities than human beings, to say the least. But Nygren's attempt to isolate God's love from any possibility of vulnerability to the beloved turns God's love, in his account, into an assertion of the lover *instead* of a relationship with the beloved. In trying to make God's love wholly independent of anything in this world, Nygren turns it into something that seems not to establish a relationship at all. This goes against his own insistence on the bestowal of fellowship with God in God's gratuitous gift of agape. It also shows why vulnerability matters to lovers, and cannot be escaped.

Lovers desire vulnerability insofar as lovers want *relationship* with their beloveds and not egoistic self-assertion or simply the realization of their own aims. For finite beings living temporal lives, this vulnerability to the beloved is also a form of uncertainty. As we've considered in other chapters, I do not know how tomorrow will go, whether my desires will change, or whether my circumstances will change around them. But as a lover, I desire to be changed by my beloved, at least in the sense that I desire not to determine everything about my time and relationship with them myself. It is the uncertainty that comes from this vulnerability that lovers *desire*; other uncertainties might be less desirable, or merely facts of temporal life. Turning to a lover outside of time—where a lack of knowledge is not a source of uncertainty—helps us see why.

The failure of Nygren's attempt to describe God's love as wholly independent of vulnerable worldly goods suggests this importance of vulnerability to lovers. The efforts of his critics to moderate his argument for a coherent Christian ethic reinforce the lessons of his failures. Where they maintain agape's perfect independence from worldly vulnerability and position it as a response to the uncertainty of our finite lives, they fail to wring out the egoism of his account. Where they treat vulnerability and uncertainty as inescapable within worldly life, they can resolve the incoherence of a perfected agape and offer a far more compelling description of what we desire in this world, and what we need.

DIVINE PERFECTIONISM

A significant strand of discussions of love in Christian ethics over the last century has been organized by two contrasts: between love and justice, competing as different "laws of life," and between *agape* and *eros*, competing as different forms of love. The competitions seem hard to score. In each, one side is characterized as definitively immeasurable, while the other stands waiting to be counted, "the 'nicely calculated less and more' of the relatively good and the relatively evil" that Reinhold Niebuhr tells us constitutes "the common currency of the moral life."[7] Justice is ready for this kind of calculation, and ready to recommend itself, in part, by the possibility of such accounting. Eros also has its eyes on the board, responding to the value of the beloved in some proportion to how much value is perceived in them. Christian love is not ready for similar measures. It flows freely and abundantly, without regard for what its beloveds deserve and against the assessments of worth that both justice and eros seek to recognize. It is not motivated by the value of the beloved nor responsive to its assessment. Agape is the love of God, and for its human emulators, a love motivated by the duty to love commanded in the Gospels and modeled on the love of Christ. While eros and justice assess and appraise, agape loves, extending itself profusely by its nature and not in measured response to its object. It creates value in its objects, by some accounts, bestowing value on the beloved in and through love for them. But the "grading criterion" of justice or eros cannot be satisfied by agape.[8] It competes with justice and eros by protesting the keeping of scores. As the love of God, it exceeds measurement and defies its possibility. As an ideal for Christians, it requires the abandonment of measurement for motivation or apportionment and demands love for its own sake.

Let me call this strand of conversation "modern agapism."[9] While identifiable by this style of tensions and contrasts with which they define the distinctiveness of Christian love, the modern agapists are also often uneasy with some of its effects. Some are concerned, for example, that too strong a distinction between love and justice might render love insufficient to address worldly problems; others, that too insistent a contrast between eros and agape misunderstands agapic attention to the beloved—issues to which I'll return in a moment. Most of the modern agapists after Nygren name his 1930s tome *Agape and*

Eros as the origin of the problems they understand to emerge from trying to hold agape too far apart from other relations. The work is a compelling culprit, from the title onward. Nygren narrows the discussion of Christian love to only two forms of love, eros and agape, with no room for *philia* or other forms of affection, attachment, or care, nor for any synthesis or complementarity of different loving relations. He defines Christian love strictly and exclusively as agape, necessary to separate from any further contamination by eros. The definitions of eros and agape that emerge from this project of distinction are markedly narrow: Nygren's eros is an appraising, egocentric love, responding to the value of the beloved and always in some way selfish or self-assertive in its pursuit of its valuable object. He defines agape, by contrast, as strictly the love of God for man, with no regard for the value of the beloved.

Nygren's strict separation of eros and agape diverges from much of Christian thought. For Nygren, there is no possibility of successful human emulation of God's love. Nygren is in these ways a compelling origin of the ideas that concern Niebuhr, among others, that Christian love is insufficiently responsive to problems in social and political life. *Agape and Eros* is interested at nearly every turn in isolating Christian love from worldly questions, whether the social problems for which Niebuhr recommends attention to justice, the promise of interpersonal relationships recommended by Walter Rauschenbusch and other proponents of the social gospel, or the concerns of erotic lovers for the endurance of their relations. Nygren's agape is wholly independent of worldly motivations, values, and interests. Its "purity" must be maintained against eros, most immediately, as well as justice, legalism, and other "attitudes to life."[10]

The extremity of Nygren's work has been the subject of substantial criticism, often in the register easily suggested by extreme views that he should soften or add more subtlety to his distinctions, entertaining syntheses or dialectical relations between some of the ideas he seeks so emphatically to hold apart. But I am most interested in the extremity of his account for a different reason: he aims for perfection, and fails in an interesting way. Nygren requires God's love to be understood as wholly independent of any worldly goods that might be construed as motivation. It must be described as perfectly spontaneous—God loving because God loves, not with any cause or motivation by anything else—so that it cannot be said that God's love has been merited by human beings in any way. To think otherwise is to risk imagining that one deserves the love of God, a "contamination" of one's understanding of agape with eros. And the mistake, for Nygren, is not only to imagine one's merit and desert, but also to imagine that God's love is thus dependent on one's value, and thereby on the vulnerable worldly goods valued in us. His distinction between agape and eros defines eros as significantly dependent on vulnerable worldly goods in this way—and agape as significantly independent from them. Worldly vulnerability appears in Nygren's work as the path to a prideful assertion that we merit God's love. Nygren then has to define God's love as strictly the assertion of the lover, and not a relationship with the beloved at all, in which the lover could be vulnerable to or dependent on the beloved. This is the connection between excess and security that must be addressed by his critics where they are concerned with the capacity for Christian love to address worldly problems. It also shows the necessity of vulnerability and uncertainty for lovers in the problems that emerge as Nygren tries to render God's love as wholly independent, invulnerable, and perfect in this way.

The Fundamental Motif of Christianity

Agape and Eros makes two main arguments: first, for agape as the "fundamental motif" of Christianity, "the basic idea or the driving power of the religion," and second, for a particular understanding of agape as the abundant, freely flowing, unmotivated, and value-creating love of God.[11] The second argument has been far more influential than the first, but it is structured and defined by the method of "motif-research" to a significant degree. Popular in the Swedish Lundensian school of theology of which Nygren was a part, the method of "motif-research" seeks the "fundamental motif" of a religion, "the basic idea or the driving power of the religion concerned, or what gives it its character as a whole and communicates to all its parts their special content and colour." The fundamental motif differentiates one religion from another, forming the "natural context" in which all other ideas and beliefs of the religion must be understood.[12] It is also described by Nygren as the concept around which a religion has internal coherence, such that the fundamental motif can be known by its removal having the effect of rendering the religion void of "all coherence and meaning."[13] This last point, according to Nygren, makes the question of the fundamental motif hardly "a matter of subjective and arbitrary choice" and instead "open to objective examination" and thus a form of "empirical investigation."[14] Nygren's definition of agape as a fundamental motif is thus offered as a claim about the coherence of the Christian religion, not a normative description of how Christians should be and understand themselves as the beloveds of God.

"Motif-research" has been the subject of withering criticism—as one commentator writes, the effort "to exemplify Christianity in a single motif, which is the aim of Bishop Nygren, invites scholarly cavil," and so it has received.[15] "Nygren's three magic words [eros, nomos, and agape] telescope centuries of religious development into a slogan which even the simplest mind can comprehend," another critic writes, and not as a compliment to the work's accessibility. "The sum and substance of church history" can then be summarized in just a few sentences, encouraging an "inadequate understanding" that "almost amounts to a falsification."[16] Whether because the "contention . . . must appear exaggerated to the historian" or because Nygren gets the answer wrong, misreading Christian history and its internal structure and content, the method, as Nygren employs it, has seemed ridiculous to many critics.[17] Many more ignore it completely, or mention it only in passing, as if an unfortunate frontispiece or obsequious dedication to a patron. But the impress of this method has not been lighter for its dismissal or neglect. It structures his inquiry by encouraging his definitions of agape and eros to be "pure" and independent of each other because this independence allows them to serve as the fundamental motifs of their traditions.

Nygren identifies three fundamental motifs in his discussion: eros as the fundamental motif of ancient Greek religion, philosophy, and culture; nomos as the fundamental motif of Judaism; and agape as the fundamental motif of Christianity.[18] Fundamental motifs need not interact at all, but eros and agape have been unfortunately entangled by history, Nygren tells us, creating the "problem of *eros* and *agape*" to which he addresses his work.[19] The problem, at its core, is that these two ideas "have originally nothing whatsoever to do with one another" but have "none the less become so thoroughly bound up and interwoven with one another that it is hardly possible for us to speak of either without our thoughts being drawn to the other."[20] More troubling to Nygren, agape has been most damaged by the entanglement, as it "entered into a world that had already received the impress of *Eros*, which therefore had the advantage of being first in the field."[21] When Christian agape "first enters on the scene," eros is "already in possession of the stage."[22] It is the fundamental motif—in a particular part of the world, for a particular set of people, though Nygren doesn't specify as much very clearly—by which all other ideas and beliefs are made meaningful. Thus agape is first encountered and interpreted by the lights of eros, a situation in which it is "bound to lose some of its original force."

Nygren describes the encounter between eros and agape in a series of dramatic metaphors. They are antagonists and combatants; they are springs, rivers, and waterways that become "united" and diluted, "the stream of the Christian idea of love" flowing "partly, at least, into the broad river of *eros*" and becoming a mere tributary.[23] They meet on the stage, as players of different parts: eros commanding the audience's attention, and agape emerging first in a "guise" that directs the audience from its true nature, "draw[ing] men's minds away from the things of sense." This is the "guise of the heavenly *Eros*," the Augustinian synthesis of agape and eros into *caritas* against which Nygren writes most vehemently. Understanding Christian love to be a supernatural, heavenly form of erotic love, as Nygren characterizes Augustine's view, is to let the "basic religious tendency of the ancient world" color Christian agape instead of receiving agape as a fundamentally different view that should color all else. To describe Augustine's *caritas* as the "guise" of agape when it enters the stage dramatizes the problem of eros and agape with theatrical obfuscation and even deceit. Nygren doesn't go so far as to say Augustine has provided the mask from the wings, but he makes clear that the audience has been duped, and he writes to disabuse them.

The "problem of *eros* and *agape*," however, is of a "very peculiar kind," Nygren tells us, because it emerges from history and practice rather than conceptual relation. This point is key to the way he comes to define the difference between eros and agape. The two ideas, he argues, should not be understood to have any conceptual relation between them. They "belong originally to two entirely separate spiritual worlds, between which no direct communication is possible." They cannot be defined in each other's terms if they are each their own fundamental motif; they are "essentially incommensurable." They do compete as "different general attitudes to life," however, requiring different ways of living and understanding all other concepts and experiences.[24]

How, then, does Nygren address this problem of eros and agape? He begins by warning against two false starts to the inquiry. One replicates the historical mistake of approaching agape through the concept of eros, a path as common as it is misleading, he suggests, and perhaps forgivable given the history of agape's emergence. It begins from the Augustinian mistake of understanding agape as a version of eros itself: "heavenly *eros*," contrasting with the "earthly" love to which eros usually refers, but forming only the more "spiritual" version of its "vulgar" cousin.[25] Agape, in this approach, follows the logic and "tendency" of eros, responding to value in the beloved but replacing valuable worldly goods with the greatest good, and a more "spiritual" one, God.[26] But an inquiry beginning from eros in this way will discover "the born rival of the idea of *Agape*" instead of agape itself, Nygren argues, by determining only the "most sublimated and spiritualised form" of eros. True Christian agape doesn't need any "spiritualizing" to lend it a heavenly cast, as Christian agape "displays a heavenly character from the beginning" and will always be thus distinct from eros, however loftily the latter is described.

Nygren then defines a second false start to the inquiry, more tempting to those who have understood the stronger distinction between agape and eros already: to begin as many of the later modern agapists do, from the dual love commandment to love God and love one's neighbor as oneself.[27] The commandment appears promising at first since it avoids the mistake of the erotic path by beginning seemingly from within the Christian tradition. But in Nygren's view, imagining the dual love commandment to be properly Christian is a mistake as well. The commandment is not native to Christianity, he argues, despite its appearance and prominence in the New Testament. Its foreignness is betrayed by its form: commandments and laws are not part of the conceptual landscape to which agape belongs in its uniquely Christian form, and as the fundamental motif of Christianity. Rather, commandments derive from the legalism of Judaism, as he describes it, where the dual love commandment originates.[28] It is "introduced in the Gospels not as something new, but as quotations from the Old

Testament."[29] The commandment is thus conceptually preceded by Old Testament legalism, in Nygren's interpretation, which forms the more fundamental motif for its interpretation. Attempting to understand Christian love from this starting point produces an Old Testament version of its object, Nygren contends, just as the inquiry into agape that begins from eros produces an erotic version of its object: something resembling agape in various ways but fundamentally determined by a foreign logic and conceptual scheme. Properly Christian agape as the fundamental motif of Christianity should instead constitute the conceptual landscape of which it is a part. Both of these other approaches cannot result in the elucidation of such a concept, because they begin by asserting a different fundamental motif.

The correct starting point, for Nygren, is Matthew 5:44, the exhortation to "Love your enemies." In his reading, this line and its surrounding verses (Matthew 5:43–48) provide "a quite definite, positive basis" for the concept of Christian love, presenting it wholly anew.[30] For Nygren, the passage emphasizes that unlike eros, this love does not require or respond to the worthiness of its object. Christians should love even those who act against them or are inferior or despising: "bless them that curse you, do good to them that hate you, and pray for them which despitefully use you, and persecute you," Christ says.[31] And unlike the commanded love of the Old Testament, Nygren argues, this indiscriminate love is made possible by God's love for human beings, as the last verse of the section suggests: "Be perfect, therefore, *as your heavenly Father is perfect*," not "because your heavenly Father so commands."[32]

God's perfection, Nygren is suggesting, is best represented by God's love of unworthy human beings, sinners as well as the righteous, which is why Christians should love their enemies as well as their friends. "The Christian is commanded to love his enemies," he explains, "not because the other side teach hatred of them, but because there is a basis and motive for such love in the concrete, positive fact of God's own love for evil men."[33] This "so intimate a connection between Christian love and the Christian relationship to God" is "no mere accident."[34] Rather, it represents what Nygren calls the "religious nature" of the Christian ethic, in which "the actual content of the ethical life is wholly determined by the religious relationship, by fellowship with God."[35] In Nygren's account, as Judaism finds its basis in the legalism of covenant and command, Christianity finds its basis in fellowship with God and, simply, in God. Both God and fellowship with God *are* agape by other terms: "God is *agape*," according to the Johannine formula, and "it is His nature to love."[36] God is love, and so God is the model for Christian love. God loves human beings, and so God's love for human beings is the model for Christian love. And God's loving relation to human beings is the model for and force behind a Christian's life, which should be lived lovingly, as God is loving, and can be lived lovingly because of God's love, without which human beings would not even have been created. Were Nygren to offer a creed to represent his idea of agape as the fundamental motif of Christianity, it would go something like that, as his claims about the "religious nature" of the tradition suggest.

This articulation of agape seems explicitly relational, defining Christianity in terms of the loving relationship of God to human beings. As Nygren develops the account, however, God's perfect love seems increasingly isolated from God's beloveds, appearing as an assertion of divine nature *instead* of a relationship—or at least raising the question of what sense of relationship is possible when formed by the assertion of love without any vulnerability to the beloved. The problem emerges in part from his ambition to distinguish agape and eros as different fundamental motifs, and is reinforced by his emphasis on the Lutheran doctrine of unmerited grace, by which he must insist on the lack of motivation for God's love in human beings' own merit or worth. We can see the beginning of the problem already in Nygren's selection of the paradigm of agape to be the "perfect" love of "God's own love for evil men." God's love is perfectly without any need for the beloved's goodness or great value to cause or sustain it—an aspect of agape Nygren emphasizes in contrast to eros, caused and sustained by the value of the beloved. In Nygren's elaboration of agape, the concept becomes increasingly isolated from both the beloved and any motivation in the beloved's value, as eros is motivated. Nygren's description of God's perfect agape thus becomes invulnerable to anything about the beloved: their sins and evil deeds, their lack of merit, and the inevitable changes to their qualities and characteristics in the course of finite lives. In the process, the sense in which agape establishes a relationship between lover and beloved at all becomes increasingly obscure.

A Spontaneous and Unmotivated Love

We are thinking here in a markedly atemporal space: God's eternal love, outside of time, is bestowed on human beings whose life within it is defined by faith that there is life beyond its constraints. The questions Nygren's discussion raises are not about certainty or uncertainty about what happens next so much as the possibility of not being changed by the beloved, including by being vulnerable to changes in them. Walking with Nygren away from time for a moment, as I suggested at the outset, will allow us to see the importance of vulnerability to love and thus the desirability I've referred to throughout this book of the uncertainty that comes from it in temporal life. But I am wary of too much time spent without any consideration of it, not least because of the problems that seem to derive from Nygren's indifference.

To see how agape becomes so distorted in Nygren's account, however, we need to return to a different question from earlier chapters: not the extraction of accounts of love from time, precisely, but the abstraction of love into definitions that promise complete, invulnerable truths. Nygren's distortion of agape is entangled with the way the value of the beloved continues to define his agape in the terms of eros—in a new iteration, perhaps, of the "problem of *eros* and *agape*" to which he addresses his work. The exhortation to "love your enemies" and the "concrete, positive fact of God's own love for evil men" emphasize the worthlessness of God's beloveds to make the point that God's love does not respond to value. What is notable about God's love in this moment of the Gospel is what God's beloveds *lack* in value, and even what they have as a kind of negative value, evil instead of good. This is emphatically not erotic love, Nygren is insisting, distinct from eros on eros's own terms. But a fundamental motif should not be distinguished on the terms of another fundamental motif, by Nygren's own description of the method, making his persistent focus on the beloved's lack of value rather strange. He seems to overcorrect for a confusion of eros and agape in this way, insisting on the beloved's worthlessness even as he attempts to describe agape's "disregard" for and "indifference" to value.[37] Disregard and indifference seem easily confused here with a reversal of valuation: love *because* of the beloved's worthlessness, a love still looking at value and loving in response to finding it wanting. His explanation of this indifference to value continues to emphasize the distinction between agape and eros by showing agape as a love for those without value or with qualities evaluated negatively, instead of showing agape's indifference to value by, say, not mentioning it further.

Nygren insists on disregard and indifference against a misunderstanding of agape as an inversion of eros, but his persistent focus on value raises the question of what exactly disregard and indifference mean in his account. Does God perceive value but disregard it, in the sense of seeing human unworthiness and ignoring it? Or does God not evaluate human beings at all? What relationship does God have to the goods of God's beloveds, indifferent to their value but not, Nygren suggests, to them?

The distinction needed to move away from further misunderstanding is between what motivates love and what the lover sees in their beloveds—a distinction we might also describe in the language of Nygren's later interpreters between regarding the beloved and love being required by what one sees. To see value in someone need not motivate love, by many accounts, let alone require love. One could love the worthy or the unworthy without one's love being motivated by the value or lack of value perceived. Similarly, seeing value in someone need not indicate that were one to love them, one's love would be motivated by the value perceived. As we've considered in earlier chapters, there are often valuable qualities and characteristics in beloveds that don't seem to matter to lovers, even if they might matter to others or matter to the beloved themselves. They don't matter in the sense that my love may not be motivated by those qualities or my evaluation of them. And even if my beloved's valuable qualities did motivate my love for them in crucial ways, we needn't say my love was somehow required by my perception of value in them. I didn't have to love them, given what I saw.

But it is the possible connection between motivation, regard, and requirement that Nygren is most worried about in his account of agape. He wants to protect agape from any idea that God's love is *merited by* human beings, and any subsequent suggestion that God *had* to love human beings given such merit. Against this concern, Nygren characterizes agape as crucially "unmotivated" and "spontaneous," a love that comes from nowhere except the lover and is caused by nothing beyond the lover.[38] God's indiscriminate love, for Nygren, is evidence not of God's appraisal of sinners, if by a different scale or with an unusual response, but of agape's spontaneity in this way. "If God's love were restricted to the righteous it would be evoked by its object and not spontaneous," he writes with a quick slip between motivation, requirement, and regard—or not even regard, but only the fact of their value, seen or unseen. "But just by the fact that it seeks sinners, who do not deserve it and can lay no claim to it, it manifests most clearly its spontaneous and unmotivated nature."[39] Unlike erotic love motivated by the value of its object, God's love is unmotivated and cannot be explained by anything beyond "God Himself."[40]

The language of "seeking sinners" muddies the water somewhat by suggesting antecedent evaluation yet again, but we might read that as a difficulty of discussing the eternal in temporal terms. God's love is both spontaneous and eternal, so God's love does not *begin*, either before or after evaluating the merit or sin of God's beloveds. The possibilities for confusion seem to lie in the tense or timing, as Nygren tries to describe God's nature and must retrace and revise his claims continuously to avoid the implication of anything other than perfect spontaneity in this sense. But his account wanders back into the evaluative language of eros in these efforts, emphasizing the unworthiness of God's beloveds in order to describe God's independence from any responsiveness to their value. Nygren insists, for example, that "the most striking feature of God's love as Jesus represents it" is the impossibility of its "explanation ... in the character of man who is the object of His love."[41] But he also insists on the importance of the negative value of the character of man, that we are "sinners, who do not deserve [God's love] and can lay no claim to it." Explanation is impossible both because agape is not the kind of love that can be explained and because human beings could not motivate the kind of love that can be. That human beings fail to deserve God's love is the best evidence, for Nygren, that "there are no extrinsic grounds for it. The only ground for it is to be found in God Himself."[42] God *is* love, agape is God's nature, and there is no other explanation for or of it—particularly not in the worthiness of its object, as Nygren insists at every turn.

This is not the first account of a "spontaneous" and "unmotivated" love we've seen. Nygren's agape bears some resemblance on these points to Harry Frankfurt's reversal of the "common understanding" of love—eros, roughly, if without an explicitly Hellenic legacy—considered in the previous chapter. Frankfurt is talking about human beings' loves for other people, not the love of God, but the conceptual resemblance with respect to motivation is instructive. Our loves are not caused or sustained by the value of our beloveds, Frankfurt argues, but are orientations of the will that make our beloveds valuable to us. We find ourselves loving the people we love not because we decide to love them on the basis of value perceived in them, or for any other reasons, nor because we are compelled to love them by anything about them, or anything outside of ourselves at all. People love, Frankfurt tells us, because it is our nature to love—it is how the will works, and how we find ourselves oriented to the world. God loves, Nygren tells us, because it is God's nature to love. Any attempt to explain God's love beyond "God himself" will fail, in Nygren's account, as any attempt to justify our loves beyond the orientation of our wills will fail, in Frankfurt's.

Neither love needs the beloved to be good, great, or even better than evil. Both loves are not reliant on anything about the beloved, nor on any external goods at all, and can continue in their decline or absence. One apparent virtue of Frankfurt's view of love, as I suggested, is that it can thus account for loves that are directed at "unworthy" beloveds, or that continue through changes in the beloved that might seem by other lights as if they deprive the lover of any reasons to continue loving. Like Nygren trying to define agape from the evidence of God's love for evil men, Frankfurt's understanding could take as its starting point the observation of people's frequent love for undeserving beloveds. And it nearly does, if we clear away his scholarly motivation in philosophical arguments about rational justification for how we should live. He would then begin, in at least one version of the argument, from the love of a parent for their children, and other loves inexplicable on the basis of the beloved's valuable qualities and characteristics.[43] His emphasis is on the lack of *knowledge* of the child's valuable qualities more than their lack of valuable qualities, but his point, similar to Nygren's, is that love is directed toward people who have little to recommend them, and so love must not require value to motivate or sustain it.

But Frankfurt's view bears a strange individualism in this capaciousness, instructive for our consideration of Nygren. Love is a way I find myself feeling, for Frankfurt, a way I find myself oriented to the world. As an orientation of the will, it provides reasons for me to do things, bestowing value and significance in the world and defining my aims by what loving my beloved entails. Among the things that love entails, for

Frankfurt, is that the lover "takes the interests of his beloved as his own," and so comes to care about things in relation to what the beloved's interests are.[44] I care about things that are important to my beloved, value those things, and value whatever is a part of the successful pursuit of my beloved's interests. Love thus determines what is important to me and what I find valuable. It directs how I spend my days and how I spend my life. But it is less clear how this love is a relationship *with* the beloved so much as a state of the self. The beloved appears in the account as the source of criteria for what I value and what I should pursue. I am vulnerable, as their lover, to changes in them that change those criteria. But this is all about me, and how I am defined by this other person, not about a relationship with them.

The lover in Frankfurt's account is profoundly vulnerable to whom and what they find themselves loving, but in the sense of how they are shaped by their loves, who they become because of them. Their vulnerability is not clearly *to* the beloved, in relationship *with* them: waiting for the beloved's response, not knowing what the beloved will do or say to them or how they will be changed by what the beloved does or says. God, in Nygren's account, is not shaped by God's beloveds, but is shaped—defined, known, and identical to—agape, God's love. Perfectly unmotivated, God loves only because it is God's nature to love. This is a circularity marked not by endlessness or an inability to reach secure foundations but invulnerability. The spontaneity of agape places God in a similar situation of non-relationship as Frankfurt's lover, though nearly inverted. Love is something the lover finds themselves doing, in both cases. It is a state of the self, not a relationship.

Independence from Worldly Goods

Encountering what would be egoism for a human lover in a description of God's love is not obviously a problem. Indeed, as a description of God's love, Frankfurt's account might appeal to Nygren precisely because of its individualism. Where Frankfurt's view of love seems most independent of the beloved, it sounds most like what Nygren argues divine love must be: independent of anything outside of the lover, explicable only by the lover's nature, and shown best by its inversion of eros with respect to value, loving the apparently unworthy and loving through changes that erotic love couldn't withstand. For Nygren, God and God's love are thus crucially invulnerable. This could be invulnerability in Kierkegaard's sense of security in the eternal, the invulnerability of something beyond our worldly senses of the possibility of change. But Nygren takes the claim in a different direction because he posits it contra eros, in terms of the value of the beloved. God's invulnerability becomes an independence from the value of the beloved, and with it, from the vulnerable worldly goods that could be valued in God's beloveds. And then he argues for one further step: agape is the creative force bestowing value. The combination of God's perfect invulnerability and God's creation of value bestowed makes God's love, in Nygren's argument, into a kind of force exerted on God's beloveds instead of forming a relationship with them. The individualism implied in agape's spontaneity becomes a kind of self-assertion. Perfectly invulnerable, perfectly independent of the value of the beloved, and perfectly bestowing instead of appraising, Nygren's agape appears to isolate God from human beings and from the vulnerabilities by which our worldly lives are defined.

The spontaneous and unmotivated nature of Christian agape forms the first of four points in which Nygren summarizes the content of the concept:

1. Agape is spontaneous and "unmotivated."
2. Agape is "indifferent to value."
3. Agape is creative.
4. Agape is the initiator of fellowship with God.[45]

The second point has much in common with the first, even seeming that it "merely restates the first," as one reviewer remarks dismissively.[46] Nygren himself begins its explanation by saying that it "does not really add anything new to what has already been said."[47] But he includes it "to prevent a possible misunderstanding" that God's love of sinners is an *inversion* of values when he actually means to describe it as a full abandonment of "*any thought of valuation whatsoever* ... in connection with fellowship with God"—an attempt to clarify the confusion we have just considered.[48] The same love that "abandons" and "excludes" value then also "imparts value by loving"—the "creative" force of point three. And so we see a new role of value emerge as the concept of agape is characterized as a matter of *bestowal* instead of appraisal of value.

Agape's spontaneity is clarified as indifference to value, and indifference is amended with the creation of value. Love of both the worthy and the unworthy is described, ultimately, as a creation of worth.

The problem here is not one of consistency, though to some readers it may be that as well. The problem is in the way Nygren's return to value defines God's relationship to worldly goods. God is not affected by the worldly beings God loves: God does not appreciate their value nor seem affected by their sin. God creates value in them, including by creating them, but this is a perfectly downward-flowing stream, invulnerable to the value of the beloved, lest it seem to motivate God's love, allowing any understanding of being thus merited by God's beloveds. God's love is perfectly spontaneous, perfectly unmotivated, because it is perfectly invulnerable to the value of the beloved, and to the vulnerability of the worldly goods that could be valued in us. Isolated from such vulnerability, God's love is indeed the steady and unchanging force both Nygren and Kierkegaard praise. But its steadiness is defined for Nygren by its isolation from anything valuable about God's beloveds and the vulnerability of what might be valued.

God's perfect invulnerability seems essential to Nygren's understanding of divine power and the nature of divine love, particularly to protect it from any sense of being merited by human beings. But we can also see in it a version of an egoism in love that seems at odds with his insistence on the bestowal of fellowship in agape, or that is at least a warning for worldly emulations of agape seeking fellowship between human beings. This is not the egocentrism of eros, in which I, as the erotic lover, want the valuable beloved for myself. Rather, it is the egoism of asserting love by bestowing it on others without regard for their participation in the relationship, or even any clear regard for them.

The contrast between eros and agape can help us see the point more clearly. Each movement of the four-part definition of agape responds directly to an aspect of eros as Nygren defines it. He identifies the "underlying rational idea" of eros with three points:

1. Eros is the "love of desire," or *acquisitive* love.
2. Eros is man's way to the Divine.
3. Eros is egocentric love.[49]

Each point emphasizes a different aspect or consequence of eros's appraising nature, its "love for the beautiful and the good." The three points together reflect its most important characteristic, in Nygren's view: that eros responds to value, pursuing the valuable.[50] We see the role of responsiveness to value in each point. The acquisitiveness of eros derives from its relationship to the value of its objects because "only that which is regarded as valuable can become an object of desire and love."[51] In its needy, desirous nature, "*Love and value belong together here; each suggests the other.*"[52] The connection between love and value suggests in turn how eros is "man's way to the Divine."[53] Finding God the most valuable, eros draws human beings toward God. God can only *be* loved, Nygren insists, and does not love erotically, for the divine has nothing greater than themselves to desire. "Since the gods have everything and need nothing, there can be no question of their feeling love" in its erotic form, as Nygren explicates from Plato. "The only relation they can have to love is to be the objects of love. In virtue of its beauty the Divine sets all things in movement towards itself; but the Divine itself is unmoved; it is absolute rest."[54] The one-sidedness of the love of human beings for the gods in Plato "is the simple consequence of the twofold presupposition of Eros-love—namely, the recognition of a value in the loved object and the consciousness of needing this value."[55] The relation to value is fundamental; eros as "man's way to the Divine" follows from it. Finally, the egocentricity of eros also follows from its definition as the response to the appraisal of value and its implication of the individual who perceives, appraises, and then desires. The entire structure of the concept surrounds the individual in this way, since eros's relation to value requires this individual. "All that matters from first to last is the soul that is aflame with Eros." It is a love defined by the perception and aims of the individual, and so bears a thoroughly "egocentric character."[56]

The defining feature of erotic love in Nygren's characterization is its appraisive, responsive relationship to value enacted as the self-assertion of the lover. But Nygren obscures the self who loves, whether God loving agapically or "the soul that is aflame with Eros," by phrasing his definitions with the form of love as the subject of the sentence. It is eros that "recognizes value" and is "man's way to the Divine," not the erotic lover. And it is agape that "is spontaneous and unmotivated" and "the initiator of fellowship with God," not God, the agapic lover, in Nygren's grammar. The identity of God and agape—God is agape, agape is God— might make a more explicit presence of the lover in Nygren's definitions technically redundant, but his language makes the lover harder to hear or see in an important way. Love is defined as a relationship doing the relating, not a relationship between beings. This is a difficulty to which anyone who has tried to write a sentence about love can be sympathetic. But it combines with Nygren's persistent definition of both eros and agape in terms of value in a particularly challenging way.

Eros and agape take objects whose value matters to their definition. If that value changes, a love dependent on it will change. We can infer that the lover might be changed in turn, but the absence of that lover in Nygren's articulation obscures their vulnerability. The vulnerability of their beloveds' value appears primarily as a threat to *love*'s continuation, in the case of eros, and not as a threat to the lover. And since agape is not threatened by changes to the beloved's value, any vulnerability of the lover is fully out of the frame. The agapic lover appears—by not appearing—to be particularly imperturbable, invulnerable to the beloved and the loving relation. God is agape, agape is God's nature, but God appears in Nygren's account less as a lover than a force asserted on God's beloveds.

It is in the terms of love's relation to value, not the lover's relationship to the beloved, in which Nygren draws the essential contrast between eros and agape: "Eros *recognises value* in its object—and loves it. Agape loves—and *creates value in its* object."[57] The transition from agape's indifference to value to the "creation" of value is strikingly responsive to the erotic conception, and to the elements of the erotic conception that are defined by the limiting features of worldly goods. The value eros recognizes is not secure: insofar as it is an evaluation of finite worldly goods, it can change, as the goods of a finite world change. As ancient Greek philosophers rarely fail to mention, beauty fades, charisma declines, and even wisdom is limited by the wise person's mortality. Eros recognizes value but is thus vulnerable to changes to that value, and so is always limited, to some extent, by the limitations of its objects. The creation of value in agape seems to extend the perfect constancy of the agapic lover to agape's beloveds in response to these erotic vulnerabilities. The decline or change of agape's beloved doesn't threaten agape both on agape's terms of disregard and indifference to value and on eros's terms of recognition of value, since value is created by the love itself. But the account shrinks back again, then, to defining agape itself, as a force asserted *instead* of a relationship between the agapic lover and beloved, and even against a relationship at all insofar as relationships suggest vulnerability between their parties.

Nygren characterizes the creative nature of agape as "the deepest reason for its uniqueness" and the "ultimately decisive feature of the idea," though "very much obscured in modern theology" by ideas of human beings' inherent worth—a question we'll return to in a moment.[58] However, it isn't clear from the scriptural passages or other sources Nygren presents why the acquisition of worth is necessary to mention or why the product of agapic love is describable in this way. He specifically isn't arguing for a bestowal of worth in the form of universal or generic human value, and unlike many of the modern agapists, he says very little about the creation of human beings in the image of God and the value thus bestowed. His description of the creative principle begins with and largely remains a contrast to eros:

> Agape has nothing to do with the kind of love that depends on the recognition of a valuable quality in its object; Agape does not recognise value, but creates it. Agape loves, and imparts value by loving. The man who is loved by God has no value in himself; what gives him value is precisely the fact that God loves him. *Agape is a value-creating principle.*[59]

Each sentence of the explanation—except the last, brief statement of the principle itself—begins with the possibility of an erotic understanding and then negates it. The negation becomes increasingly constructive, without much explanation or argument except his mention of the idea that "the man who is loved by God has no value in himself." How this serves as an explanation of the creation of value is not obvious, but it does at first seem to offer something beyond the negation of eros. Yet this principle, too, Nygren derives against eros. The idea that "the man who is loved by God has no value in himself" is important, Nygren explains, as a correction to the idea of human beings' inherent value—a major misunderstanding in Christian theology, in his view, since "value . . . belonging to man by nature" would set God's love in an uncomfortably erotic light, and challenge the Lutheran doctrine of unmerited grace.[60]

Here we return to Nygren's core concern: to protect the perfect love of God from any hint that it was merited by God's beloveds, required by this merit, and thus may be dependent on the value of human beings.

Were human beings inherently valuable, Nygren suggests, God could be said to love in some response to this value. God's love would still be unique in its forgiveness and disregard for "the manifold faults and failings of the outward life," but it might constitute an erotic response nonetheless to the "inward, imperishable value which not even sin has been able to destroy."[61] God's forgiveness and love of both the worthy and unworthy would then be "merely the recognition of an already existing value."

But it is evident enough that this is not the forgiveness of sins as Jesus understands it. When He says, "Thy sins are forgiven thee," this is no merely formal attestation of the presence of a value which justifies the overlooking of faults; *it is the bestowal of a gift*. Something really new is introduced, something new is taking place. The forgiveness of sins is a *creative work of Divine power*.[62]

God's forgiveness of sins is the paradigm of God's love, for Nygren, providing a perfect negation of eros in a kind of mirror to eros's appraisive, responsive, and acquisitive aspects. But understanding divine love to be creative, bestowing, and even a gift doesn't require that it be a *"value-creating principle."* Nygren never explains why agape would bestow value, and there is much else to give—most immediately, in light of his interpretation of the "religious nature" of Christianity, the gift of fellowship with God. When finally Nygren arrives at the fourth characteristic of agape, that "agape is the initiator of fellowship with God," it seems as if he could take the creative principle in this direction. Agape initiates fellowship from God to man, graciously loving and not based on a human recognition of God's greatness or a divine recognition of some value, positive or negative, in human beings. Rather, God's love is initiated by, and as, God's loving nature, and offers fellowship with God to undeserving human beings. The gift bestowed by agape seems as if it could be the fellowship between God and human beings on which Nygren argues all of Christianity is based. But Nygren continues to describe agape's creative power as a bestowal of value on the beloved, without connecting fellowship to this creative act.

In addition to questions of consistency, the presence of value in Nygren's account of agape poses a broader problem of what Nygren thinks the term "agape" should describe, what it should do, and how it can serve as the fundamental motif of Christianity. Part of Nygren's characterization of agape as a fundamental motif has to do with its independence from externally constraining, defining terms. It should not be trying to meet the demands of divine command or erotic appraisal, to take Nygren's two main examples, lest it be described through other motifs and thus governed by their worldview. These examples generalize to an emphasis on the idea that definitions of terms set or reveal the criteria by which those terms are judged and constrained—similar to the Euthyphro problems we considered in the previous chapter. This is true of definitions on the whole, but it takes on a special significance in the "motif-research" method because fundamental motifs are supposed to set the criteria through which all else is judged. Their definition, then, either constitutes the fundamental motif or undermines it by asserting another set of criteria as more fundamental. A proper definition of agape, in Nygren's view, thus should not be defined by anything but itself. It should be used to understand much more—all of Christianity and its worldview, no less—but it should be self-sufficient and self-consistent to the point of self-definition.

This independence of definition is related to the independence of agape from worldly motivation: Nygren defines agape as unmotivated in both content and form. Agape is not motivated by anything in the world, because it is God's nature and not the result of any cause. It is also unmotivated in this formal, conceptual sense that it cannot be defined by other terms. The combination of these two arguments in Nygren's work makes for an extreme account of agape, and one easily criticized for its lack of interest in worldly problems or provision of much guidance to Christians at all. Its extremity, however, allows the issue of agape's independence from other things—worldly goods and conceptual criteria—to come to the fore. He is describing a perfection of divine love, agape, as wholly independent and invulnerable, untouched by worldly problems and not beholden to their possibility. He wants to describe the loving God as strong and endlessly powerful in a way that renders God's love an assertion of God rather than an opening for relationship.

Nygren argues for the perfection of divine love by insisting on its invulnerability to worldly change and lack of dependence on the value—and persistence of value—of God's beloveds. Other modern agapists, as we'll see in the next section, argue for an understanding of agape that addresses worldly vulnerability by saying, roughly, we may change, we will change, we have changed, and God still loves us. Nygren argues, in contrast, that we may change, we will change, we have changed, but God's love won't be affected at all: spontaneous and unmotivated, agape is secured against the changes and vulnerability to change that plague other relations—and the vulnerability that promises the depth and growth of many relationships, as well.

This account of agape's perfect independence is part of where later modern agapists focus their critiques of Nygren, but largely in ways that don't attend clearly to the connection between independence from motivation and independence from vulnerability, nor to the one-sided assertion of agape that emerges from it. The vulnerability of God's beloveds, however, should be at the center of their ethics given what they say agape should do and be in the human experience and emulation of it. Nygren's divine perfectionism must be overcome more fully, by correcting its mistaken response to the vulnerability of this world.

LOVING THE VULNERABLE

A spontaneous and unmotivated love, "defined by love" and not by anything outside of it, is insulated from a certain kind of vulnerability: to changes in the beloved that could change the lover's perception of their value, and thus change a love dependent on it. As vulnerable beings in a finite world, to be loved in this way seems a gift of a high order. But Nygren's account raises the question of whether such invulnerability to changes in the value of the beloved is also, necessarily, an invulnerability in or to relationship *with* the beloved. What kind of relationship is possible with a lover who is indifferent and invulnerable in the ways Nygren describes?

The question takes on a different significance in a more traditional interpretation of agape as both the love of God and the love commanded by God to be practiced by Christians—an interpretation to which all of the modern agapists except Nygren are committed. As a description of God's love, agape as an invulnerable force may not trouble many interpreters. But as a worldly ethic, the forceful assertion of agape without clear regard for the beloved, let alone vulnerability to them, is a dangerous ideal.

Agape bears a substantial constancy in both contexts, evident in God's love of sinners and the command by God to love one's enemies and love one's neighbor as oneself. Whether practiced by God or human beings, agape does (or should, as an ethical ideal) not discriminate among beloveds on the basis of their value, and thus should not change if the value of the beloved changes. It constitutes a kind of response to worldly vulnerability in this way, and contrasts with loves made uncertain by the vulnerability of the worldly goods on which they depend. But as a worldly ethic, to be practiced by human beings loving other human beings, agape's invulnerabilities seem both especially marvelous and especially strange. What does it mean to be loved by a person who will not stop loving you if you change? Is that desirable—an "unconditional" love, as we sometimes ascribe with admiration to human relationships—or a limitation of connection, tending toward the bestowal of generic benevolence and blunting the possibilities of relationship? And what does it mean to emulate this kind of love as a lover? Is it an invitation to greater commitment, the defeat of half-heartedness and other wavering of the will? Or a temptation toward egoistic self-assertion, inattentive to the other or even dominative, however well-intentioned, in the force of love and care?

A Worldly Ethics of Agape

When Protestant Christian ethicists began arguing with Nygren about agape after the publication of his work, one target of their criticisms was his lack of interest in agape as an ethical ideal for human beings. Although he names the exhortation to "love your enemies" as the starting point of his inquiry, he makes sure to finish the citation quickly— "Be perfect, therefore, *as your heavenly Father is perfect*"—to argue for the restriction of agape as the perfect love of God, not a love practiced by human beings. For Nygren, the focus of other Christian ethicists on agape's role in worldly ethics is a key failure of efforts to understand agape as Christianity's fundamental motif. For many readers of him, however, his lack of interest in worldly ethics is a key failure of his account, inconsistent with the teachings of Jesus as well as conceptually confusing, and confused.

To understand the other modern agapists' handling of vulnerability and agape, let me first say a few words about the structure of their conversations overall, particularly those parts of them to which Nygren's approach is most substantially outlying. Most of the modern agapists begin their inquiries from two questions long central to Christian ethical reflection, both rejected by Nygren as false starts to the inquiry into agape as the fundamental motif of Christianity. The first is about the meaning of the imperative to love cited by Jesus in Matthew 22, Mark 12, and Luke 10. Jesus is asked by a lawyer which commandment is the greatest of all (in Matthew), the "first" of all (in Mark), or what he must do "to inherit eternal life" (in Luke). Jesus responds,

> "You shall love the Lord your God with all your heart, and with all your soul, and with all your mind." This is the greatest and first commandment. And a second is like it: "You shall love your neighbor as yourself." On these two commandments hang all the Law and the Prophets.[63]

The Greek word for love used in these lines and elsewhere in the Gospels is *agape*, hence the consideration of agape as Christian love as opposed to other forms of love named by other Greek words like *eros* and *philia*. The basic distinctions among these words in ancient Greek usage hover over the interpretation of the scriptural passages, as Nygren warns.[64] Many questions emerge from these classical definitions and the New Testament passages in which agape, but not eros or *philia*, is used to talk about love. The one that most occupies the modern agapists other than Nygren is what kind of imperative the second commandment to love the neighbor must be. Does it require or recommend actions or attitudes, or should it primarily constrain us from certain actions and attitudes when we are tempted toward them? What kind of ethics and politics does it encourage, or demand? What must a Christian do to pursue this commandment?

The second question concerns the relationship between this commanded love of neighbor and the loves we find ourselves having, like romantic love, friendship, and familial love. Do these "natural" experiences of love, as Kierkegaard calls them, offer any instruction in what the Christian should be doing when loving the neighbor as God commands? Or do they lead us away from understanding what it would mean to love agapically? Is the love of neighbor in tension with these other loves—should a person give them up, or restrain them, in order to love according to the commandment? Or might a person

Christian Agape and the Vulnerability of Worldly Goods 99

love agapically alongside other forms of love? And should our love for family, friends, and romantic lovers be transformed by the love of neighbor? Must it be, given the constraints of time and energy on how we pursue and sustain relationships in the finite world?

These are questions about the uniqueness of Christian love as opposed to worldly relations. They are also questions about the ethics and politics that emerge from taking love as the "greatest of all" commandments. An ethics and politics interested in love need not take love as the "greatest of all" imperatives, commanded or otherwise, nor as an imperative at all. It could be treated as a form of relation that can be enacted more or less virtuously, or with greater or lesser potential for cruelty or domination—as something that happens, in other words, like so many things that happen in life, that can be pursued or responded to in better or worse ways. The commandment to love the neighbor sets Christian ethical reflection on a different course. It outlines an ethic that starts from love and "holds that there is only one basic ethical imperative—to love—and that the others are to be derived from it," as William Frankena describes the view.[65] *Love* might refer to many experiences and relations we find ourselves having or desire in different parts of life, but *agapism* focuses on an imperative to love, and to love certain people in certain ways that might be very different from loves we experience or hope for in families, friendships, and romantic relations. The modern agapists are concerned primarily with the nature of this imperative and its connection to, and difference from, other worldly relations. This is one of their significant criticisms of Nygren's account of agape: that his diminishment of agape as the commanded love of neighbor mistakes the role of Christian love in Christians' lives.

The dual love commandment also introduces a new character to the discussion of love, whose significance Nygren diminishes but the other modern agapists center in their accounts. Where the ancient Greek philosophers refer to the "beloved," the "beautiful," and the "friend" as the objects of love, defined by their attractive qualities and the lover's recognition of them, Christian love of neighbor defines a new beloved by, perhaps paradoxically, their being undefined by any qualities or characteristics. The neighbor is "every man, unconditionally every man," in Kierkegaard's description, a view endorsed by all of the modern agapists (with varying degrees of interest in less gendered language) and echoing much of the history of Christian thought.[66] Modern agapists have been especially interested in the "unconditional" qualifier. "All distinctions are indeed removed from the object" because of it, Kierkegaard continues. The neighbor is not selected among others for their beauty, intellect, or good humor. Love is extended to the neighbor for their own sake, regardless of their merit, worth, or any other conditions of these kinds. The neighbor is sometimes referred to as simply the "other" in this sense, because the neighbor is any and every other person, and for many modern agapists, also oneself. The people to whom one has special attachments—family, friends, romantic lovers—are neighbors as well, though not by virtue of those attachments or anything that recommends them. The people to whom one has special disdain, enmity, or hatred are neighbors, too—and perhaps the most important to mention, some argue, because it might be the love of enemies that best exemplifies the distinctiveness of Christian love. We saw Nygren argue for the importance of the love of enemies as well, but against the elevation of the commandment to love as a paradigm of agape.

The definition of the neighbor is a key place that the contrast between agapic love and other forms of love is often made in terms of the value of the beloved, and thus raises the questions of vulnerability that accompany it. A love for "every man, unconditionally every man," cannot arise from or be sustained by the valuable qualities and characteristics of a person. Its object is not selected in this way; it should not be selective nor discriminating at all, as opposed to loves like eros and *philia* that are defined by their discrimination among potential beloveds. Agape is an "identification with [the neighbor's] interests in utter independence of the question of his attractiveness," in Karl Barth's description, and thus "does not arise from and is not proportioned to anything a given neighbor individually possesses or has acquired," in Gene Outka's.[67] It is extended "regardless of any merit perceived in the beloved or any utility produced for the lover," Timothy Jackson writes; given "gratuitously," in Nicholas Wolterstorff's language, uninterested in what is deserved and ready to go beyond whatever might be.[68] The neighbor is not defined by their value, and the love of neighbor is not dependent on that value.

But this is not to know precisely what agape's relationship to value must be, and the moderation of Nygren's view by later readers takes up his understanding of agape's relationship to value as a significant locus of critique. Nygren emphasizes the worthlessness and sins of the beloved to define agape's indifference to value, wary of any implication that the beloved might merit love. For others, however, the constancy of agape is indicative of the constant value of the beloved, or at least the constancy of the value that agape bestows and regards. For Outka, for example, agape is known to be "independent and unalterable" not because it is bestowed even on the worthless, but because it is commanded as a love of neighbor, not a love of some neighbors, family, or friends.[69] Part of what it means to have a love "determined by love" in which "all distinctions are indeed removed from the object," as Outka quotes from Kierkegaard, is that what happens in life to make us different from each other, and from earlier versions of ourselves, shouldn't alter agapic love. The possibility of change shouldn't alter agapic love either, nor be feared by the agapic lover or beloved. The Christian must love the neighbor "prior to his doing anything in particular" and beyond anything he does to his credit or shame.[70] "One ought to be committed to the other's well-being independently and unalterably," Outka writes. "*Agape* enjoins an equal consideration that is independent of changes in the particular states of the other, and unalterable in that some attitudes toward the other are never set aside; on no conceivable occasion are they out of place."[71] Changes in one's beloved might dramatically affect erotic love or friendship; changes in the neighbor should not change agapic love. And the value of the neighbor, Outka argues, should be defined by the equality and constancy of agapic love, instead of those features defining or displaying the beloved's worthlessness. To find the beloved "irreducibly valuable" is "the corollary to such independent and unalterable regard."[72]

Outka's argument for agape as independent and unalterable "equal regard" is made explicitly against Nygren, as part of a critique of Nygren as overly invested in an idea of value individually acquired, possessed, and appraised. Others criticize Nygren on similar grounds, suggesting that his understanding of a person's value is overdetermined by his interpretation of the Lutheran doctrine of unmerited grace, as we considered in the first section.[73] If grace is an unmerited gift, it is important to specify that God loves human beings without human beings deserving this love because of something we've earned or are due. God's love cannot be understood in any way that suggests it is merited by human beings—God cannot be said to be required to love human beings because of what we are worth, or something we have done. Nygren is so engaged in defining God's love as unmerited, however, that he seems unable to conceive of a love that regards a person's value in any other sense: as something a lover could regard and respond to without their love being required by it or dependent on it.

In one common sense of "a person's value," as we've considered in other chapters, value refers to qualities and characteristics of a person evaluated in comparison to others, and judged better or worse, greater or lesser on these grounds. Some of these qualities and characteristics are acquired through intention and action, others by accident or fortune, and others by something like nature or biology, which might be to say, accident of birth. Many emerge from a combination of these sources, and are also defined by the preferences and perception of those assessing them. Your beauty or intellect is some complex product of biology, what has happened to you as you've lived, and what you've done to cultivate it. It is also "in the eye of the beholder," famously, assessed by people whose own qualities and characteristics affect how yours are valued.

This last point introduces the possibility that there could be some distinction between the value of your qualities, characteristics, and other things about you, and the way you are in fact valued in the world. In some contexts, it might be meaningful to say that you have value even if it is not in fact being valued. It might be meaningful, for instance, to say that you *are* beautiful even if you are not in fact *being seen* or *assessed* as beautiful by anyone around you. It could be that there is a fact of the matter that you are valuable in this way, even if no one in fact values you.[74] "Valuable" refers most directly to the *possibility* of valuing, however, and someone could insist that you still don't *have* that value until someone values you, realizing the possibility. But it could also imply the existence of goods that can be called your "value" even without the historical circumstance of their being valued. A person's value in this sense might refer to qualities and characteristics, present in them always or acquired during their lives. More often in the modern agapist conversation, a concept of a person's value independent of the historical fact of someone's valuing them is present in the form of what Outka calls "generic endowments." We each and all have inherent value, in this sense, even if we are horribly disdained or utterly ignored by all who encounter us. We have this value as human beings. If no one in the world, in history, ever in fact recognizes it, that doesn't mean it isn't there, in this view. And this form of value, for most of the modern agapists, belongs to us as beings created in the image of God.[75] It is the form of value qua human existent bestowed by God's love. In this way, God is the being who values and has valued us, and so we have value even if no one else values us. This value might then be what the Christian should love in the neighbor, making their love responsive to value, just not the kind of value we tend to recognize or discuss in our romantic loves and friendships.

A Christian love of neighbor that is responsive to this kind of value qua human existent in this way might then have more in common with eros than Nygren, at least, would like, suggesting the next set of issues to clarify in the discussion. Part of the disagreement between Outka and Nygren is about the differences mentioned in the previous section among love *regarding, responding to,* and *being required by* value—differences we can now see more clearly, and consider in the very different context of a worldly ethic. By defining agape as "equal regard" for all persons qua human existents, Outka is defining a sense of Christian love that sees the generic value of each beloved and responds to it. But what are the roles of "regard" and "response" in this relation? What does it mean to be commanded to regard and respond—is this love then required by a person's value qua human existent, or strictly by the commandment, bypassing the value of the beloved as motivation, if not in other ways? Does its regard allow "the serpent of requirement" to "have wriggled its way into the garden of pure *agape*," as Wolterstorff so vividly describes Nygren's concern?[76] And must agape be kept "pure" from requirement when human beings are its subjects, not God? These questions get to the heart of the tension between agape and eros that the modern agapists explore. They also get to the heart of the question of agape's independence from the vulnerability of worldly goods—to what it means to love the vulnerable with the constancy of agape.

On the question of regard, most modern agapists agree with Outka contra Nygren that Christian agape, like classical agape, cannot ignore the value of the beloved if to do so would be to ignore their particular qualities and characteristics. The classical interpretation of agape is as a love that does not appraise but bestows value, as in the love of parents for children or teachers for students. But parents and teachers must be able to see the qualities and characteristics of their beloveds. Their ability to love them well requires that they know who they are and the particularities of what they need, like, and aspire to. Their love cannot ignore their particularities; those particularities just aren't the object of their love, or the motivation for it. All of the modern agapists except Nygren define Christian agape similarly, in that the particularities of the beloved must be seen to know what it would be to love them for their own sake. A lover who never turns to the neighbor and tries to see them as they are cannot love them well, no matter how well-intentioned the lover may be.

We all, of course, fail to see our beloveds well from time to time. I think my student would benefit from one thing, but have misunderstood them; parents try to do what they think is best for their child, and later see that they were wrong. But the lover must try to see the beloved, *this* beloved, to have a credible claim of trying to act for their sake. To do otherwise would be at best to offer some kind of generic benevolence, as might be expressed when packing identical lunches for charity, with no sense or way of knowing of the particular individuals who will eat them. That kind of charity isn't bad, and might even be derived from an attempt to pursue the dual love commandment within the limitations of our finite world, but it isn't what the modern agapists are talking about, primarily, when they talk about the love of neighbor.

This kind of regard—to see the neighbor in their particularities—is endorsed by all the modern agapists except Nygren as a part of agapic love and not a threat to its definition in the dual love commandment or its distinction from an appraising eros. Nygren's position is less clear, mostly because he doesn't treat the issue of regard separately from the question of love's motivation and dependence on worldly goods in the value of the beloved. The entanglement, if not its obfuscating effect, is also part of what I find interesting in Nygren for our discussion here. Value regarded is for Nygren value appraised, and value appraised is value that motivates, in the sense of being the cause of love instead of love being given freely by the lover. A love that regards value cannot be trusted to be independent of it, in his view. If the value of the beloved fades or vanishes, the love may vanish as well. The serpent of requirement is thus also a source of vulnerability: a love that depends on value is vulnerable to changes in worldly goods in a way that an unmotivated love is not.

But this train of thought tightly connects concepts that need not be held so closely together, as we saw in the first section. Regard for the beloved's particularities need not imply an appraisal of their value. Appraisal need not motivate love such that love is no longer freely given by the lover. And motivation need not imply enduring dependence: love (of many kinds) might be motivated in ways on which it is not continuously dependent, as in the simple, familiar cases of falling in love with someone knowing one set of things about them and finding, as the relation continues, that those things seem not to matter anymore at all. These are the kinds of shifts we considered in the first chapters, and the kinds of shifts that I think must be prominently considered in an account of love. They suggest more room in these categories and their relations to one another than the modern agapist discussion sometimes encourages us to see, especially when it hews closest to Nygren's arguments for the distinctiveness of agape.

A Human Problem, If a Divine Marvel

One way to think about the modern agapist discussion, as I have thus far, is through the definitions of its key terms, as part of a project of definition: the possible meanings of value and regard, appraisal and bestowal, motivation and requirement, selection and discrimination, and so on, that compose the definitions of agape and eros and define the contrast between them. Another way to think about the discussion, however, is through the dynamics of motivating and making claims on each other and ourselves, for and against different relations and actions within them in the effort to love as God commands. As Nygren and Outka disagree over the agapic lover's regard for the value of the beloved, we can see that the motivation and moment for inquiry is different in each discussion. Nygren is concerned with the implication that value could be said to merit agapic love, such that the beloved could take themselves to have had something to do with agape being bestowed on them. This is love considered from the perspective of the beloved, trying to interpret how they came to be loved and what this love is. Outka writes of a moment of alteration or discrimination, when the qualities of the (potential) beloved present themselves to the discouragement of the (potential) lover. This is love understood from the perspective of the lover, at a moment when their love or will to love is being tested: when they need encouragement, a reason to keep loving, or a way to motivate themselves to love at all. The question of the relation between love and value looks very different at these different moments of inquiry, and from the different perspectives of the lover and beloved. The differences suggest that we should revisit, in this very different context, the concerns of the previous chapter about what questions definitions of love aim to answer. Are they to help us understand love that exists, or help motivate love to exist? Do they seek to contest failures of love? Are they corrective, motivating, or serving some other purpose? Will they work?

One reason to define agape is to try to understand what exactly God commands, and for many of the modern agapists, the use of agape in a commandment is what gives it its clearest definition. As a worldly relationship, in these accounts, the constancy of agape as practiced by human beings derives from its commandment, not from its indifference to value nor its bestowal on the worthless and sinful. None of the modern agapists other than Nygren takes God's forgiveness of sins as the singular paradigm of God's love. Each takes seriously that one marvel of divine love is the love of sinners, and one marvel of Jesus's teachings on love of neighbor is the love of enemies. These are extraordinary forms of love, not just in a world that has "already received the impress of *eros*" but to anyone who has experienced basic forms of attraction and aversion, desire and dislike, let alone enmity toward someone who has wronged them, or great want for someone who delights them. But for the other modern agapists, the love of sinners and enemies should not encourage us to think of the beloved as worthless, nor of agapic love as unmotivated. It should encourage us to think of agape's stability and constancy as derived from its motivation in God's command, as we saw Kierkegaard describe at the beginning of this chapter. In human relations, agape is not unmotivated, in these accounts. It is motivated differently: by duty, instead of the value of the beloved.

The transformation of love into a duty *is* the securing, stabilizing force of the commandment to love for the modern agapists other than Nygren, allowing lovers to relinquish the insecurities of erotic love and friendship because their love is no longer dependent on its object. "Only when it is a duty to love," Kierkegaard writes, "only then is love eternally secured against every change, eternally made free in blessed independence, eternally and happily secured against despair."[77]

In this way the "You shall" makes love free in blessed independence; such a love stands and does not fall with variations in the object of love; it stands and falls with eternity's law, but therefore it never falls. Such a love is not dependent on this or on that. It is dependent on the one thing—that alone which makes for freedom—and therefore it is eternally independent.[78]

Because this love is secured in the eternal love of God, through God's commandment, it is secured beyond the vagaries of worldly goods. It is not dependent on the endurance of any good qualities in the beloved nor on the endurance of the lover's appreciation for them. It is not dependent on worldly goods at all. It is dependent on the eternal law, which is to say, according to Kierkegaard, that it is eternally independent, as the eternal law will not change, and so the love that flows from it will not change. The lover who loves in accordance with the commandment can weather changes in worldly conditions because their love is not defined by worldly conditions.

However, the duty to love is still dependent in practice on the persistent motivation of the lover to follow God's command. Kierkegaard's account of the stabilizing force of the commandment emphasizes the challenge of the lover's motivation—a different source of vulnerability than the value of the beloved, but one no less threatening to worldly relations.[79] Agape as a duty to love commanded by God places the difficulty for lovers in the realm of faithfulness and obedience to God, instead of the vulnerability of the valuable qualities and characteristics of the beloved. Christians must still motivate their love through faith and obedience; commanded love is still vulnerable to the inconstancy of human beings, though as lovers of God instead of lovers of their neighbors. The isolation of agape from the vulnerability of worldly goods in the beloved thus addresses only part of the vulnerability of worldly love. A love defined by love, as practiced by human beings, can still fail or be absent. Love may end, even if it is not dependent on the value of the beloved to continue. The commandment to love addresses this potential by the force of eternal law, but it thus calls attention to the problem of the lover's motivation. This is a problem of the will. And the human will is not always so steady—we lack God's constancy, to say the least. An invulnerable love is a human problem, if a divine marvel.

One reason some of the modern agapists are interested in distinguishing a robust concept of justice—twinned to eros with respect to evaluation and desert—from Christian love is because of the way justice provides a place to turn when the ethical ideal of a freely given, constant, unwavering agape requires correction: when love isn't given at all, doesn't endure, or otherwise fails. Nygren's insistence on an agape radically distinct from justice doesn't offer very much to someone struggling with injustice or with a lack of love from their neighbors. He doesn't suggest it will: his paradigm of the contrast between love and justice is Jesus's parable of the vineyard laborers, in which Jesus criticizes those who complain about generosity on the grounds of its injustice.[80] But sometimes people need to complain, and need grounds to contest their conditions in ways that a bestowed agape doesn't obviously provide. As Reinhold Niebuhr argues, injustices are frequent enough and harmful enough that Christians must have a social ethic that aids in their contestation and correction. Injustice does not appear in the world primarily in the form of a vineyard owner paying fair wages to those who have worked full days, but the same amount to those who have worked half days. It might be true, as Nygren argues, that such injustice can only be understood through the lens of agape, and that we should not complain of injustice where people are only being generous. But that simply isn't the kind of problem we tend to face in the world. Failures to be generous are far more common, and failures to be more basically fair or to avoid harm are more urgently in need of redress.

Niebuhr writes that his interest "in making a sharper distinction between justice and love ... was prompted by the growing awareness of the defect in the social gospel in its analysis of human behavior, derived from its rejection of the doctrine of original sin."[81] In the "liberal movement" of the social gospel most prominently put forward by Walter Rauschenbusch, Niebuhr argues, the unfortunate realities of human nature in this world and the injustices that result from them are insufficiently considered. Agape struggles, he suggests, to provide a way to contest situations in which value, worth, or due is disregarded in the sense of disrespect or violation. This is a different kind of concern about agape's regard or disregard for the value of the beloved than we've seen thus far. The question is not whether the agapic lover sees value, idiosyncratic or generic, but what to do when we wish people saw us as valuable, or wish they treated us better however we appear to them. These are questions about recourse and correction, how to make claims on each other for better treatment and the reduction of harm, which need something beyond a love "defined by love" to be asked coherently and answered persuasively. A "pure" agape, unmotivated and bestowed, cannot be demanded as justice can be demanded. For Niebuhr, this requires Christian attention to justice in addition to love, and attention to the distinctions between them. For Nygren, it shows the radical nature of agape, and its distance from worldly concerns.

The difficulty of recourse and correction is one manifestation of the problem with the human emulation of divine love when it is construed as a perfectly invulnerable, assertive force. What God lacks as a lover in Nygren's description is any way of being affected by God's beloveds. Love is one-sided, not a relationship so much as an ever-given gift. A human love seeking to emulate the constancy this invulnerability makes possible may not be affected by the beloved either—not by changes in their value, for better or worse, nor by their complaints or other indications as to how this gift of love is being received. Bestowal seems marvelous unless what it being bestowed is undesirable. The capacity to complain, to describe misrecognition of needs or desires, or otherwise to have an effect on someone who claims to love you is essential for ethical relations in a world where human needs and desires are diverse. I cannot always know what my beloveds need or how best to love them, even if I am committed to love them whatever they do or are. I cannot let the commitment to constancy override the need to listen, correct for misrecognition, and otherwise be in relation *with* them without creating significant opportunities for injustice, domination, and abuse.

It isn't clear, however, why agape should be understood in a way that makes it so distinct from justice to the point of defining a relationship in which the demands of justice cannot be made effectively. Strong versions of the contrasts between agape and justice and agape and eros allow agape to be useless for worldly contestations, and justice and eros to be wholly disconnected from something bestowed for the other's sake. Outka, Jackson, and Wolterstorff each argues against making these contrasts so extreme, suggesting that trying to keep the terms too perfectly distinct from each other leads to incoherent and even ethically repulsive versions of them. For Jackson, a synthesis of eros and agape—not a muddied agape as "heavenly eros," as Nygren decries, but a synthesis of their distinct qualities—is necessary lest we forgo the charity and compassion we require or ignore the inherent value of our fellow human beings, and ourselves. We need more than an appraising form of love, he contends, since "we all live by the service and mercy of strangers whose love outstrips anything explicable in terms of reciprocity or desert or natural impulse."[82] Our feeble bodies are both vulnerable and unable to motivate consistently the care that this vulnerability requires. The "just and rational eroticism" of love caused and sustained by the value of the beloved "is not enough to keep physical vulnerability or moral culpability within livable bounds."[83] But in order to develop the kind of charitable, neighborly love that we require, Jackson argues, we must attend to the intrinsic worth of others in more than the practical perception of needs allowed by a narrow definition of agape. We cannot assume that the value of our beloved is entirely bestowed by our love for them, and we cannot love without a recognition of inherent worth.[84] Thus love should not be understood as *either* appraisal *or* bestowal of the value of the beloved. This is a false choice, ethically dangerous and easily misguiding.

Vulnerability appears in Jackson's account as part of the worldly conditions agape addresses, and that agape is needed to address. But agape, for Jackson, is not a consolation to these conditions nor should it be understood to respond to them by offering their escape. It should attend to them, seeing what change is possible and what is feared. And it should respond to them by offering more than we fear we will deserve or motivate in others by only the force of their desire. Of all of the modern agapists, Jackson most clearly corrects Nygren's isolation of agape from the vulnerability of worldly goods in this way, and suggests how a worldly ethic of agape could approach the vulnerabilities of both lover and beloved without the isolation of "indifference," the paradox of inconstancy in the fulfillment of duty, or the turn away from love to justice in order to pursue a social ethic that actually responds to the problems we find in the world. The perfect invulnerability of Nygren's agape is replaced with the constancy of *excess*. Agape offers always more than could be deserved, is always bestowed beyond motivation in the beloved's value, and is always offered past norms of requirement or regard. It responds to the vulnerabilities of worldly love and life by making them essential to the relationship, and positing the limitations they represent not as something to be escaped but as the definition of where to begin.

Vulnerability must be only the beginning, however, and the agapic lover's response to it must not be the end. The agapic lover must be in relationship with the vulnerable beloved such that the beloved, and others around them, have the opportunity for effective recourse where what is bestowed is unwanted, harmful, or simply missing the mark. Otherwise, agapic love as an ethical ideal for human beings becomes a project of self-fulfillment or achievement, similar to the projects of the "achievement subject" we saw in the first chapter. Well-intentioned domination and abuse are constant specters in any relationship of care. Their possibility is exacerbated where the constancy of care is idealized and secured by the invulnerability of the caregiver to changes in the person they care for.

Most of the modern agapists argue for a moderation of agape's invulnerability to changes in the beloved, at least as far as it would prevent the lover from being affected by the beloved's concerns and complaints. They see the problem with such a failure of relationship and are careful to define the ideal of agape so that it is not so extreme a bestowal, not the force asserted of Nygren's divine agape. But these risks in an ethics of agape are obscured by promises of constancy. Where the ethical ideal of agape is described as too perfectly constant, too perfectly invulnerable, too perfectly secure apart from the beloved, it hides the need for due consideration of the opportunities for the beloved to affect the lover and the vulnerability of the human lover's own will. Yet these are the essential problems of so much of vulnerable human life: to be seen and heard in relationships with others, including to ask for, direct, or correct their attention and care. Perhaps we "live by the service and mercy of strangers," as Jackson suggests, but only where we can direct and correct it to respond well to who we are and what we need.

The problem is not only that people will get the things they do and offer in love wrong, and need to be able to hear what is actually desired and required. The problem is that agapic love bestowed as an assertion of the lover makes what relationship with the beloved might have been possible into a project, undertaken by the lover, of escaping worldly vulnerability. The effort to define an ethical ideal of love more constant than human beings seem to muster otherwise mistakes the importance of vulnerability *in* loving relationships, necessarily facing an unknown and uncertain future in the finite world. God, in the Christian agapists' understanding, is not subject to such uncertainty. But human beings seeking its escape in love will find themselves without a relationship with another at all. Denying the uncertainty of the future in how their beloved will change their life and affect their love, they will turn love into another project of the self, only made slightly imperfect by the limitations of finitude. Instead, the limitations of finitude should define what love for human beings is and can be: a constant confrontation with uncertainty, made marvelous—not perfect—by the possibility of its continuation into the unknown.

◦ 4 ◦
Promises and Obligations: On Loving the Dying

I have argued in the preceding chapters for a view of love that emphasizes the lover's want for more time with their beloved, not knowing what that time will bring. But sometimes we know all too much about how our time is likely to be determined, as the possibilities of life cede to the expectations of illness and decline toward death. What happens to love when the future together seems no longer promising, not as a matter of the desire of the lover but the reality of what they can expect? How does love continue in these conditions—and how do we think about cases where it may not?

These are questions about love's continuation under duress, and about the ethics of caring for the people near us. They concern the possibility that love might end at times when we think it should continue, and that we might fail our loved ones in other senses just as they need us most. They are also questions about where our obligations lie, and what obligations to care have to do with love. In finding time with my beloved promising, have I *made a promise* to them, to care for them in times of need?

I will argue in this chapter that finding time together promising is different from making promises, though we often do make promises to our beloveds alongside our professions of love. It is important, however, to disentangle the promises that obligate us in care from the happy promise of an uncertain future in love, lest we mistake the indeterminacies of love for the indeterminacies of care. When we love someone, we want more time with them, not knowing what that time will bring. When we care for someone, we commit ourselves to provide for their needs, not knowing what those needs will be. Each relationship is uncertain and indeterminate, but in significantly different ways. Where we mistake desire in love for commitment to care, we may be easily disappointed and left devastatingly alone. Where we assume caregiving commitments to be happily undertaken with desire for a future together, we neglect the work of caregivers on the pretense that it is the work of love.

I will look at these questions in two relationships that reach us through their depiction in art: a painter and his model, lovers and new parents, whose love is represented—perhaps—in a series of portraits he paints of her as she dies; and a fictional couple in Tony Kushner's *Angels in America*, lovers once and maybe still, as one man dies of AIDS and the other cannot seem to bear his illness. Each relationship is strained by the determination by illness of what time together they have left. The sick need care, and their lovers struggle to provide it. They also struggle with their love: whether they love and how, how to keep loving, what is required where they feel less desire than fear. They may not be exemplary lovers. But they offer illuminating examples of the limits of love—and an outline of what else is needed in our fragile, finite lives.

VALENTINE GODÉ-DAREL, AS SHE WAS DYING

In late January of 1915, the Swiss symbolist Ferdinand Hodler painted a stunning portrait of his lover Valentine Godé-Darel shortly after she died of ovarian cancer. She lays in bed, in the painting, on top of the sheets and propped on pillows, with her hands grasping each other over her lap. Her head is tipped back, as if she were sleeping, and her mouth is open like someone trying to sleep with a bad cold. Her skin is painted in beautiful, ghostly tones of deep yellow and green; her legs shadowed in bright blue where her pale yellow bedclothes fold over themselves. The background of the painting is a vivid, warm pink with visible brush strokes and cheerful, rich red dots resembling roses floating over the scene. She lays in the posture of a saint, or even of Christ—the composition resembles Hans Holbein the Younger's *The Body of the Dead Christ in the Tomb*, prone in death, swathed in a simple shroud, mouth gaping toward an unknown ceiling, or sky.[1]

Die Tote Valentine Godé-Darel is one of eighteen paintings and at least 120 drawings that Hodler made of his lover throughout her illness and in the days surrounding her death. The portraits depict the decline of a woman he loved and so loved to paint, often in vigorous health. Hodler and Godé-Darel had met eight years earlier when she began modeling for him and became the figure of some of his most famous celebrations of the female form. She appears in his 1908 *The Splendour of Lines* in dynamic vitality, her back to the viewer as she moves in a kind of dancer's step forward past the frame. A year later, in 1909, she was the subject of *The Joyful Woman* in a similar pose, a painting infused with a symbolist's sense of vivacity in its rich blues and golden yellows, the musculature of her body visible under a thin dress, and the simultaneously strong and graceful motion of her arms and chest: joyful, as we know from the title, and also steady and controlled, a picture of health and strength even more than joy in its senses of happy abandon.

It seems nearly cruel that the model for these lively compositions would be diagnosed just a few years later with ovarian cancer, shortly after the birth of their daughter, Paulette, in 1913.[2] Early in her illness Hodler began to paint very different portraits of Godé-Darel than the prior pieces, including striking frontal compositions reminiscent of the Fayum portraits painted to cover the faces of bodies mummified for burial in first-century Coptic Egypt. The faces of the Fayum dead stare out directly from their boards with large black eyes and little expression but a sense of identification, a portrait of precisely that person, now recognizable to all who see the piece. Godé-Darel stares similarly at the viewer, as if the paintings were records to use to find her later. The paintings and drawings from these early days of her illness mark a turn in Hodler's depictions of Godé-Darel, and perhaps his relation to her. Where earlier she appeared as allegorical Woman, she is now a subject of portraiture: a particular face, herself and not another, with compositional reference to the identification and commemoration of the dead.

As she got sicker, Hodler began to visit regularly, often daily, spending hours by her bedside painting and drawing her. In many of these pieces she looks directly at the viewer, or the artist, in discomforted gazes that seem to form a relation, or ask for it, while also fading from it. Her direct stares emphasize the distance between herself, as she suffers, and her onlooker, while also marking the onlooker's presence with her. And the "onlooker" here seems to be Hodler more than the viewer. These are not the outward stares of a Mona Lisa or the portraits earlier in her illness that seem to look to an audience. The angle of the gaze, the pathos of her expressions, and, most of all, the agony evident on her face make it hard not to think of the person *in the room* who could attend to her pain. It is then hard not to imagine the eyes she was looking into, how Hodler looked back at her, and what relation was formed, or transformed, in the exchange.

Her weakness and pain become increasingly evident in these pieces as the series continues, and soon, more often, her eyes don't meet ours, or Hodler's: her head buries itself exhausted into the pillow, her cheeks gaunt, her hand appearing to rest, but nearly to clutch, at her heart. An article published in the *Journal of Clinical Oncology* describes the portraits as having "documented her wasting and eventual extinction without mercy and yet with intense sympathy," identifying a kind of medical accuracy in what the author describes as "a series of paintings that force the viewer to face the process of dying." The portraits may thus be "helpful to an oncologist to sense his or her reactions to these visual stages of suffering"—a curriculum of decline and death, made as the two lovers followed it themselves, in real time, together.[3]

Unfinished Love

I was first captivated by Hodler's work when I saw one of the final portraits, *Valentine Godé-Darel on Her Deathbed*, at the Met Breuer's *Unfinished* exhibition in the summer of 2016. The composition of the painting is the same as the painting first described above: Godé-Darel lies horizontally on the bed, her feet nearly touching the left edge of the canvas, her head just a bit farther from the right edge, propped on pillows, face tipped back, mouth open. But unlike the other painting, there is no vibrant pink background or red dots suggesting flowers floating above her, nor are the folds of her dress accented in bright blues and greens. The colors here are far more muted. The wall behind her is a slightly dirty white; the shadows showing the folds in her dress painted in quiet blue-grays, and in the sheets, a slightly grayer gray. The most saturated colors in the painting are the black of her shoes and stockings and the darker olive tones of her skin, sickly and deeply shadowed in sunken cheeks.

I was drawn to the spare composition and its vague horror from across the room, but also to its apparent "finish" in a collection of supposedly "unfinished" works, loosely collected though they were by that theme throughout the show. The didactic panel seemed written in reference to this concern, describing the piece as "executed in an incomplete and sketchy style" that "conveys [Hodler's] silent anguish as well as a sense of finality." It continues:

> Created under extreme circumstances and at the end of an unprecedented series in which he recorded his lover's illness and physical decline, the painting raises fundamental questions regarding the transitional nature of the moment of death and the inherent "unfinishedness" of human life.[4]

I liked this description, though the idea of the portrait as unfinished because of its sketchy style or of life unfinished as human life is "inherently" unfinished seemed hard to defend, or define. What could it mean for life to be "inherently" unfinished? By what standards, and in whose telling—or, conversely, as opposed to what? A successfully completed life?

With respect to the piece itself, I could imagine a painter having precisely the intention to finish the painting as it appears, at this level of looseness in the brushstrokes and colors, the remnants of the compositional grid left unerased. I think these are quite interesting aspects of the painting, laudable to be intended as its "finished" state, instead of laudable at best as accidents of incompletion. I could also imagine the moment of death being captured by the painting precisely as a kind of completion, or in the words of the didactic, a "finality," "finished" in that sense. The Fayum funerary portraits seem like potential examples of such work. The grammar of a "finished" life is still a bit odd, but it seems possible as an intention of the artist or a decent interpretation by the viewer of the painting's subject.

It seems possible, that is, if not for learning that the artist and subject were lovers, and that the painting is part of a series of portraits painted as she was dying, not a singular memorial at her death. The possibility that it is a "finished" work—even the idea of a "finished" work—

provokes a different set of questions by these lights. What would it mean for the artist to "finish" a painting of his beloved, now dead? What would it be to *want* to finish it? Would that desire be a desire for a kind of end to the relationship, to time spent with Valentine, whether with her physical body or with her in only painted form? We may desire endings of some kinds after our beloveds' deaths, forms of closure to end forms of pain, but these desires seem far from the lover's mind at the moment of passing. And maybe they are far from a lover's mind altogether, qua lover, or so I want to consider here.

Learning that the artist and subject are—or were—lovers makes it hard to imagine the possibility of a "finished" version of the work because it is hard to imagine a lover seeking to exhaust their engagement with their beloved, as that might imply. Some forms of desire pursue exhaustion of certain kinds, but not the forms that bring a man to his lover's bedside as she dies, to be with her for hours, painting and drawing her. It becomes harder to imagine any possibility of "finishing" the work in this setting, not because of an inherent "unfinishedness" of life, but because lovers desire more time together.

We might find some further suggestion of this reading by comparison, because this was not the first time Hodler had painted a deathbed scene of a lover. In fact, he painted a previous lover in death in a very similar composition around the time he first met Godé-Darel. This deathbed portrait, of Augustine Dupin, resembles even more than those of Godé-Darel Hans Holbein the Younger's *The Body of the Dead Christ in the Tomb*—an unfinished life in a very different sense, depicted as such in still-open eyes and mouth, not closed by mourners nor yet reopened in the resurrection. Hodler's portrait of Dupin in a similar pose is painted on a large, nearly square canvas, with a vast wall colored a deep ocher in the space above her figure lying in bed. At the top of the canvas, Hodler painted three bold blue lines, which he described to a friend at the time as "intended to symbolize her ascending soul."[5] But the verticality of ascent is thus represented horizontally, an "insistent horizontality" that some have understood to "foreshadow" his portraits of Godé-Darel.[6]

A striking painting, Hodler's deathbed portrait of Dupin is relatively singular, with some other sketches made surrounding its development but not any extended series documenting her decline or the days and hours surrounding her death, as Hodler made of Valentine. It is also not actually quite a portrait of a lover, by all accounts, or someone with whom he was still in love. Dupin and Hodler had been romantically involved some thirty years earlier, in the 1880s, but were no longer lovers by the time of her death. The affair had produced a son, Hector, with whom Hodler was close, and thus a connection that continued past the end of the romantic relationship. It was Hector who called Hodler to her bedside, to sit with them both as she died.[7] He may have loved her still, as the mother of his son or otherwise, but the relationship, it seems, was very different by the time of her death than the relationship he had with Valentine as she was dying.

The paintings are different as well: the paintings of Valentine in the same position are composed on more rectangular canvases, "coffin-like," by one description, without the more ample space for the soul's ascent.[8] Many of the sketches are composed entirely differently, capturing strange angles of her head as she rests in pain, and seemingly drawn from different angles at her bedside. Most significantly, Hodler's deathbed portraits of Godé-Darel represent not only his lover at the end of her life, in the tradition of deathbed portraiture undertaken also with Dupin, but the next entry in a series, and then the next, and the next—a series that doesn't quite end at her death, as if in some disbelief or denial that the end of her life might be an end to their time together. In this way, they recast our understanding of the earlier portraits of Valentine. Where it was tempting to think primarily of the suffering and pain depicted as she becomes sicker toward death, the temporality of the portraits now comes to the fore, setting the relationship of artist and model *as lovers* into relief. The portraits depict a woman dying in intimate relation to the artist, her lover of nearly a decade and the father of the child she was leaving behind. We see that not in the quality of her gaze or the beauty of her depiction, in compositional choices or the vibrancy of the paint, but because they represent many hundreds of hours spent together as she rests, suffers, dies, and then lays dead. We might now imagine her suffering through the lens of these days by her bedside, Hodler's trips back and forth between his house and hers, his drawing and painting her as her days dwindled, almost as a way of multiplying the days they had left by rendering them in oil or ink. The portraits represent time spent together, and so Hodler's want for more time, the hours together never sufficient and the relationship always incomplete.

This was what captivated me in that initial exposure, and continues to captivate me about the series—as a series, significantly, and not as single works. Paintings notoriously struggle to depict the continuation over time that defines many relationships, but as a series, these seem to do something of the kind.[9] They depict not just the beloved as her lover sees her, but his desire to keep looking at her, and in this sense at least, his want to spend more time with her. They are not an attempt to complete a depiction of her in some sense of mastery, having fully and finally drawn what he sees. They are the depiction of time together, and even the unsettling in that time of prior depictions. The "melodic" movements of allegorical Woman in earlier paintings no longer under the painter's compositional control, Hodler seems discomposed, the canvas determined on the horizontal plane by her illness, her waning strength, and eventually her death.[10] He cannot capture that, if to capture is to control. He must be seeking to capture it, on canvas, in a different sense.

Hodler was evidently frustrated in his attempts to capture her during this period. Swiss author Hans Mühlstein, an intimate of Hodler's at the time, describes Hodler destroying sketches of Valentine after his visits to her while she was hospitalized, exclaiming "It just doesn't represent what I have seen!" and later "kicking one of his paintings of the sick Valentine in frustration."[11] Drawing on Mühlstein's records, the historian Jill Lloyd describes Hodler in this period "bitterly disappointed by the two-dimensional insubstantiality of his drawings and paintings," apparent in his turn briefly and uncharacteristically to sculpture in 1914 to attempt a better rendition. He produced a small bronze bust of Valentine showing her sunken cheeks and thinning face, in what Lloyd calls "a desperate attempt to duplicate the reality he knew was slipping away from him."[12] He returned to painting, however, as she grew closer to death, the pace of the paintings and drawings quickening and the repetition of their compositions suggesting repetition itself as a response to the inadequacy of the two-dimensional form.

As a series, then, they also suggest a lover's defiance of reducing the beloved to some set of valuable qualities and characteristics, information about her grasped and held. The repetition recalls the continuous narration of the beloved discussed in the work of Adriana Cavarero in the first chapter, the impossibility of finishing the story lest it suggest there is nothing left to discover or learn. Hodler paints and paints, draws and draws, without letting any one piece be the full and final depiction of Godé-Darel. Her irreducible particularity seems displayed in the repetition, each piece losing its claim with the next to being *the* depiction of her. It is as if each painting, as part of a series, ends with Alexander Nehamas's "and so on"—of our loved ones, there is always more to say, and somehow something always still left out.

Accounts of love defined by its relationship to the value of the beloved would tell us that the valuable qualities he's depicting in the portraits are why, or among the reasons why, he loves her, or conversely, that her beauty in the portraits might be the result of his love, or could be read as such were we to learn, for instance, that in fact she was much less beautiful in life. They would define his love within the frame by what we can see of her fine qualities—her beauty, her bold features, her gracefulness even in exhaustion. But little inside any particular painting shows us his love and not, say, an interest in depicting the finality of death or the agony of illness. He could be an oncologist's illustrator, in any one painting, or Holbein the Younger depicting the "unfinished" life of Christ, or himself, just a few years earlier, depicting the death of another woman in a singular, static memorial image. He seems to be doing none of those things in these paintings, however, when considered in the plural. Their beauty, their pathos, the many qualities of the portrayal of his beloved do not indicate his love for her. We know him as a lover not because of the way he paints her, or the things about her that he is showing us. We know him as a lover because his paintings never seem complete. They insist on the next image, and the next, and thus on the inadequacy of any one. They represent time together, his want for it, and his want for *more*.

The Promise of Unhappiness

The paintings seem to form a record of Hodler's love in this way, their repetition representing the impossibility of finishing her depiction, and the sheer quantity of the work representing many hours spent at her bedside. But their story of illness and decline suggests a need to reconsider the terms on which I've been describing love. At the time of her diagnosis, Hodler and Godé-Darel learned that their indeterminate future together would be far more predictable than they might have thought. It would be determined unhappily, in pain and suffering, weakness and withering decline. Happy uncertainties turned to terrible likelihoods. Could time together in these conditions still seem promising?

I argued in the first chapter for a clarification of Alexander Nehamas's formulation of our response to a beautiful work of art, a new friend, or a beloved as finding "a promise of happiness" in its inversion, a "happiness of promise." My argument was that the feeling of happiness is present in the desire for time together: I feel happy to find the future promising, to desire a future without knowing exactly how it will turn out. I suggested as much in part to avoid the implication that the future together promises something specific—value deferred, but still tabulated as a determinate motivation for love—and to emphasize the lover's desire for a future they cannot know, or even well predict. My interest in the reformulation, however, also aims to address the possibility that the future the lover finds promising is not itself a happy one, but may still be desired by the lover—and the lover might still be happy to desire it, in this sense. This might be how Hodler feels when he learns of Godé-Darel's illness. Let's look more closely at what this could mean.

One suggestion of "the promise of happiness" is that the promise could be unfulfilled: that it could turn out to be *only* a promise, in that the time we spend together could turn out to bring less to my life than I had thought and hoped it would. It is "only a promise" in this sense in that it is not a guarantee, and it might disappoint us. Our beloveds could turn out not to be as wonderful as we thought they would be, or their great qualities might fade, or time together may be simply far less pleasant than we expected it to be. If only we could guarantee that all their valuable qualities would never be diminished, that all promises would be fulfilled—that is the wish implied in this line of interpretation. It's not an unreasonable wish: I don't want my beloveds to turn out worse than they promised to be, or for our time spent together to be anything less than I imagined it would be. But if it is, and the promise is unfulfilled, that doesn't make it less true that I found the prospect promising, nor should my love at that time be redefined by what I know now of what happened next. Whether the promise is fulfilled or disappointed is not a relevant referendum on whether it was love that I felt when I found time together promising, nor even whether my love continues despite some disappointments. Hence the confusion of "the promise of happiness," if it implies, as many promises do, that it should be judged by its fulfillment. Our beloveds might disappoint us. Life might turn out badly because of it. But I was happy to have had people I wanted to spend it with.

The disappointment of promise in this sense, however, isn't the only disappointing possibility of a future together. We may also experience the promise of *unhappiness*, without the loss of promise itself. Hodler's case might be one example. His beloved is diagnosed with a terminal illness, one that will bring pain and agony and much less time together than he might want. The future seems no longer uncertain, or no longer happily uncertain, promisingly so, because even the best-case scenarios are horrible. And the uncertainty itself seems to have changed: he may feel he's loving with a clock ticking, without the pleasure of losing track of time that one might feel in love in the happy promise of an indeterminate future. But the lover does not respond by abandoning his desire for the future, as if the promise itself was gone. He wants more time with his beloved, even if it promises mainly sadness and suffering. Time together is still desired, even if it is not desirable by other standards. He spends time with her, daily, hourly, because he desires time together and knows there will not be enough. He even tries to spend more time with her after she dies, unwilling to leave her side as he paints the final portraits of her body in death.

Hodler seems in this way like a paradigmatic lover on the terms I've sought to describe: he wants to spend more time with his beloved, even as that time seems increasingly certain to be unhappily determined. But it's not quite so easy. By another version of the story, he's a cad: he sends her away to be cared for elsewhere, then starts seeing other women while she's sick, even painting coy self-portraits to send to a woman he becomes seriously interested in romantically.[13] He leaves care for their child to others, and eventually to his own wife, Berthe. He lives somewhat rambunctiously as a bachelor, despite his professed attachments elsewhere both to Valentine and to his wife. None of this means he doesn't love her, though by the standards of their community documented in letters among friends, it suggests they at least suffered what Lloyd delicately calls "stormy interludes," including, perhaps most significantly for my discussion here, "a period at the height of Valentine's illness in 1914 when Hodler stopped seeing her for a number of months."[14] He spends a lot of time *not* with Godé-Darel, and spends at least some of that time entangled in other romantic ventures that might indicate shifts in his desire or attention. And the time he spends with her isn't obviously, actually, about her, if we think back to where we began.

When I first encountered the series of paintings, I was struck by their fervent temporality *as loving*, imagining that painting her portrait would be a way nearly to multiply their time together in depiction, or at least to spend the many hours with her that it takes to draw and paint so many pieces. But we might also see the paintings as objectifications of her, where what he loves and wants to spend time with is the image of pain and illness she presents, the opportunity to paint this series of paintings, not *her*. Hodler might, in other words, be in love with an *idea* or *project* that time with her allows him to spend time with in turn. The criticism of him as her lover, in that case, might be that he's turning love into a project of the self, or that he is in love with the wrong thing—and, perhaps more urgently, that he is failing also because he is failing to attend to *her*, and to care for her as she suffers and dies.

That is the question the paintings might demand most of all: Are the eyes she's looking into, when she stares out from the frame, the eyes of a lover who is concerned for her? Who provides for her needs? Who soothes her pain? Or are they the eyes of a painter, focused on the project at hand? Or, perhaps, is he focused on her, but finds painting her, not caring for her, to be his way of responding to her illness? Would that be enough? Would it be contemptible? Would he, in that case, be failing to love—by failing to fulfill a kind of promise?

These are questions about their—and our—expectations of the relationship between love and care, and about what these paintings show us of either. They are questions, then, in part about what it means for us to look at her, suffering, in his depiction, and what it meant for him to look at her, suffering, and depict her. There are ways to narrate his painting and drawing as evidence of his love for her, as I've suggested. It is also easy to assume some necessity to his endeavor because of its necessity for us to see and know of their relationship. But he could have spent his time with her differently. Would it have been better if he had? Would he have been a better lover? Could he have had a better response to her pain?

OBJECTIFICATION, ATTENTION, CARE

A detail about Hodler's methods painting Valentine as she died has haunted me since reading of it shortly after the Breuer exhibition. In many of his works, Hodler used "Dürer glass," named for the great fifteenth-century artist Albrecht Dürer, credited with developing a version of the tool and technique.[15] In Hodler's use of it, the artist takes a pane of glass, sometimes marked with a light compositional grid and often the full size of the intended work, and places it between himself and the person or scene to be depicted. He then sketches the image in outline directly onto the glass with a brush and ink or paint. The technique allowed Hodler to do a kind of tracing from life instead of needing to look at the desired image and then depict what he saw. He could then trace the outlines from the glass onto paper, and trace from paper onto canvas. It's not an uncontroversial technique, sometimes criticized as a kind of cheating—an escape of artistic skills and talents in seeing and representing what one sees.[16]

It also erects a pane of glass between the artist and the subject of their work. As the historian Oskar Bätschmann has described it, Hodler's version of Dürer glass is thus "an apparatus that simultaneously permits a distancing from the model and a precise tracing thereof."[17] The glass is intended to enhance a kind of *accuracy* in the depiction, as in Dürer's original technique, which aimed at a more realistic representation of a three-dimensional object onto a two-dimensional surface through the use of perspective. But it separates the artist and his subject, and maybe enhances a sense of her as only an object to view: it renders her, in the room, a flattened image for Hodler to trace. The paintings may represent many hours at her bedside, but at least some of those hours were spent with a pane of glass between Hodler and the bed, the better to see her on the two-dimensional plane.

I say that this method has haunted me because it seems both understandable, even appealing, as an artistic technique and defies any behavior I can imagine undertaking at the bedside of a sick loved one. It sharpens questions of what his painting and drawing is doing *for* her, and *to* her: whether he is taking advantage of her condition, putting her on display in the wrong ways, and what this has to do with any responsibilities he has to care for her, or otherwise respond well to her as she suffers and dies. I have tried to imagine that it was something Hodler resorted to out of his frustration at being unable to capture what he saw, grasping for a mechanical solution to what was really an existential problem. I've tried casting him as obsessive in his distress at her illness, fixating on achieving some impossible "accuracy" in her depiction to escape confrontation with the devastating reality of her disease. I've tried also to imagine that the Dürer glass was simply so routine in his work, and thus in their relationship as artist and model, that it seemed to them far less intrusive than it seems to me. But it continues to shatter my want to understand Hodler as wanting to spend time with *her*, and frames him instead more insistently working, ever absorbed in artistic pursuit, next to a woman suffering and in need of care. It makes me wonder if in seeing his love in the paintings I am seeing only my own romantic imagination reflected in the pane, and should find troubling assumptions within it about who is responsible for care, whose egoism is blameworthy and whose can be ignored, and what forms of disengagement are excused—even exalted—in the name of genius, or its attempt.

The Heroic Artist

There is a line of criticism against Hodler that reads the portrait series as primarily an objectification of Godé-Darel, evidence of his disengagement with her and egoistic self-assertion in response to her suffering. Most deeply developed by the literary theorist Elisabeth Bronfen, the claim is that the paintings objectify Godé-Darel and her suffering by flattening a real person into images that glorify the artist while subordinating, and effacing, the life and death they depict.[18] Representation, in this interpretation, does not serve to witness her suffering or extend their time together in its repetition, nor is it a suitable form of care or attention itself. Rather, it serves to render Godé-Darel's suffering a spectacle, enacting a form of violence that runs parallel to the harm she suffers from her disease.

For Bronfen, Hodler's depictions of Godé-Darel as she dies sacrifice the real death, the real suffering, and the real woman Valentine Godé-

Darel to an aestheticization, refocusing the spectator's attention on the paintings themselves. We do not see Godé-Darel's suffering as such, she argues, but instead see the qualities of the paintings, and thus the qualities of the painter. "For do we ask ourselves," Bronfen writes, "are these paintings skillfully done? Or do we ask ourselves, does the woman suffer? Do we see the woman's pain? Can we really see this pain?"[19] To the extent that we can, she argues, it serves a vision of the "heroism" of the painter precisely by its erasure of his subject. We praise Hodler's attempt "to recognise death over the body of his dying beloved, to fulfil his mourning through painting this body ... marking the site of his prowess, his imagination, his creativity."[20] He is praised by critics and art historians as Nehamas's "philosophical man" might be praised, for transcending the real horror of her particular death to represent a universal Death, "rescu[ing] the particular from its finitude," in Cavarero's words, "and uniqueness from its scandal."[21] And for Bronfen, the proliferation of this representation in series serves not to display their time together or suggest the inescapable partiality of the depiction of a unique being, but to reinforce the violent transcendence of Godé-Darel's real suffering and death by encouraging an "allegorising gaze." She is turned into a *story* across the series of paintings, Bronfen argues, and thus becomes a "*figure* of death," instead of a real person, really dying.[22] "Effaced in each case is the subjectivity of the dying woman, her position within the death process, her body and her pain," Bronfen writes. At best, she is "deindividualized into the 'beloved' in the classical tradition of the muse, comparable to Dante's 'Beatrice' or Petrarch's 'Laura.'"[23] She is not herself, a particular person, unfolding, ever incompletely, in her lover's narration of her. She is a story to be told, for him to tell, to express himself.

Part of Bronfen's criticism suggests a larger danger of hearing or seeing a person from only a lover's point of view: we might know little of them in the telling, and what we think we know is only the assertion of what the speaker says they see. We should be suspicious of the speaker's control over the narrative and the painter's control over the depiction. We don't know if the beloved would want to be described or depicted in this way, or whether their desires have had much impact at all on the person now showing or telling us of them. We don't even know what they would think of the lover portraying themselves as such—they might have never imagined the relationship as it is being narrated or displayed, let alone having desired or reciprocated it. Their subjectivity is subsumed by the lover's determination of their story.

This concern should chasten some of my earlier discussions of the narration by lovers of the beloved. Narration is important, and there is much to learn from what we hear. But there are questions to ask as well, sometimes with suspicion or skepticism, about exactly what we're listening to. Bronfen's discussion suggests that we ought to be particularly skeptical of supposed lovers telling us of their beloveds where it lets them speak of the *theme* of love—or pain, death, longing, or some other idea—such that they seem to express *themselves*, on that theme, more than the irreducible beloved. We can't know if they are indeed in love with the person or are really in love with the idea they want to talk about or the accomplishment of its narration or depiction. And we should notice that this ambiguity serves the "heroism" of the lover precisely as it effaces the particularity of the beloved. They are praised for what they say about the theme, not about the beloved, as the audience is listening for the universal story and not the ever-partial narration of some person important only to the speaker. Bronfen might be sympathetic to Cavarero's account of lovers narrating each other to each other, as a private activity of loving relationships, but she is skeptical of artists and poets, at least, portraying their beloveds for an audience beyond themselves.

Hodler marked many of the drawings of Godé-Darel from this period "p.a.v.," or "pas à vendre," "not for sale."[24] He showed some of the drawings and paintings to close friends, but he did not circulate them widely or offer them for public exhibition. They were first gathered for public display by Jura Brüschweiler in 1976, more than sixty years after Godé-Darel's death and nearly as long after Hodler's.[25] "This means that we see these images always detached from their original context," Bronfen writes, and "their 'private' quality for us as belated viewers is not reconstructable."[26] The violence of putting Godé-Darel's suffering on display might then be "on the part of the exhibition organisers" more than Hodler, though this should direct our attention primarily to the way "that in our spectatorship we are always already dealing with a cultural construction of a painter and his paintings."[27] This cultural construction encourages the "fictionalization" and objectification of Godé-Darel, Bronfen argues, as she becomes the character of the story the paintings tell, instead of a real, particular person, suffering and dying.[28] We focus on Hodler's skill and role as the painter, the narrator of the story, according to a cultural script of the heroic artist who transcends grief for the sake of art—or, in a neighboring story, the artistic genius who can do no other than paint in response to his lover's devastating illness. Godé-Darel recedes from either plot by becoming the allegorical Beloved in each of them, her decline and death a trope instead of real suffering, confronting the viewer of the paintings as such.

I have now taken some steps away from the relationship between Hodler and Godé-Darel, into a set of questions about our own viewing of the paintings, as outsiders to their relationship meeting them through these works. These questions cast a skeptical light on whether we can know much of Hodler's love from the portraits, while illuminating some of the social and cultural assumptions that we—I—may have brought to an interpretation of them. If Bronfen is right about the way we interact with them as cultural formations, we find them embedded in social scripts about art, its revelation of emotion, its orientation toward universal truths, and its creation by artists. And the artist himself is a figure of our social imagination as well: passionate and brilliant, assessed for "his prowess" and "his creativity," not his ethical sensitivity or responsiveness in care. Reinforcing expectations of prowess and disinterest in care, the heroic artist in Western culture is also paradigmatically male, Bronfen argues, and the image of the dying woman depicted by him is a gendered paradigm as well, imposed on Godé-Darel as we look at Hodler's depictions of her. She becomes a figure in a story of a woman dying and a man transcending his grief to depict universal truths about Death and Love. Care doesn't figure into it, because she isn't a real person with needs and vulnerabilities, or at least because those needs and vulnerabilities aren't relevant to the story being told. The story is about her relationship to the artist, or more precisely, about his relationship to her, and to art, love, death, and truth itself. She serves a story of masculine strength and feminine weakness, creative potency and its powers to capture the sublimity of pain and death. Hodler may not have intended the portraits to suggest as much, but our encounter with them may be defined far more by our expectations and assumptions than by his actual feelings, desires, and concerns, or hers. *We* objectify her in this way—Hodler is not the only culprit.

The Attentive Viewer

As an argument about the ethics of viewing these portraits, I am sympathetic to Bronfen's critique of the cultural constructions through which we encounter them. She traces the trope of the dying woman through many examples in modern European art and literature, and as she does, the images of Godé-Darel begin to blur into other women's corpses, becoming a "*figure* of death" instead of a particular person dying. But I experience this "allegorising gaze" as *Bronfen* places her in a series of other depictions of other dead and dying women, not from viewing the series of Hodler's paintings of her. Perhaps this indicates only how unaware I am of the cultural formations I bring with me as I look at Hodler's work, but I find their proliferation demands something else of me as a viewer. They do tell a kind of story, but it is not a readily plotted fiction subsuming its characters into allegorical play. Rather, they are repetitive. They require the viewer to endure the repetition. It's more nearly *boring* than a drama of death and Hodler's heroic confrontation with it. Viewing image after image of her lying in bed, we are made to sit with her, there, always there, suffering across many hours and days.

This endurance might help me resist some objectification of Godé-Darel where it resists acculturated expectations of story, event, and the portrayal of characters. But does it bring me into better relation with *her*? And does it tell us anything about Hodler—as a lover, as a painter, as a person sitting next to a woman in pain?

In his analysis of the Godé-Darel portraits, literary theorist Harold Schweizer argues that the repetition of her depiction across the series requires of the viewer an *ethical* attention to her particularity as a suffering person.[29] As I have suggested as well, Schweizer understands the repetition of her depiction to present her irreducible particularity by suggesting that she cannot be captured in any singular depiction. He then connects this depiction of particularity to ethical responsibility, drawing on Emmanuel Levinas's account of the exposed face of the other, as informed Cavarero's arguments in the first chapter as well. The face of the other calls forth responsibility for them because of their vulnerability as radically particular:

> Such a face in its innermost vulnerability cannot be grasped *thematically* or *conceptually*. It must therefore be painted *repeatedly*, every day

from November 1914 until the end of January 1915. It is as if in this unceasing labor Hodler literalized Levinas's injunction that he who seizes his obligation "at the approach of [the other's] face, is never done with the neighbor."[30]

Description and obligation come together here: where the description is suitably endless—suitable to a person's particularity—it might allow the forms of attention to the other that particularity requires ethically as well. For Levinas, the obligation to the particular other is as endless as their description. To set boundaries on our responsibility to and for them is to reduce them to something less than themselves, an object or story with a beginning and end. Where the lover does not *want* their beloved's story to end, the caregiver, or the person ethically enjoined, in Levinas's terms, by the face of the other, cannot *allow* the story to end. They are responsible for more than they can ever specify, or say.

Are we, as viewers of these portraits, ethically enjoined by the face of Valentine? Are we thus implicated in her suffering, even responsible for her care? For Schweizer, the repetition of her depiction is most significant for its effect on *us* in this way. Schweizer argues that the paintings "reflect—and require of us," their viewers, an ethical practice of *attention* as Simone Weil defines the term.[31] For Weil, "attention to a sufferer is a very rare and difficult thing; it is almost a miracle; it *is* a miracle."[32] It requires us to relinquish any other motivation or intention other than attention to the sufferer, attended to as themselves, not a member of a needy class or type. To attend to them is to see them particularly, as they are, and to be with them however their time suffering proceeds. It is a matter of "proximity and sympathy," responding to "a sufferer whose need . . . [is] that someone is there."[33] Attention to the sufferer is thus a form of *waiting*, Schweizer argues, in which one's "identity is nothing but his waiting."[34] To wait with the sufferer requires one to reorient to time itself from the ways the modern world teaches us to understand it: to abandon our common understandings of *using* time, *spending* time well, and not wasting it, in which we are keeping time in relation to other purposes. "Waiting-as-attention," by contrast, returns to time itself, accompanying the sufferer as they endure it and recognizing suffering as something marked, significantly, by duration.

The miracle of attention for Weil does not lie in this rejection of time's *use* specifically, but Schweizer's definition of it is instructive. It suggests one way that suffering is "out of sync" with modern life, "outside of the 'moral' and economic community of those whose time is productive and synchronized."[35] We might recall Byung-Chul Han's critique of consumer society here as well, oriented toward productivity and achievement without anything beyond the reach of these measures. The professional caregiver, at least as their jobs are defined, fits well into this world, their time "productive and synchronized" to shift changes and specified levels of care, duties defined by protocols, checklists, and their successful completion. But suffering is not well defined in this way. It is unproductive, unhurried, and unscheduled. The sufferer does not know what they will need, or when they will need it, with certainty. Their needs are particular to them both as the people they are, suffering from their particular ailments, and in time, enduring their illness on a schedule unknown until it has been lived. To attend to them is to wait with them, without knowing what that time will bring.

Attention in this sense is significantly different from *care*. Schweizer writes that attention, for Weil, "is this kind of waiting one offers to a sufferer whose need, Weil notes, is not primarily that *something gets done* but that someone is there."[36] He permits in his description that some activities may occur during the wait, but they are not the project of the person attending:

> To wait with the dying is not a matter of length or efficacy but of proximity and sympathy. If bedpans have to be emptied, sheets changed, and drugs administered, such activities derive their quality entirely from the proximity and the sympathy of the person who performs them. What matters is that one gives one's presence to the sufferer not as an activity but as the substance of waiting.[37]

Schweizer's argument here is again reminiscent of Han's "achievement subject" of consumer society, always planning projects to accomplish instead of living with others who might defy our intentions, intrude on our plans, and demand more of us than we could know or say. To wait with the dying is not to care for them if their care is a project of this kind, for Schweizer or for Weil. We might do things for the dying as we wait, but these activities cannot subsume the purposelessness of true attention. To determine our purpose as something other than attention—understood as presence and proximity over time—would be to overdetermine the other, by this account, rendering them no longer other to oneself but a creation of one's own determinations.

It is *attention*, not care, that Schweizer argues the paintings require of us. They ask for proximity, not activity; they allow us to be close to Godé-Darel in her endurance of suffering instead of asking us to use the paintings to learn something or do something, to hurry something to an ending, a task performed or a lesson acquired. "Each painting, to say this differently, is structured not by a waiting with an object and a purpose, but by waiting *as such*," Schweizer writes. "Each painting is to be conceived as an empty interval that, since it cannot be filled with a future, can only be filled with the proximity of one who waits with the person who suffers."[38] We cannot foreclose the time in which suffering must be endured. It is an "empty interval" that we can know in neither length nor quality before its duration. It must be endured by the sufferer, and we can only wait with them, attending to them as they endure it. The paintings call us to this attention, in Schweizer's interpretation, because they allow us to be with Godé-Darel over time, as a person who appears not in allegory or coy portrait, not as object or achievement, but as a particular person, suffering and enduring her suffering over time. They look at their subject "in the realm of *sympathy* that cannot be reduced to spatial categories or modes of objectification"; they are not "merely done as things that need to be done in the order of bedpans."[39]

But the work of emptying bedpans, changing sheets, administering drugs, and so on, *does* need to be done. Where attention is set too far from these activities, it suggests their ethical insignificance in a way of which I think we should be wary. Grouped with strictly purposeful activity and achievement in this way, the activities of caregiving are cast into the shallow, selfish, or cynical realm of modern economic culture, as part of the work we do for the realization of only ourselves as achievement-oriented, consumer subjects. Acknowledged but diminished in a concept of attention as something one does *while* waiting with the suffering, but shouldn't *aim to do*, they appear incidental, insignificant to our relations with the suffering instead of essential to their endurance and what we are enjoined to do by their vulnerability and pain. These activities are too determinate, it seems, for the indeterminacy of attention, in Schweizer's account.[40] Where we provide care intentionally, he suggests, intentionality itself disrupts our attention to the person we care for.

But care is indeterminate in its own way. It cannot be reduced to a list of tasks, though it requires plenty of tasks that may be well organized by lists. It is repetitive as well, and endlessly so. Cleaning is never *finished*; feeding is never *over*. The responsibilities of a caregiver do not end so long as they live to care for a living person, and they recur in mundane and tedious ways.[41] They are also disrupted by new needs and changing conditions, as unpredictable as other tasks are monotonous. They require the commitment of a caregiver who promises to provide for whatever the other needs, or at least commits themselves to try, without knowing exactly what they are committing to.

There is a similarity, then, between love and care that the temporal approach I've developed helps us to see. Each is oriented toward a future that cannot be fully known or named, and in each we take on that uncertainty not as the simple, regrettable reality of the future itself but as a defining feature of the relationship. When we love someone, we want more time with them, not knowing what that time will bring— and want that time to be determined, at least in part, by our beloved, not only by our own intentions. When we care for someone, we commit ourselves to provide for their needs, not knowing what those needs will be. Both prospects may be disappointed: our want for more time with our beloveds might seem, in retrospect, unfortunate or misplaced, and our efforts to care might fail or falter, inadequate to what the other needs or incorrectly assessing what they require. As love is not defined by whether the promise of a future together was ultimately fulfilled, however, care cannot be defined by its successful completion. It is not a task to be done, or not only that, in the sense that it is not an *achievement* of the caregiver to be proposed, pursued, and then accomplished. It is a commitment to respond to unknown vulnerabilities, wants, and needs.

Who Cares for Godé-Darel?

Valentine Godé-Darel seems to have been well cared for during her illness. She received treatment at an advanced clinic in Lausanne for several months, and then seems to have lived in the company of people taking care of her needs. Some accounts suggest Hodler paid for these caretakers, and her treatment overall.[42] But very few critical or historical accounts of the portraits, Hodler, or Godé-Darel offer specific information about the arrangements, even where copious evidence is provided to paint detailed pictures of Hodler's artistic endeavor and the relationship that brought him to it. Hodler is always described as her *lover*, never her caregiver. His care for her is described as evident in the paintings, and their proliferation. Care that responds to her needs, however, is hardly mentioned at all.

When I have discussed the portraits with colleagues and students and raised the question of Godé-Darel's care, I have been surprised by how certain most people are *that* she is being cared for—including by my own certainty as I try to talk through the story. Different people are certain of different versions of it, however: some assume Hodler is caring for her, others that he is paying for care by professionals, and others that there must be caregivers around, paid or unpaid, or else Hodler wouldn't be painting but instead attending to her needs. The last version suggests Hodler *would* provide care for her if no one else was, and that his paintings are actually a kind of evidence that she was so sufficiently provided for that he was free to paint and draw. I'm not sure the social scripts of "heroic artists" require as much, though I appreciate the implication. As with the figure of the heroic artist, however, there do seem to be gendered scripts about caregiving at play, in assumptions, for example, that his responsibility is to *pay* for caregivers and not to *be* a caregiver, or that he doesn't have a responsibility to provide for her care at all. This responsibility is somehow outside the frame, though the suffering that demands it is centered within it.

To look at a dying woman requires some question of whether she needs help, whether she is being made comfortable, and what work there is to do for her. As only viewers of paintings of a woman long dead, we can do none of this work. But we can be interested in who did it, and whether it was done. The question of *whether* responds to her vulnerability and suffering directly. We should care about whether she was cared for because we should be responsive to a person in evident need. Hodler's caregiving, or lack thereof, matters to us as viewers, then, because his possible failure to respond to her suffering with care might be a failure of basic ethical responsibility. It might make him contemptible not as her lover but simply *the person in the room with her*. The horror of the paintings in this vein would be that he responds to her pain by painting and drawing, without providing care, comfort, or other aid to her endurance of her disease. And if his failure to care is being excused, in our reception of the paintings, because of his artistic prowess, we should ask whether such privileging of prowess over the provision of care is something to condemn in our cultural imagination. On this interpretation, his lack of care indicts *our* assumptions about the situation, particularly our exultation of the figure of the artist and relative disinterest in caregivers, left out of view.

The question of *who* cared for Godé-Darel, however, informs our judgments of whether the people around her behaved as they should by fulfilling their roles appropriately. It is a question of social expectation beyond the fulfillment of the primary ethical injunction to care. Should her lover be the one who changes her bedpans? Who pays for someone to do the work of care? Is love what makes him responsible, if he is? Or should love have nothing to do with these responsibilities?

Alongside cultural constructions of the heroic artist and his romantic figure of Death, we can find social expectations that entangle love and care: that to love someone is, or should be, also a commitment to care for them. This is a view I reject, as I will argue in greater detail in the next section. It might be good—practical, convenient, and perhaps complementary to other goods of a loving relationship—to commit to care for the people we love. But the commitments of care are different from the commitments of love, and we should not insist that one necessarily leads to or is a part of the other. Commitments to care have a different orientation to the future than love's want for more time with the beloved, not knowing what that time will bring. If we mistake the lover's orientation toward the future for the caregiver's, we will struggle to account for failures to care and failures in love, as we will see in a moment in the relationship between Louis and Prior in *Angels in America*.

Love does not necessarily motivate the commitments of care, and care should not be understood to emerge from love in a way that imagines the caregiver's desire for the relationship—and depends on it. Hodler may have been a disappointing lover during Valentine's illness, his attentions wavering and his time with her mediated, often, by panes of glass. We may judge him to be a bad caregiver as well, where he did not provide care for her himself. But such failures to care are not failures to love. They would be failures, significantly, of a different sort.

LOVE AND CARE

The feeling of promise in love as I have described it thus far can begin and end without reason. It is a desire, an orientation of the will, that the lover finds themselves having, sometimes to their surprise, and may find themselves not having just as unexpectedly. It orients the lover to the future, but it is not a commitment to continue to be oriented in this way, to feel as one feels now in time to come. My desire for a future together is a feeling I have now, or did have then, or may have in the future—it is a description of my desire, not of my want for that desire or my sense that having such a desire would be a better fulfillment of a duty. Considering love in this way sets it apart from commitment, recognizing—and seeking to describe—that whatever our intentions may be, we sometimes find ourselves no longer loving. Commitments to care might be good promises to make for a variety of reasons— ethical, political, religious, practical—but they are of a different order and mode than the lover's finding time together promising. That is still a *desire*, not a commitment to continue to desire nor a commitment to provide for the other in that time. These are orientations to the future of different kinds.

And yet we often have the intuition that they go together. That seems to be the intuition, and ultimately the judgment, of both Louis Ironson and Prior Walter in *Angels in America*.[43] When we meet Prior Walter, he is in the early stages of experiencing significant symptoms of AIDS. Visible signs of the disease are beginning to appear on his body; he spends much of his time in bed, too weak to go out except for visits to the hospital, where he stays for days on end for treatments and therapies he has little hope will work. Louis, his lover of many years, has left him, or is in the process of doing so—or of coming back, or of trying to figure out what he's doing. Louis isn't sure if he is still in love with Prior, and simply unhappy, or whether he has fallen out of love with him, and that's why he wants to leave. What he does know is that he feels tremendously guilty about the thought of leaving his partner of many years when he's sick, even if he has other caregivers, and even if moving out of their apartment may be an accurate representation of the way Louis feels about him *now*.

Louis isn't sure where his responsibilities lie, and what his feelings have to do with them. He loves Prior, or he did. He doubts whether he still loves him given that he doesn't want to be around him when he's sick, but he doubts these doubts, in turn, as superficial and shameful. He's tangled in questions of how to account for his feelings and whether he still even counts as a lover, or as loving, if he doesn't want to be there as his beloved declines. "What does the Holy Writ say about someone who abandons someone he loves at a time of great need?" Louis asks a rabbi in one of the play's early scenes, at the burial of Louis's grandmother. "Why would a person do such a thing?" the rabbi replies. Louis responds:

> LOUIS: Because he has to.
> Maybe because this person's sense of the world, that it will change for the better with struggle, maybe a person who has this neo-Hegelian positivist sense of constant historical progress towards happiness or perfection or something, who feels very powerful because he feels connected to these forces, moving uphill all the time... Maybe that person can't, um, incorporate sickness into his sense of how things are supposed to go. Maybe vomit... and sores and disease... really frighten him, maybe... he isn't so good with death.
> RABBI ISIDOR CHEMELWITZ: The Holy Scriptures have nothing to say about such a person.[44]

They have nothing to say about him, Kushner seems to suggest, because to abandon a loved one in a time of great need is never acceptable, *even if* the happiness of promise, the delight in the possibility and indeterminacy of the future, or some "neo-Hegelian positivist sense of constant historical progress towards happiness or perfection or something" is gone, and one's love in the sense of a desire to spend more time together has ended. You still have to stick around and care.

Louis wants to know whether he has to care for Prior and also whether he has to *want* to care for Prior. He describes Prior in this conversation as "someone he loves," but he describes elsewhere that he might have stopped loving, or must have stopped loving given his want to abandon his supposed beloved. He wants his love to motivate caring for Prior, in some moments, or for a sense of obligation to care to reinvigorate his love. He is worried about the judgment of others were he to abandon Prior, and also about what his want to abandon Prior tells him of himself. Is he a bad lover? A bad person? Has he failed as a lover, ambivalent in his intentions, not "so good with death"?

Louis's confusion suggests an important distinction between finding time together promising in love and *making a promise* to care. It also raises a crucial concern about what we think of lovers who disentangle these promises in practice: the lover who ceases to love, the lover who doesn't stay when care is needed, the lover who loves but won't provide care, or the person who stays and provides care but only out of obligation, with no desire. Do we condemn them, as Louis so sharply condemns himself?

Love's Failure and Love's End

One of the reasons to understand love in time, as I have suggested, is the clarity it affords to understanding when love ends. Love ends when the lover no longer desires more time with the beloved. The beloved doesn't have to change, the lover doesn't have to discover something terrible about them or the prospect of life with them; nothing has to be different than the moment before except the lover's desire for a future together. In the cases we have been considering in this chapter, however, something does change, which seems to change the happy promise of more time together considerably. What if love ends in the discovery of these changes after all? Is that a failure of love, an unhappy coincidence, a contemptible run from responsibility? Or a reasonable response to a future that no longer seems promising, through which love might persist, but also might not?

At the time Prior Walter would have been diagnosed with AIDS, in 1985, symptoms of the disease had been observed by doctors across three continents for seven years. Its progression patterns were becoming better known in the medical community, such that Prior's diagnosis would have come with a relatively confident prediction of what his coming year, or few years, were likely to look like. The play begins as he finds his first external signs of the disease on his body, lesions caused by Kaposi's sarcoma. He has already started not to look like himself in other ways. He is getting thinner, with hollowed cheeks; his energy levels aren't high. Louis and Prior live in New York City in the midst of the AIDS epidemic's devastating run through the gay community there. They know many others who have been infected, suffered, and died. For all that wasn't known about AIDS at the time, Louis and Prior know a lot about what to expect for their future together: more pain, more lesions, less energy, more infections, slower recoveries, ordinarily minor ailments bringing him to the brink of death, or past it. "This is my life, from now on, Louis," Prior says during a scene in his hospital room. "I'm not getting 'better.'"[45] The future is clearer than ever, and it is not what either lover wants.

Louis isn't sure if he is still Prior's lover, or if he still wants to be, or if maybe he has to be, whatever that might mean, even if his love has ended. He seems certain, however, that in wanting not to be with Prior in his condition, he has *failed* as a lover. In an early scene, Louis describes this sense of failure to Belize, Prior's best friend and nurse, while Prior sleeps in his hospital bed beside them:

> LOUIS: Mathilde stitched while William the Conqueror was off to war. She was capable of ... more than loyalty. Devotion.
>
> She waited for him, she stitched for years. And if he had come back broken and defeated from war, she would love him even more. And if he had returned mutilated, ugly, full of infection and horror, she would still have loved him; fed by pity, by a sharing of pain, she would have loved him even more, and even more, and she would never, never have prayed to God, please let him die if he can't return to me whole and healthy and able to live a normal life ... If he had died, she would have buried her heart with him.
>
> So what the fuck is the matter with me?[46]

The stage directions note a "little pause," and then Louis asks, "Will he sleep through the night?" His brief, nervous, caring question seems to peek out from under the weight of what he's admitted he's thinking about Prior earlier in the monologue. In comparison to Mathilde, he casts himself as a failed lover, not ready to endure the suffering of his beloved. He is not devoted. He does not want to wait for his beloved to return, and he does not want his beloved to *change*. He suggests, by contrast to Mathilde, that he has wished and maybe even prayed—though elsewhere he says he's unfamiliar with prayer—that his beloved would die rather than be so sick, mutilated by infection, anything other than "whole and healthy and able to live a normal life." The life he wants to be able to expect is gone with Prior's diagnosis, and he finds he has none of the feelings he thinks a lover should have in response.

The feelings Louis praises in Mathilde are some of the ones that made the value-responsive accounts of love we considered in the first chapters unconvincing: love that endures past changes in the beloved, past great declines of the qualities, capacities, and characteristics their lovers once valued in them. Love does endure through such changes, sometimes, and value-responsive accounts struggle to account for its endurance. But where endurance through change perplexes those understandings of love, love's end in the face of changes in the beloved horrifies Louis. It might also horrify others. We often praise love's endurance past change as admirable devotion, loyalty, and commitment, as in the story of Mathilde's love for William the Conqueror. And we might be particularly inclined to think it praiseworthy—and the alternative horrible, and wrong—when we are the beloved in question, when we are faced with changes to ourselves and worried the people who love us might stop loving us because of them. Louis is not alone in his worries about love changing. Prior has much to say about Louis's ambivalence, as well.

Repeatedly in his conversations with Louis, Prior turns to the language of justice and judgment whenever they start to discuss love. "Tell me some more about justice" he asks of Louis in an early scene. "You are not about to die," Louis answers, as if the question asked for last rites. But he presses him again, starting the sentence, "Justice..." and Louis picks it up, "is an immensity,... a confusing vastness. Justice is God." Then Louis reaches the point:

> LOUIS: You love me.
> PRIOR: Yes.
> LOUIS: What if I walked out on this?
>   Would you hate me forever?
>   (Prior kisses Louis on the forehead.)
> PRIOR: Yes.[47]

Prior is wounded by Louis's abandonment, and condemns him for it throughout the rest of the play. Their wrenching arguments tend to return to the language of justice, perhaps even more than the language of love. In one exchange, Prior says, "You have no right to do this... It's criminal," and Louis responds, sarcastically, "There oughta be a law."

Prior responds, seriously, "There is a law. You'll see."[48] In a play with fearsome angels seen judging the world below them continent by continent, the prediction sounds like a threat. But we return to a worldly court just a little later in the same conversation, as Prior interrupts Louis's refusal of his judgment:

> LOUIS: I won't be judged by you. This isn't a crime, just—the inevitable consequence of people who run out of—whose limitations—
> PRIOR: Bang bang bang. The court will come to order.[49]

Louis then suggests that they "talk practicalities, schedules; I'll come over if you want, spend nights with you when I can," seemingly a gesture toward caregiving in the absence of love. Prior cuts in, "Has the jury reached a verdict?"

The question of the case, it seems, is whether Louis has failed as a lover. But the terms shift as they enact the trial, or as Prior enacts the trial and Louis tries to escape the conceit. "I'm doing the best I can," Louis protests. "You can love someone and fail them. You can love someone and not be able to . . ." Prior interrupts him, "You *can*, theoretically, yes. A person can, maybe an editorial 'you' can love, Louis, but not you, specifically you . . . A person could theoretically love and maybe many do but we both know now that you can't." Louis says he loves him. Prior rejects the claim: "I repeat. Who cares?" And this time playing the jury foreman, "We have reached a verdict, Your Honor. This man's heart is deficient. He loves, but his love is worth nothing."

We might imagine some defense, perhaps from these pages, that Louis has loved, but his love has ended. He *wants* to continue loving, but finds himself no longer desiring time together. He wants to offer care in the absence of love, fulfilling his obligations, as he understands them, even if he does not desire time together with Prior any longer. He doesn't express, or maybe understand, these commitments to care particularly well—"I'll come over if you want, spend nights with you when I can" is not a commitment of a primary caregiver so much as an occasional, and maybe reluctant, helper—but he wants not to abandon Prior entirely. He wants to do the right thing, even in the absence of love.

But to define desirous love and obligations to care apart from each other would be a weak defense in Prior's court. Prior accuses Louis not of failing to fulfill his obligations or some promises made long ago, but of having a "deficient heart," love "worth nothing" because of its inability to imagine life together as something other than the "whole and healthy... normal life" Louis longs for Prior to have. Louis fails as a lover, in Prior's view, because he can't love the future they're likely to have. Perhaps he loved only one possible future, a "normal life" as he imagined it. Or perhaps he simply can't love *this* future. He cannot imagine its uncertainties to be anything other than horrible, nor can he imagine any other way time together might be desirable from here. He can only imagine the future's certain suffering, its duration toward death, and he finds himself unable to desire these determinations of the time. He wants a way to think Prior will "get better." Prior needs him to imagine life together without that possibility—but with others, promising in other ways.

This is how Prior seems to define a failure of love: a lack of imagination, even more than a failure of commitment or care. Louis fails Prior because he *cannot imagine* the future with him, not because he does not desire it. To not desire it would be the end of love. To find it unimaginable is his failure as a lover. "Failing in love isn't the same as not loving," Louis says to Prior in a conversation near the end of the play. "It doesn't let you off the hook."[50] The relationship continues, as the failing lover continues to want a future together of some kind. He just can't imagine it in a way that he desires it, or can't accept what he imagines as the future that awaits.

If a failure to love is a failure of imagination, it is significantly different from the end of love as an end of desire. Failure might then be differently judged, and condemned, than the end of love. We might have a sense that our imagination can be constructed differently with effort and the help of others, in a way that desire cannot be so effectively changed. If what I need is an image or a story I haven't been able to imagine, you could show me the image or tell me the story. If what I need is to desire that image or story, there is much less that either you or I could say.

A failure of love as a failure of imagination may also be condemned as making a mess of one's own desires, as a kind of self-sabotage or self-defeat. Louis seems to want more time with Prior: he loves him, as he says repeatedly, he just also wants to leave. He can't imagine how to want *this* time together, but at some moments, at least, he seems to want time together overall. His desires are frustrated by what the future promises because *some* future still seems promising. Maybe this frustration, this failure of imagination, will infect his love enough to end it. But to find himself no longer loving would be different than these tortured failures in love.

Promises of Different Kinds

The other failure at stake is the failure to care. Louis's abandonment of Prior might be not only the abandonment of his beloved, but the abandonment of someone who needs him to care for him as he suffers and dies. We return here to questions raised by Hodler and Valentine's relationship as well, about the entanglement of love and care and possible obligations to care for the people we love.

One reason we might think the people who love us are obligated to care for us is because they are the people nearest to us, often, when we are in need. They are the people we spend our time with, if we're lucky, as we want to spend our time with them. As I need care in that time, it might be most convenient if the person I'm spending time with provided that care. They are the people in the room. They are the people, therefore, who must respond to my vulnerability and pain. But on this description, their response would be obligatory insofar as we are ethically enjoined by proximity to need, or in Levinas's terms, by our encounter with the face of the other. That their face is also the face of a person we love is not the reason we must care for them. If we were otherwise indifferent to them, or even hated them, we would still be obligated to respond to their needs, by this account, if they are the people we encounter. My obligations to care may thus seem entangled with love in practice, because in practice I may be near my loved ones more often than others. I encounter their faces more often; I am next to them, more often than others, as they cry out in pain. I may be responsible for them, then, more often than I am responsible for anyone else.

The question raised by the two couples we have considered in this chapter, however, is whether a lover's obligation to care should emerge not from this kind of bare ethical responsibility in encounter but from love itself. I admit a suspicion about entangling love and care in this way on feminist grounds: if care is the necessary work of love, caregiving labor, performed in our society still more often by women, can continue to be uncompensated and unrecognized as nothing more than action stemming from happy desire. Philosophically, however, arguments for the entanglement of love and care more often rest on definitions of love in which the lover wants the good of the beloved, and is thus obligated to act for their good.[51] If to love is to want the good of the beloved, then I should want my beloveds to be well cared for, throughout their lives and particularly in times of need. If I am obligated to *act* for their good as well as wanting it, I would be obligated to care for them, or act to ensure they are cared for.

Associating the lover's want for the good of their beloved with the activities of caregiving, however, suggests the elision between love and care that I think lies beneath Louis's confusions, and the difficulty of understanding Hodler's obligations. Care and love start to seem like nearly the same thing: to love someone *means* caring for them, or means you would care for them, if you are able. The association of love and care is strong enough in such a view that not providing care seems like not loving at all, or seems like evidence of love's end, in Louis's case, or love's failure, in Prior's view of it. Someone whose heart was not deficient would stay and care—or so the argument might go.

Holding love and care together so closely, however, misunderstands the relation between them—both why they seem similar, and what makes them distinct. Care and love seem similar, in part, because indeterminacy and promise play critical roles in each, but in different configurations. In love, the indeterminacy of the future together is promising: I want to spend more time with you, and time together seems somehow desirable. I may imagine that time will bring happiness of kinds I can't yet imagine. I may think I have a good idea of what time will bring, for better or worse, and desire that. I may know of many likely determinations that are far from happy indeed, but as a lover I desire time together nonetheless.

In care, by contrast, I am making an indeterminate promise: I will care for you, whatever you may need, even if I can't yet imagine what you will need or how demanding it will be, and even if I will fall short of what your needs demand. I may fail, but I am committed to try to respond to your needs, whatever they may be. This is the difference many ethicists of care define between a primary caregiver, as we often expect people who love us to be, and a professional caregiver.[52] The professional caregiver has boundaries to their promises. They have specified duties and hours on duty, and thus time off duty and tasks they are not responsible for. The primary caregiver, by contrast, has promised to care however the content of that promise may be determined by the other's needs. They are never really "off duty," and they are responsible for needs far from what they might be able to provide. Their commitment is to care, whatever that might require, not to provide a set of services specified in advance.

The role of indeterminacy in love as I have argued for it can then be seen to mirror, and illuminate, moments of incoherence in similarly structured accounts of care. Corresponding to the value-responsive account of love, discussions of care ethics (or discussions more generally of ethical obligations to the other) sometimes define someone's value, dignity, or vulnerability as what makes them *worthy* of care, as the valuable beloved is *worthy* of love because of their valuable qualities and characteristics.[53] But such accounts tend to fall short of their own ambitions to obligate us toward the vulnerable, whether by naturalizing the possibility of invulnerability or overidentifying vulnerability with helplessness, and a passive participation in the caregiving relationship because of those "care-worthy" qualities. Conversely, care often goes awry in practice when it resembles volitional or bestowing accounts of love: when the care of the caregiver is allowed to define the needs of the cared-for without attention to them particularly, and their ongoing revelation of qualities, desires, capacities, and needs. These problems in caregiving might be said to objectify the person cared for, turning them into only the object of care and a passive recipient of it without agency in the relationship. It might also render them imparticular in a significant, specific sense: they are still themselves and not another, but they are not attended to as sources of how their stories should be determined. The caregiver is the only narrator; what they say of the other becomes the full story of who they are.

Overdetermining care is an easy path to well-intentioned domination. We imagine we know what the other needs, and we impose it on them without listening for—or being able to hear—their views of what we provide. We talk about care being "provided" like a gift and we ignore that gifts are sometimes impositions, both of the gift itself and the definition by the giver of what the recipient wants and needs. And care is often needed in situations where people lack the abilities to assert themselves in ways that many may be more accustomed to noticing, hearing, or respecting. It can be easy not to hear when a voice is faint, and easy to overdetermine the story of someone who cannot speak for themselves. The indeterminacy of care is important to emphasize against such possibilities. The people we care for have needs we cannot predict and may never know. In committing to care for them, we take on these needs as our responsibility. But we must not imagine that we ever grasp them fully, lest we render the other merely whatever we have said them to be: *what* they are, in our assessment, instead of *who* they are, endlessly revealing themselves to us, to others, and to themselves. The ideas of indeterminacy and the insufficiency of description that we've considered in love may thus be an important guide to the indeterminacies of care. They encourage a kind of epistemic humility as well as a resistance to transforming care into an accomplishment to be finished, instead of an ongoing relationship determined over time. Care is a promise to provide for an ever-unfolding set of needs, indeterminate throughout the ever-unfolding life of any human being. In love we find the future with our beloveds promising. In care we promise the future to the people we care for.

Condemnation and Expectation

To find the future together promising is not to make a promise, but we might still *want* the people who love us to be committed to care for us, as well. The conceptual distinction between love and care should encourage us not to overdetermine care and not to assume that care is provided out of love. It also reminds us that love is not a firm ground on which to demand care where love has faltered, as we can't demand the continuation of desire.

But any account of love would probably provide a weak defense in Prior's court because Prior is charging Louis with failing to love *him*, not an abstract moral failure or a violation of principle. He appeals to the language of law and divine judgment, the "immensity" and "confusing vastness" of justice, as he loves to hear Louis describe it, in a parody of the particularity of Louis's offense. Because while Louis appeals to Scripture, to God, to the march of "constant historical progress towards happiness or perfection or something," Prior traces his sarcomas like constellations, shuddering at their proliferation seemingly cell by cell. His problems are close at hand, not in the heavens. And he wants Louis to be held accountable to *them*: to him, to his transformation in illness, to their relationship, and to its transformation in illness, in turn.

This is the court that matters. Conceptual distinctions and philosophers' definitions are worth little when the people we love expect better of us or we expect better of them. And sometimes such expectations have already promised more than we have, and without our assent. If our loved ones expect us to care for them because we love them—a commitment to care in the future, no matter how our desires change—we are accountable to their expectations so long as we are in relationship with them. If our love ends, if we are "freed," in Louis's terms, we might be "let off the hook" in a bare sense of no longer caring in the same way what *that person* thinks—though even when love ends, the judgment of someone we've once loved might still matter to us significantly. We are also embedded in webs of relationships that make the transformation of one less a severing than a reweaving. We remain accountable to others who love our former beloved, and to people we care about who took our love of them seriously. If they expect us to care, regardless of our desires, we remain accountable to their expectations. Disentangling love and care conceptually can only go so far.

Social expectations of the entanglement of love and care might offer a kind of security against the instability of lovers' desires, or at least suggest an answer to the question pressed by both Godé-Darel and Prior's stories of who is left to care for us if our lovers do not. The most immediate concern raised by their suffering is who will respond to it, provide for it, not abandon them in need. The question of whether their *lovers* will care for them in these ways is important where we expect it of lovers, and where there is a social reliance on them as primary caregivers for the suffering. But social expectations could be configured differently, such that care is not part of the question of what lovers do in response to their beloveds' suffering. Care might be held far apart from love, in some communities, or could be, were we to want our communities to be remade in this way.

It matters, in this vein, that Louis and Prior's relationship is depicted both between the two of them and situated in a larger queer community, negotiating urgently emerging needs to care for the sick and dying through networks of relationship defined also by desire and love. Louis's abandonment of Prior doesn't leave him without care, it leaves him in the hands of his best friend and nurse, Belize, a former drag queen who administers his medications, tends to his lesions, and negotiates to get him into an experimental drug trial that allows him to live far longer than his initial prognosis. The expectations of love and care are crucially at stake in all of these relationships, negotiated among their participants both prospectively and retrospectively. Belize fiercely condemns Louis for his failure as a lover, but less for his failure as a caregiver. Louis defers to Belize as both a professional and primary caregiver for Prior, but contests Belize's judgments of him as a lover, and whether Belize has the right to judge him in this role. Accountability for failures to care and failures to love is distributed, and constantly negotiated, in the webs of relationships depicted.

Among Louis, Prior, and Belize, the expectations of love and care are also negotiated largely without the assumptions of female caregiving, to be fulfilled or unfulfilled, that we see in the heterosexual relationships of the play—and that we might understand to surround Hodler's relationship to Godé-Darel and their daughter, Paulette, as well. Love and care are often entangled by social expectations that are significantly gendered, particularly where the social paradigms of loving relationships are between men and women or in families with a mother and a father. The entanglement then can serve another role: to devalue women's labor in caregiving as the happy work of love, expected and even obligatory, but commended as a desired pleasure—and uncompensated as such. To disentangle love and care may help to resist these elisions in social norms and expectations. It should help much less to respond to our beloveds' claims, asking us to account for our love, and our failures.

The people we love are particular to us, and their claims on us are particular, as well. Their claims may not accord with social expectation—sometimes a joy of loving relationships—or they may follow social scripts fully assumed by everyone involved. If our beloveds act against these scripts or we fail to fulfill them, we may struggle with social condemnation, a sense of our wrongdoing judged from beyond the relationship itself. The Holy Scriptures may have nothing to say about us, in the words of Louis's rabbi. And the people we love, once loved, or who love us will have something to say, suffering these failures personally and not only socially, or in the "immensity" of divine justice and other ultimate goods. It is in these interpersonal failures that the differences between love and care matter most to us. We discover, as Prior discovers, that we indeed cannot demand that someone love; desire is not persuadable in this way. But we can demand care, and imagination. Prior tries to do both, pulling Louis away from his lofty images of love and into a room in which the sick need care, the future will be determined badly, and they must still imagine, together, what its endurance will demand of them both.

Afterword: Ethics Without an Ending

In Carol Gilligan's now-classic studies of moral reasoning in psychological development, the "different voice" she hears from girls instead of boys asks about the continuation of relationships beyond the scenarios of moral dilemma the children are asked to resolve.[1] Given the story of a "Mr. Heinz" who cannot afford the medicine his wife needs and is contemplating stealing it to save her, boys were observed to mature into the capacity to abstract the concerns of the scenario into questions of justice, fairness, and obligation, seeking their triumph over unreasoned desires for the people one loves and the dangers of such preferential inclinations. Girls were observed to go through periods of thinking in these terms as well, but as they matured, they were more likely to ask whether Mr. Heinz could appeal to the pharmacist for a payment plan or charity, or whether there were other people in their community he could ask for help. They sought relationship, Gilligan argues, while male subjects sought abstraction from relationship, the better to diminish its potential dangers and pains. This "contrapuntal theme" became a foundation of the feminist ethics of care of the last half-century: problems of relationship can be solved with more relationship, not less. Strengthening relationships might be a better solution than severing or escaping them. Ethical problems that seem intractable as situations or "dilemmas" might open up in relationships that extend beyond them, and offer more than the original situation ever seemed it could bear.

A core insight of the feminist ethics of care is that the continuation of relationships can be ethically promising, even as the unknown future poses significant risks. This is not a cheerful reminder that the future might not be so bad, or an argument for some kind of fearlessness in the face of vulnerability. It is an argument for the continuous negotiation of relationships lived in time, where others' responses—for better or worse—are not guaranteed. It is also an argument against the foreclosure of future possibilities because of uncertainty about what lies ahead. The ethics of care imagines that one mistake of philosophical abstraction in ethics is its abandonment of time, and all we cannot know in a life lived within it. Ethical theory is too often resistant to unknowing. Related to this resistance, it is often eager to avoid prolonging interactions with others, in which we are always vulnerable and cannot know how or when they will end.

The understanding of love I have pursued in these pages recovers its experience in time on similar terms. We've seen that the project of foreclosing future possibilities to escape uncertainty runs against the desires of lovers. Lovers desire their beloveds without knowing exactly who they are or will be in time to come. They desire a future with them, sometimes in grand senses and sometimes in the simple want for a moment to see them again, to know them further, to hear their reply. We cannot know how this time will be determined: it is uncertain, in the most basic sense of not knowing what will happen. In desiring it, lovers desire its uncertainty, lest they reduce what time they might have with their beloveds to an assertion only of themselves.

There is a version of this discussion that says next: "and so we learn from love not to foreclose our futures in other contexts," not to try to skip to the end but to embrace uncertainty as we desire it in love. The lover's want for endlessness, in this view, responds to our experiences of risk and attempts to control it by teaching us that endlessness is sometimes desirable, or at least that our attempts to control the future are often likely to diminish life in ways we should not allow. We learn from love, then, that we can and maybe should desire our uncertain futures, or at least not prize control over them in the ways we sometimes do. There might be things we imagine in them that we would like to avoid, but we should desire uncertainty more than ethical theory tends to encourage, or afford.

This lesson belongs to a different discussion than mine. I don't think that we should learn from love to embrace uncertainty, nor that we can learn from love, as such, how to relate to uncertainty well. What we can learn, instead, is something like the formal insight of the ethics of care: relationships happen over time, continuing in ways we cannot predict and likely beyond whatever end we narrate or imagine. Every story we tell of what we should do, what we desire, and what we think we know of either is incomplete. Our unknowing will likely have some effect on our thinking about how we should live. We should not underestimate it or look for a theory that can overcome it entirely. Anyone who says they've found such a thing has proven themselves untrustworthy by the claim.

My own view is that this unknowing means we should be sympathetic toward each other's fears of the future, and our own. We should watch out for the mistakes of rushing to the end, but not because people who want to do so are unwise or insufficiently courageous. Rather, we should watch for these mistakes because vulnerability is hard to bear. Its foreclosure is tempting, even at great costs to other goods. It is easy to act for the protection of what we know instead of acting for the possibility of something unknown. It is often right to do so. We need help imagining the future, then, and help responding to what we imagine well, without blindly privileging fear over desire or pursuing desire as if we had no fears. But these are not imperatives learned from love as such. They are imperatives to learn from time, where tensions between desire and fear emerge, never to be escaped.

Acknowledgments

This book began on a walk in Arcadia with Jeff and Sally Stout. My first writing on the topic came a few months later, after Jeff suggested the words might come more easily if I focused on love instead of its ineffability. The project owes more than I can say to his teaching, guidance, and generous conversation.

What virtues it may possess are due also to the other extraordinary people I have been lucky enough to study with and think alongside. My public school education formed me as a writer and reader, and I am particularly grateful to Saladin Ambar and John Baxter for their instruction in argumentation in comments on hundreds of essay drafts; to Barbara O'Breza for her reading lists and undue support; and to John Kavalos, whose high standards and tremendous knowledge made art and art history obvious places to think about every question. I wish we could have seen Hodler's paintings together, and talked through the ferocious edits you would have made to my writing about them. Susie Wilson, Nora Gelprin, Ellen Papazian, and the other staff and students at the Network for Family Life Education taught me the importance of thinking seriously about relationships, and made me skeptical of any ethical or political discussions that seem uninterested in them. Without our work together, I would not have written this book.

As an undergraduate at Princeton, I wandered into a religion department filled with ideas and arguments I immediately knew I wanted to understand, and a faculty brilliantly engaged in teaching their students how. I am especially grateful to Kwame Anthony Appiah, Sarah Arvio, Leora Batnitzky, Maria DiBattista, Sophie Gee, Eddie Glaude, Eric Gregory, Marie Griffith, Kevin Hector, Yusef Komunyakaa, Elaine

Pagels, Al Raboteau, Tracy K. Smith, Cornel West, Amanda Irwin Wilkins, C. K. Williams, and Michael Wood, and the community of graduate and undergraduate students I studied alongside, including Shira Billet, Molly Borowitz, Stephen Bush, Lily Cowles, David Decosimo, Molly Ephraim, Molly Farneth, Yarden Fraiman, Rachel Gross, Elizabeth Jemison, Sarit Kattan-Gribetz, Jordan Kisner, Michael Lamb, Isabelle Laurenzi, Rachel Lindsey, Levi McLaughlin, Fiona Miller, Anthony Petro, Bill Plevin, John Raimo, Elias Sacks, Terrance Wiley, Joseph Winters, and Kevin Wolfe. Kerry Smith brought inordinate joy and kindness to the religion department and my time in it. At the very end of those years, a conversation with Alexander Nehamas made me think I might have questions worth asking about love and time that even a specialist without obligations to listen could be interested to hear. I remain grateful for his time that afternoon, and for the writing he does when not meeting with extraneous students.

My graduate training allowed me to explore a broad range of texts and traditions that took me far from this project and helped me see I was rarely very far from it at all. Stephen Bush, Mark Cladis, Bonnie Honig, and Tal Lewis were each extraordinary advisers and interlocutors. I am deeply grateful for their guidance, example, and continuing conversation—and significant comments on drafts of this project at critical stages. I am also thankful for the community of faculty, students, and staff at Brown at that time, particularly Nic Bommarito, Karida Brown, Niki Clements, Sarah Cooke, Chris DiBona, Nicholas Friesner, Alexis Glenn, Susan Harvey, Nechama Juni, Nancy Khalek, Alex King, Caroline Kory, David Lê, Ferris Lupino, Megan McBride, Caleb Murray, Paul Nahme, Daniel Picus, Noga Rotem, Kerry Sonia, Jon Sozek, Yana Stainova, Andrew Starner, Nicole Vadnais, and Andre Willis. Fellowships from the American Association of University Women, the Pembroke Center, and the Cogut Center for the Humanities generously supported my training and research, both materially and intellectually.

Washington University in Saint Louis and the Danforth Center on Religion and Politics have provided the space, time, and resources required to realize this project in its current form. My colleagues here have provided much more. I am particularly grateful for conversation and collegiality—and many hours of reading each other's work—to Tazeen Ali, Heather Berg, Nancy Berg, Rachel Brown, Talia Dan-

Cohen, Ben Davis, Abram van Engen, Marie Griffith, Clarissa Hayward, John Inazu, Elena Kravchenko, Frank Lovett, Joe Lowenstein, Laurie Maffly-Kipp, Zach Manditch-Prottas, Lerone Martin, Melanie Micir, Leigh Schmidt, Kit Smemo, Mark Valeri, and Rebecca Wanzo. Debra Kennard and Sheri Peña keep the Danforth Center running with astounding expertise, and make life here—and life generally—a joy. The postdocs who come through the center have been fantastic colleagues as well: thank you particularly to Christie Croxall, Dana Lloyd, Dana Logan, Cody Musselman, and Cyrus O'Brien for rich conversations about parts of this book. Presenting work from this project at the Danforth Center Colloquium and the Workshop in Politics, Ethics, and Society provided helpful and generous feedback. A fellowship at the Humanities Center provided the time to finish the manuscript (and start the project they were funding), as well as the gift of writing in the company of Elizabeth Hunter, Stephanie Kirk, and Anca Parvelescu. And I have been lucky to teach remarkable students whose intellectual creativity and ethical sensitivities contributed substantially to this book. Thank you especially to Amber Aarsvold, Sofie Adams, Jennifer Greenberg, Akua Owosu-Dommey, Micah Sandman, and Celia Stern—I look forward to many more years of conversations to come.

I presented portions of this work at a number of conferences, workshops, and invited lectures, and I am grateful to the participants at each for their thoughtful engagement of these ideas. My deep thanks to Amy Hollywood and Jim Wetzel for reading and discussing a full draft of the project at a manuscript workshop, and to Marie Griffith for organizing and funding the event. Nic Bommarito, Stephen Bush, Mark Cladis, Ashleigh Elser, Nicholas Henke, Bonnie Honig, Kate Moran, Neha Nandakumar, Robert Niles-Weed, Gillian Steinberg, Elisheva Urbas, and Ludger Viefhues-Bailey read significant portions of the manuscript and provided very helpful feedback at different stages of its development. Martin Kavka, Laura Levitt, Larisa Resnik, and Sarah Stewart-Kroeker each asked questions that significantly changed my thinking about the project, and have been remarkable colleagues in many other ways. Mara Benjamin provided exceptional wisdom, perspective, and support through a critical period of trying to figure out what this book would be, and what I could be—thank you.

It has been a privilege to work with the University of Chicago Press. Kyle Wagner saw the book as it could be well before it got there, and

I am deeply grateful for his exceptional editorial work and wisdom at every stage. I am also grateful to the anonymous reviewers for the press who offered particularly insightful readings and suggestions for revision. Nathan Petrie, Kristin Rawlings, and Mark Reschke have brought this book into existence with brilliance and expertise. Gwyneth Henke and Mazie Drummond have been outstanding research assistants at the beginning and end, respectively, of turning these ideas into a book. Emily Cosgrove and Safa Khatib have been invaluable interlocutors about every word of the manuscript, as well as extraordinary colleagues, students, co-teachers, and friends. If this book offers anything to either of you, I will be satisfied.

Most of the words of this book were written during the COVID-19 pandemic. Writing about love alone in my apartment would not have been possible without friendships that always promised to persist through trial and distance, and stand for much more than having passed this most recent test. Lora-Faye Åshuvud, Alda Balthrop-Lewis, Shira Billet, Stephen Bush, Pannill Camp, Dave Christie, Joshua Dubler, Emily Dumler-Winkler, Travis Dumler-Winkler, Molly Ephraim, Molly Farneth, Arlo Fosburg, Richa Gawande, Elizabeth Kassler-Taub, Jordan Kisner, Callie Lefevre, Steve Marcus, Carly Margolis, Daniel May, Paige McGinley, Kate Moran, Amber Musser, Evan Nicholas, Jon Niles-Weed, Robert Niles-Weed, Stephanie Palmer, Jocelyn Parr, Halcyon Person, Josh Schenkkan, Andrew Walker-Cornetta, and Kay Zhang: thank you. This is a book, in part, about how hard it is to put love into words when narrating it to other people. There will be more to say when we can next spend time together.

Friends and neighbors in Saint Louis provided extraordinary joy and support while writing this book. I am grateful for wonderful meals, conversations, and hundreds of favors not yet mutually exchanged with Livia Arnal-Woods, George Brell, Xena Colby, Matt Elia, Ashleigh Elser, Katie Garland, Carson Monetti, Rachel Sachs, Gavriel Savit-Woods, Eloise Schlafly, and Paul Sorenson. Special thanks to Noah and Tammy Arnow, Emily Balestra, Clari Bowman, Melissa King, and Kevin Konzen for making Saint Louis a warm and happy home.

My brother, Max, has taught me more about love than he might know, and I love him more than I can say. Thank you for finding me an amazing sister in Brittany, and for Solomon, who gives me hope for the future and overwhelming happiness in the present. June and Willa, Gabe and Silas, Natalie and Oren, Claire, Greta, and Zia: thank you for being such wonderful extra nieces and nephews, and most of all, for being yourselves.

This book is dedicated to my parents, William and Charlotte. Their love for each other was the first I saw in the world, and their love for me has been the good of my days since long before I had any words to name it. They also, as my grandmother would say, have a particular talent for having a good time.

PREVIOUSLY PUBLISHED MATERIALS

Chapter 4 and portions of chapter 1 are adapted from Fannie Bialek, "The Happiness of Promise: Ferdinand Hodler and Alexander Nehamas on Love and Care," in *Faith, Hope, and Love*, edited by Troy Dujardin and David Eckels (Springer, 2022). Reproduced with permission from Springer Nature.

Notes

PREFACE

1 Some of the most significant work of the last century on differentiating types of love can be found in Carrie Jenkins, *What Love Is and What It Could Be* (New York: Basic Books, 2017), bell hooks, *All About Love* (New York: William Morrow and Company, 2000), Alan Soble, *The Structure of Love* (New Haven, CT: Yale University Press, 1990), and C. S. Lewis, *The Four Loves* (London: Geoffrey Bles, 1960).

CHAPTER ONE

1 Plato, "Phaedrus," in *Lysis, Symposium, Phaedrus (Loeb Classical Library)*, trans. Chris Emlyn-Jones and William Preddy (Cambridge, MA: Harvard University Press, 2022), 230e. All references to the *Phaedrus* are to this translation and edition unless noted otherwise.
2 Plato, 231a.
3 Plato, 234e, 235b.
4 Plato, 235c.
5 Plato, 264a, trans. Carson, quoted in Anne Carson, *Eros the Bittersweet: An Essay* (Princeton, NJ: Princeton University Press, 1986), 126; Plato, 264b.
6 Plato, 264c.
7 Plato, 231d.
8 A version of "trading in" and "trading up" *is* what Socrates offers in his speech on love, quoting Diotima, in the *Symposium*. Diotima's famous image of the "love ladder" represents a view of love in which it is the lover's task to be drawn to greater and greater goods, eschewing lesser loves as they go. Alcibiades briefly encourages these kinds of comparisons by saying that Socrates has managed "once again" to sit next to the most handsome man in the room (he sits between Alcibiades and

Agathon), but his role in the *Symposium* is ultimately disruptive to this kind of thinking about love. He is defied by Socrates's particularity, unable to consider him as commensurable to other goods. Though in the *Symposium* "trading in" and "trading up" are not anathema to Socrates—as they are not anathema to Lysias's discussions of love—the Socrates of the *Phaedrus* is more troubled by love that can be so immune to particularity. For more on the disruption of Alcibiades in the *Symposium*, see Martha Nussbaum, *The Fragility of Goodness* (Cambridge: Cambridge University Press, 1986), chap. 6. For more on Socrates's shifts toward the incommensurability of beloveds, see Nussbaum, chap. 7.

9 The most prominent recent proponent of this view is Harry Frankfurt, whose work I will discuss at greater length in the next chapter. He reaches this reversal of the relation between love and value through an understanding of love as an orientation of the will, directing us to care about some things and not others. People and things in the world have value to us insofar as we care about them, he argues, so no further assessment is needed, nor would it change the way we feel. Harry Frankfurt, *Reasons of Love* (Princeton, NJ: Princeton University Press, 2004).

10 Susan Wolf, "The True, the Good, and the Lovable: Frankfurt's Avoidance of Objectivity," in *Contours of Agency: Essays on Themes from Harry Frankfurt*, ed. Sarah Buss and Lee Overton (Cambridge, MA: MIT Press, 2002), 236, 234.

11 Wolf, 232, 231, 237.

12 Wolf, 238.

13 A choice *not* to buy, voluntarily, is cast as countercultural, a statement against consumption that might be pursued for environmental or other principled reasons, or as a kind of novelty, emphasizing the assumption that consumer life is the dominant way of being.

14 Byung-Chul Han, *The Agony of Eros*, trans. Erik Butler (Cambridge, MA: MIT Press, 2017 [2012]), 2.

15 Han, 2.

16 Han, 41.

17 Han, 10.

18 Han, 9.

19 Han, 10.

20 Han, 14.

21 Han, 2.

22 See, for example, the abrupt transitions at 232b, 232e, and 233a.

23 Han, *The Agony of Eros*, 35. We might think also of the proliferation of choice in terms of reproductive options, greater acceptance of different kinds of family structures and relationships, and shifting norms—in a variety of directions—about the relationship between personal and professional pursuits. Not everyone has access to these greater ranges of options, but we encounter them as possibilities in the world and thus possibilities we can want to achieve.

24 Han, 15.

25 Han, 50.
26 Alexander Nehamas, *Only a Promise of Happiness* (Princeton, NJ: Princeton University Press, 2007).
27 Nehamas, 3.
28 Nehamas, 6.
29 Nehamas, 7.
30 Adriana Cavarero, *Relating Narratives: Storytelling and Selfhood*, trans. Paul A. Kottman (London and New York: Routledge, 2000), 53.
31 Cavarero, 109.
32 Cavarero, 110.
33 Nehamas, *Only a Promise of Happiness*, 45.
34 Nehamas, 47.
35 Nehamas, 137.
36 Nehamas, 52.
37 Nehamas, 131.
38 Nehamas, 132.
39 Nehamas, *On Friendship* (New York: Basic Books, 2016), 135.
40 Nehamas, 133.
41 "Finally—here comes the reversal of Aristotle's view—we are more likely to be friends not because we recognize in one another some independently acknowledged virtues but because we take the features we admire in one another, whatever they are, to be virtues, whether or not they are such in the abstract." Nehamas, 28.

CHAPTER TWO

1 Anne Carson, *Eros, the Bittersweet* (Princeton, NJ: Princeton University Press, 1986), xi.
2 Carson, xi.
3 Carson, xi.
4 Harry Frankfurt, *Reasons of Love* (Princeton, NJ: Princeton University Press, 2004), 28.
5 Carson, *Eros, the Bittersweet*, xi–xii.
6 Nussbaum, *The Fragility of Goodness* (Cambridge: Cambridge University Press, 2001), 25.
7 Nussbaum, 26.
8 The resemblance has been noted in print by Ronald de Sousa and Alan Soble and repeated with reference to them in many other places. See Alan Soble, *The Structure of Love* (New Haven, CT: Yale University Press, 1990), and Ronald de Sousa, *The Rationality of Emotions* (Cambridge, MA: MIT Press, 1987).
9 Plato, *Euthyphro*, 10a, trans. Harold North Fowler, 1 vol., Loeb Classical Library (Cambridge, MA: Harvard University Press, 1914) (quoted from the 1995 reprint ed.).

10 Massimo Piggliucci, "Love and Reason?," in *Rationally Speaking*, May 20, 2013. http://rationallyspeaking.blogspot.com/2013/05/love-and-reason.html.

11 The ethical theories of Christian love that I'll discuss in chapter 3 have organized their questions somewhat similarly in discussions of the contrast between eros and agape. In the work of Søren Kierkegaard and Anders Nygren particularly, the right understanding of God's love and the love commanded to be practiced by Christians, agape, is defined against the erotic love of classical thinkers like Plato, for whom eros is a form of love responsive to the value of its object. With eros, we love what we love because it has value, to paraphrase Piggliucci; eros is a response to the perception of value inherent in the object of our love, independent of our relation to it. Agape, by contrast, should not depend on the value of the beloved nor even regard it for more than practical purposes. The paradigm of agape is God's abundant, gratuitous love for humanity, not deserved because of any inherent value of human beings. Nygren insists that agapic love "has nothing to do with the kind of love that depends on the recognition of a valuable quality in its object," and is displayed best in God's forgiveness of sinners who clearly do not deserve what they receive. Christians should love likewise. But for Nygren and many influenced by him, the value of the beloved is not then left out of the conversation entirely. It is a critical term of contrast, rendering a somewhat Euthyphronic structure to these discussions as well, as Nygren displays: "Eros *recognizes value* in its object—and loves it. Agape loves—and *creates value in its object.*" Anders Nygren, *Agape and Eros*, trans. Philip S. Watson (London: SPCK, 1982), 78 and 210.

12 Plato, *Euthyphro*, 4e.

13 Plato, 5a. On Plato's and Socrates's roles in rendering Euthyphro the fool of the dialogue, see Alexander Nehamas's *The Art of Living*, especially chap. 1, "Platonic Irony: Author and Audience" (Berkeley and Los Angeles: University of California Press, 1998). As Nehamas notes, the circularities of the conversation are mocked even in Euthyphro's name, which translates literally as "straight thinker."

14 One of the conflicts of "competing claims to right" that are "repugnant to reason" to which Nussbaum refers.

15 Plato, *Euthyphro*, 7b–7c.

16 Plato, 7d.

17 Plato, 10b.

18 Plato, 10b.

19 Frankfurt, *Reasons of Love*, 3.

20 Frankfurt, 4.

21 Frankfurt, 38.

22 Frankfurt, 38.

23 Frankfurt, 24.

24 Frankfurt, 26, 28.

25 Frankfurt, 28.

26 Frankfurt, *The Importance of What We Care About*, 83. I use "care" in this section in Frankfurt's sense of the orientation of the will, "caring about" something in a way that directs one's life. Frankfurt's use of the term generally corresponds to many colloquial uses, but it is not the sense of care that I will discuss elsewhere: caring for the sick, the dying, the needy, the vulnerable, and so on, caring in the sense of *providing* care. Frankfurt is speaking of what a person cares about, not what care other people require. Caring about someone or something might lead me to care for them if they need care, but caring about them, for Frankfurt, first orders *my* life, not theirs.

27 Or at least his account of "part of that range" of what "the term 'love' is customarily made to refer." He does not seek to provide a comprehensive account of everything we call love, but the subset of the things we call love in which those loves direct our lives. Fleeting desires would be generally excluded, as might loves that, on reflection, seem to be something like lust—a desire for the possession or use of another for one's pleasure, in which the person is instrumental to what I care about instead of being someone I care about themselves. It's tempting to say he's referring to "real" loves or "important" loves, since the phenomena that fall outside of his discussion seem to do so because of their relative unimportance to the larger trajectory of our lives—and, perhaps, because of a sense that they are relatively shallow, brief, and thus immature. I think we should resist that description, however, and I appreciate Frankfurt's own resistance to it, except tautologically. Love, as Frankfurt considers it, orders our lives. Our loves—in Frankfurt's sense—are, by definition, important to the trajectory of our lives because they determine that trajectory. But any further judgment of their value or importance, significance as opposed to shallowness, maturity or immaturity, is premature, and likely smuggles in assumptions about who is worth loving and what loves are worth pursuing that Frankfurt's account specifically undermines. We will consider those assumptions further in the next section. Frankfurt, *Reasons of Love*, 32.

28 Frankfurt, 39.

29 Frankfurt, *Necessity, Volition, and Love*, 131.

30 "About certain things that are important to him, a person may care so much, or in such a way, that he is subject to a kind of necessity. It is not that he cannot muster the necessary power. What he cannot muster is the will." Frankfurt, 111.

31 Genesis 22:1–20. A very brief summary: God calls Abraham to sacrifice Isaac, his son with his wife Sarah. Abraham, Isaac, two unnamed servants, and a donkey leave their home for the designated location of the sacrifice on Mount Moriah. On the morning of the third day of their journey, Abraham instructs the servants to stay with the donkey as he and Isaac go up the mountain for the sacrifice. When they reach Mount Moriah, Abraham binds Isaac and lays him on the alter, picking up his knife to kill him. A messenger of God—at the crucial moment—calls to Abraham to spare the child, Abraham having shown by his willingness to sacri-

fice Isaac that he fears God. Abraham looks up to see a ram in the bushes, whom he sacrifices in the place of his son.

32 *The Contemporary Torah*, ed. David E. S. Stein (New York: Jewish Publication Society, 2006), Bereshit 22:6.

33 Bereshit, 22:8.

34 Or what is sometimes described as an ultimate test of faith. The story might also be read as an ethical failure, of Abraham to his son, or as a divine failure, of God to Abraham, among many other readings.

35 Kierkegaard (writing as Johannes de Silentio) describes Abraham as the "knight of faith" in this vein, through his experimental retellings of the story in *Fear and Trembling*. Significantly, Kierkegaard names the *voluntary* nature of Abraham's actions here as part of what makes him a knight of faith; if he had been compelled by other people or a coercive power of God, we should not be so impressed. This is a very similar sense as Frankfurt's that the compulsion of our wills—finding ourselves unable to do otherwise—is in fact a kind of freedom, as an expression of the will. Abraham voluntarily goes up to Mount Moriah, though he may be unable to do otherwise because of the orientation of his will toward the love of God. Søren Kierkegaard, *Fear and Trembling*, ed. and trans. Howard V. Hong and Edna H. Hong (Princeton, NJ: Princeton University Press, 1983), and *Concluding Unscientific Postscript*, ed. and trans. Howard V. Hong and Edna H. Hong (Princeton, NJ: Princeton University Press, 1992). An excellent set of essays reading "Kierkegaard After Frankfurt" does not contain discussions of this example, though it offers many others connecting Kierkegaard's interest in necessity to Frankfurt's. See Anthony Rudd and John Davenport, eds., *Love, Reason, and Will: Kierkegaard After Frankfurt* (New York and London: Bloomsbury Academic, 2015).

36 Or against what others expect to be love, that is discovered not to be love at all. One interpretation of the story is that Abraham discovers that he doesn't love Isaac, not that he doesn't love Isaac *as much as* he loves God. This interpretation displaces the ethical challenge of the story into the question of whether one is supposed to love one's children—what I argue later in this chapter is a matter of social norms and not truths about what love is—rather than placing the ethical challenge within Abraham, in a tragic contest between loves.

37 See, among other places, "Identification and Wholeheartedness," in *The Importance of What We Care About*, 159–76.

38 Frankfurt, *The Importance of What We Care About*, 94.

39 Susan Wolf, "The True, the Good, and the Lovable: Frankfurt's Avoidance of Objectivity," in *Contours of Agency*, ed. Sarah Buss and Lee Overton (Cambridge, MA: MIT Press, 2002), 229.

40 Wolf, 229.

41 Wolf, 236.

42 These are taboos that seem prevalent in many societies, including my own, but there are many other examples worth considering. Homosexual love is still considered "wrong" in many places, as is the love—romantic, friendly, or other-

wise—of people of different religions, races, ethnic groups, or nations. Taboos proliferate easily and social norms can change quickly, exemplifying part of the problem with trying to define "right" and "wrong" loves universally.

43 Some people who hold the views discussed in the previous paragraph would still disagree with this statement, through arguments such as some Kantian understandings of rationality or other anthropologies in which human beings, by nature, can reason our way to certain truths. My argument doesn't begin from or lead to such ideas about either reason or human nature, and I do not think someone who holds them would find much to agree with here about these issues. What they might find compelling, however, is to read this account as descriptive of certain social practices and tendencies of relationships that a social ethics is likely to need to contend with.

44 Frankfurt, *Reasons of Love*, 28.

45 Frankfurt, 29.

46 Some of these interrogations may fall into the realm of questioning the actions they take (or fail to take) for their children, and are thus properly questions about what they *do* because of their love and not *whether* they love them. Some are questions about caregiving and obligation that don't require love at all—we might think here of the large category of interrogations by state authorities into parental actions—though those lines of inquiry may be entangled in assumptions about love in ways that make such distinctions cold comfort to the parent (or others). I will discuss that entanglement further in chapter 4.

47 Parents may also ask these questions of themselves. The example that comes most easily to mind is the questioning of one's parental love shortly after the child's birth. That uncertainty may be intermingled with postpartum depression, for birthing parents, or with other struggles to adjust to a new configuration of life. Such situations are worthy of careful consideration and are poor illustrations of any particular point given their complexities.

48 Richard Rorty, "Religion as a Conversation-Stopper," in *Philosophy and Social Hope* (London: Penguin Books, 1999), 168–74.

49 Rorty, 171.

50 Stout draws the concept from Robert Brandom, *Making It Explicit: Reasoning, Representing, and Discursive Commitment* (Cambridge, MA: Harvard University Press, 1994). In Jeffrey Stout, *Democracy and Tradition* (Princeton, NJ: Princeton University Press, 2004), 86.

51 Stout, *Democracy and Tradition*, 86–87.

52 Stout, 87.

53 As some people seem to offer religious claims in political conversation, as well.

54 Stout, 90.

55 Richard Rorty, *Contingency, Irony, and Solidarity* (Cambridge: Cambridge University Press, 1989), 73.

56 Rorty, 73.

57 Stout, *Democracy and Tradition*, 90.

CHAPTER THREE

1 Søren Kierkegaard, *Works of Love*, trans. Howard Hong and Edna Hong (Princeton, NJ: Princeton University Press, 1995), 29.
2 Kierkegaard, 30.
3 Kierkegaard, 33.
4 Kierkegaard, 29.
5 Kierkegaard, 66.
6 Kierkegaard, 66.
7 Reinhold Niebuhr, *An Interpretation of Christian Ethics* (Louisville, KY: Westminster John Knox Press, 2013), 103.
8 Gene Outka, *Agape: An Ethical Analysis* (New Haven, CT: Yale University Press, 1977), 77.
9 Here I follow Nicholas Wolterstorff's characterization of "modern day agapism" as a movement in twentieth-century Christian ethics that he defines primarily by the tension it explores between love and justice, not the contrast of eros and agape with which I am most interested here. "Modern day agapists" are interested in "that distinctive form of love that is *agape*" with which Christians are commanded to love their neighbors, distinctive in part because of its possible disregard for or tension with justice. By Wolterstorff's definition, "All modern day agapists held that agapic love is a species of that sort of love which consists of seeking to promote the good of someone as an end in itself, provided one does not do so because justice requires it." They offer a discussion of Christian love that is interested in the way it might come into practical conflict with justice, and must not be motivated by justice. They also tend toward a style of contrasts—love *versus* justice, eros *or* agape—that might be resolved by syntheses or moderations of tensions, instead of a larger resistance to distinguishing Christian love in contrasts of these kinds at all—as in Paul Tillich or Martin D'Arcy, where different forms of love are not defined against one another in this way. I will define modern agapists primarily by this style of interest in tensions and contrasts to define the distinctiveness of Christian love, instead of the positing of agape's tension with justice particularly. To identify modern agapists in this way is to include Wolterstorff himself, as an advocate for a reduction of tensions or a resolution of them but still someone interested in the way they have been staged. It is also to include thinkers like Gene Outka who offer what they consider primarily descriptive accounts of what the concept of agape has been in Christian ethics before giving their own (relatively brief) normative arguments for what it should be and how it should be understood. And it is to include Nygren—centrally—though he differs from the others in an important way by defining agape as strictly the love of God and not a love belonging to the practice of human beings, though it should be emulated in the Christian's love of neighbor. These inclusions make for a diverse group, and not one that I propose has substantial diagnostic value. I name the conversation mainly to avoid treating it as the occupation of Christian ethics as a whole during

its period. It was an important strand of some (prominent, even dominant, and institutionally powerful) parts of Christian ethics, but treating it as "Christian ethics" in this period or even "Christian ethics of love" obscures the diversity of the field.

Wolterstorff names Kierkegaard, Nygren, Karl Barth, Reinhold Niebuhr, and Paul Ramsey as the central figures of the movement he defines. I add Gene Outka and Timothy Jackson, as well as Wolterstorff himself, to the conversation in my discussion here, and largely neglect Barth and Ramsey, not in contestation of their inclusion but because of a difference in emphasis. There are many ways to contest the list, of course—it is easy to argue about exclusions and inclusions in any identification of a movement that does not define itself, and even then. But Wolterstorff is right to group a set of discussions about Christian love in North Atlantic, Protestant Christian ethics in the twentieth century (with a nineteenth-century predecessor in Kierkegaard) engaged by these authors as sharing something, and something distinct from discussions of love in Christian ethics over the same period that were more interested, for example, in the loving relationship of human beings to God that characterizes, in different ways, Martin D'Arcy and Paul Tillich's work on Christian love over the same period. Nicholas Wolterstorff, *Justice in Love* (Grand Rapids, MI: Eerdmans, 2015), 1, 21, 23. See also Paul Tillich, *Systematic Theology* (Digswell Place: James Misbet and Company, 1968), and Martin D'Arcy, *The Mind and Heart of Love: A Study in Eros and Agape* (New York: Meridian Books, 1956).

10 Nygren, *Agape and Eros*, 34.
11 Nygren, 35.
12 Nygren, 35.
13 Nygren, 37.
14 Nygren, 37.
15 Philip Rieff, "Eros Cross-Examined," review of *Agape and Eros* by Anders Nygren, trans. Philip S. Watson. *Kenyon Review* 16, no. 4 (1954): 645–48, 650–52, http://www.jstor.org/stable/4333533, 646.
16 Lowell D. Streiker, "The Christian Understanding of Platonic Love: A Critique of Anders Nygren's 'Agape and Eros,'" *Christian Scholar* 47, no. 4 (1964): 331–340, http://www.jstor.org/stable/41177405, 331, 333, 334.
17 Rieff, "Eros Cross-Examined," 646.
18 Nygren's treatment of Judaism is starkly antisemitic throughout this text. He describes it is a religion of law and not of faith, necessarily superseded by the incarnation of God in the person of Jesus Christ. The problems with his discussion on these grounds are beyond the scope of my argument here, but worthy of further examination.
19 Nygren, *Agape and Eros*, 54.
20 Nygren, 30–31.
21 Nygren, 54.
22 Nygren, 30.

23 Nygren, 54.
24 Nygren, 31.
25 Nygren, 50–51.
26 Nygren, 51.
27 Nygren, 61. Matthew 22:37–40; Mark 12:28–34; Luke 10:25–28.
28 For a relevant refutation of this interpretation of Judaism and Christianity as religions of law and love, respectively and exclusively, see Shai Held, *Judaism Is About Love: Recovering the Heart of Jewish Life* (New York: Farrar, Straus, and Giroux, 2024).
29 Held. Not only is it quoted from the Old Testament, but it is also "a lawyer, a representative of Old Testament religion [and its legalism], who combines the commandments," Nygren argues, quoting from Luke 10:25. But he fails to address that in both of the other introductions of the dual love commandment in the Synoptic Gospels, it is introduced and combined by Jesus himself (Nygren mentions this fact in Mark, in passing, though not in Matthew and without any mention of the significance of its articulation in this way in two out of three appearances in the gospels). He also reads the scene in Mark as portraying Jesus strongly referencing the Old Testament with the commandment, "while a scribe is represented as heartily agreeing with Him," suggesting the connection to legalistic Judaism (Nygren, *Agape and Eros*, 62; Mark 12:25). But in both Mark and Matthew, Jesus offers the commandment in reply to a lawyer such that it seems offered as a replacement of the law, and thus might seem to mark Christ's departure from the intricate legalisms of the Old Testament more than his connections to it. See Matthew 22:37–40; Mark 12:28–34; Luke 10:25–28. The problems with Nygren's argument do not rest in his interpretation of the Gospels nor does it seem from the structure of his text that he would concede the larger claims were someone to convince him on these others. This is one example, however, of the way his interpretations of Scripture are often less than convincing.
30 Nygren, *Agape and Eros*, 66.
31 Matthew 5:44, King James Version.
32 Matthew 5:48, quoted from NIV. Emphasis mine.
33 Nygren, *Agape and Eros*, 66.
34 Nygren, 67.
35 Nygren, 67.
36 Nygren, 47 and 75.
37 Nygren, 75.
38 Nygren, 77.
39 Nygren, 77.
40 Nygren, 75.
41 Nygren, 75.
42 Nygren, 75.
43 Harry Frankfurt, *Reasons of Love* (Princeton, NJ: Princeton University Press, 2004).

44 Frankfurt, 80.
45 Nygren, *Agape and Eros*, 75–80. Quotations, numbering, and ordering original.
46 Streiker, "The Christian Understanding of Platonic Love," 332.
47 Nygren, *Agape and Eros*, 77.
48 Nygren, 77. Emphasis in original.
49 Nygren, 175. Quotations, numbering, and ordering original.
50 Nygren 175, paraphrasing Plato. I focus here on Nygren's derivation of the concept of eros from Plato for the sake of brevity, though Nygren argues for it as the most important version of the concept: "Neither the dry theorizing of Aristotle's treatment of the subject, nor the abstruse mythological notions of Plotinus and still more his successors, whereby the universe is populated with a multitude of Erotes which furnish a link between earth and heaven, can successfully compete with Plato. Plato is both the creator and the perfecter of the classical idea of Eros.... All the essential features of the Eros motif—everything necessary for determining its structure—can be found in Plato. For our immediate purposes, therefore, of comparing and contrasting the Eros motif and the Agape motif in respect of their constitutive principles, it might suffice simply to take the idea of Eros in its original Platonic form" (182). Nygren goes on to consider other forms of the concept from Aristotle and Neoplatonist authors because of their influence on Christian theology, but his readings of these authors do not change his own conclusions in a way that bears on my reading of him here.
51 Nygren, 176.
52 Nygren, 176. Emphasis in original.
53 There is a difficulty in his explanation of this point as he slips between eros as it should be understood in a Christian context, colored entirely by the concept of agape; how it is mistakenly understood by Augustine and others describing a "heavenly eros" in a Christian register overtaken by the terms of ancient Greek religion and philosophy; and ancient Greek religion and philosophy, in which "the Divine" to which eros draws human beings is the multiple gods of ancient Greece. I use the plural "gods" here to refer to the gods of ancient Greece where I take Nygren to be referring to them, and "the Divine" and "God" where Nygren uses the singular, apparently in reference to the singular God of Christianity.
54 Nygren, 177.
55 Nygren, 178.
56 Nygren, 178. Nygren's discussion here bears some similarity to Aquinas on desire, want, and need and the role of the individual in these phenomena. He gives no suggestion that he has these passages in mind, but the connection might be made in reference to recent work using Aquinas in discussions of love and the value of the beloved, similar to mine here. See Eleonore Stump, "Love, By All Accounts," *Proceedings and Addresses of the American Philosophical Association* 80, no. 2 (2006): 25–43, http://www.jstor.org/stable/27645191.
57 Nygren, 210. Emphasis in original.
58 Nygren, 78.

59 Nygren, 78.
60 Nygren, 79.
61 Nygren, 79.
62 Nygren, 80. First emphasis mine, second in original.
63 Matthew 22:37–40 (NRSV).
64 Generally speaking, eros is a desirous response to the beauty or other value of the beloved; *philia* is the love of friends, desirous of company and mutual endeavor; and agape is the bestowing love of parents, teachers, and other superiors, love that extends from a greater party to a lesser one, given instead of deserved. For further discussion of the continuity between Greek and Christian forms of love in modern Christian thought, see Terence Irwin, "Conceptions of Love, Greek and Christian," in *Love and Christian Ethics*, ed. Frederick V. Simmons and Brian Sorrells (Washington, D.C.: Georgetown University Press, 2016), 36–50.
65 William Frankena, *Ethics*, 2nd ed. (Englewood Cliffs, NJ: Prentice-Hall, Inc. 1973), 56.
66 Kierkegaard, *Works of Love* (1995), 66.
67 Karl Barth, *Church Dogmatics IV/2*, trans. G. W. Bromiley (Edinburgh: T&T Clark, 1958), 75, quoted in Outka, *Agape*, 11.
68 Jackson, *Love Disconsoled*, 65. Wolterstorff, *Justice in Love*, x.
69 Outka, *Agape*, 12.
70 Outka, 10.
71 Outka, 10 and 11.
72 Outka, 12.
73 See, for example, Irwin, "Conceptions of Love," and Streiker, "The Christian Understanding of Platonic Love."
74 For this to be the case, one would need to believe that there are "facts of the matter" of this kind, independent of people's relation to them. Not everyone believes that, including me. But for people who do believe there are facts of this kind, the value of a person need not be an exception.
75 See Jackson, *Love Disconsoled*, chaps. 1 and 3.
76 Wolterstorff, *Justice in Love*, 45.
77 Kierkegaard, *Works of Love* (1995), 44.
78 Kierkegaard, 53.
79 Kierkegaard is significantly attentive to other forms of vulnerability in love in other texts, including in his references to his relationship with Regine Olsen and use of seduction metaphors in *Either/Or* and *The Seducer's Diary*. I focus here on *Works of Love* for the most direct connection to the Christian ethical accounts of the love commandment that Nygren and his interpreters are considering, and regret that his interest in desire and its possible end(s) is beyond the scope of this discussion. See Kierkegaard, *Either/Or*, trans. Howard V. Hong and Edna Hong (Princeton, NJ: Princeton University Press, 1988), and *The Seducer's Diary*, trans. Howard V. Hong and Edna Hong (Princeton, NJ: Princeton University Press, 2013). For a consideration of Regine Olsen herself, as well as her representation

in Kierkegaard's writings, see Joakim Garff, *Kierkegaard's Muse: The Mystery of Regine Olsen*, trans. Alastair Hannay (Princeton, NJ: Princeton University Press, 2017 [2013]). I am grateful to an anonymous reviewer for the University of Chicago Press for suggesting the richness of these other texts on these themes. I am also grateful to my brother, Max Bialek, for first introducing me to the story of Kierkegaard's relationship with Regine Olsen with the wise suggestion that "no matter your metaphysics, the abstract is grounded in reality."

80 Matthew 20:1–16.
81 Niebuhr, *An Interpretation of Christian Ethics*, xxxi.
82 Jackson, *Love Disconsoled*, 64.
83 Jackson, 64.
84 Jackson, 139.

CHAPTER FOUR

1 Hodler's encounter with Holbein's 1521 *The Body of the Dead Christ in the Tomb* (translated also as *The Corpse of Christ in the Tomb*) at the Kunstmuseum Basel in 1875 has been well documented as a significant influence on his larger body of work and the Godé-Darel pieces particularly. The painting was displayed above a painting of Holbein's wife and children, a connection Hodler continues as he examines death most intensely in the portraits of Godé-Darel, his lover and the mother of their child. In the year after seeing Holbein's Christ, Hodler painted two portraits of dead bodies that experiment with similar compositional choices as Holbein's painting (*The Dead Farmhand*, 1876, and *The Dead Peasant Woman*, 1876). Holbein's haunting lighting of the corpse of Christ from below the face, illuminating the neck, upper lip, bottom of the nose, and top of the eye sockets is recreated in these two 1876 paintings, which also imitate Holbein's naturalism. In the portraits of Godé-Darel, the style is generally sketchier and the source of light less clear, but the postures of the head and body are the same, drawn at inanimate angles, sharp profiles fallen just to the side as the neck no longer holds the head. In addition to the compositional similarities, Hodler made frequent comments later in life about the influence of Holbein on his work. See Oskar Bätschmann, "Ferdinand Hodler the Painter," trans. Michael Johnson, in *Ferdinand Hodler, Views and Visions* (Zurich: Swiss Institute for Art Research, 1994), 26–65, published to accompany an exhibition at the Cincinnati Art Museum, National Academy of Design NY, Art Gallery of Ontario, and Wadsworth Atheneum, 1994–95; and Jill Lloyd, "Valentine Godé-Darel: Time and Eternity," in *Ferdinand Hodler: View to Infinity*, ed. Jill Lloyd and Ulf Küster (Ostfildern: Hatje Cantz Verlag, 2012), 40–53.

2 Biographical sources differ on the timing of the diagnosis in relation to Paulette's birth. Jill Lloyd cites the diagnosis to a time after Paulette's birth, but with symptoms beginning prior to the birth and suspected at first to be tuberculosis. This

account is the best grounded in documentary evidence, including letters between Hodler and his friend Oskar Miller discussing her illness. Lloyd, "Valentine Godé-Darel: Time and Eternity," 44–45, n12.
3   Bernhard C. Pestalozzi, "Looking at the Dying Patient: The Ferdinand Hodler Paintings of Valentine Godé-Darel," *Journal of Clinical Oncology* 20, no. 7 (April 2002): 1948.
4   Kelly Baum, Andrea Bayer, and Sheena Wagstaff, *Unfinished: Thoughts Left Visible* (New York: Museum of Modern Art, 2016). First seen in exhibition: Metropolitan Museum of Art (The Met Breuer), "Unfinished: Thoughts Left Visible," New York, March 18–September 4, 2016.
5   Lloyd, "Valentine Godé-Darel: Time and Eternity," 44.
6   Lloyd, 44.
7   Esther Driefuss-Kattan, "Ferdinand Hodler: From the Vertical of Life to the Horizontal of Death," in *Art and Mourning: The Role of Creativity in Healing Trauma and Loss* (New York, Routledge, 2016), 81–100.
8   Driefuss-Kattan, 81–100. In a few of the paintings of Valentine, including *Die Tote Valentine Godé-Darel*, 1915, the three blue lines representing the soul do appear at the top of the painting. But they are much closer to the body of Valentine than they were to Augustine, because the body of Godé-Darel is placed nearly in the middle of the frame, with the lower half of the painting filled with stripes of gray, white, faded pink, and brick brown, seemingly depicting her mattresses, the bed, and the floor. Critics have interpreted this changed shape to enhance the horizontality of the paintings as something oppressive, creating a constraint from true ascent into an open space above. See Dreifuss-Kattan, "Ferdinand Hodler: From the Vertical of Life to the Horizontal of Death," and Lloyd, "Valentine Godé-Darel: Time and Eternity."
9   Louis Marin argues for this idea in his discussion of the resistance to telling a story that extends over time in Caravaggio's paintings. For a critical discussion of failures of temporality in painting, see Adriana Cavarero's discussion of Leonardo daVinci's *Virgin and Child with St. Anne* and Bonnie Honig's reply in *A Feminist Theory of Refusal*. Louis Marin, *To Destroy Painting*, trans. Mette Hjort (Chicago and London: University of Chicago Press, 1995); Adriana Cavarero, *Inclinations: A Critique of Rectitude*, trans. Amanda Minervini and Adam Sitze (Stanford, CA: Stanford University Press, 2016); and Bonnie Honig, *A Feminist Theory of Refusal* (Cambridge, MA: Harvard University Press, 2021).
10 Vasily Kandinsky described Hodler as having "revitalized" the "melodic composition" of paintings, by which he meant a "simple composition, which is subordinated to a clearly apparent, simple form" characterized by "primitive geometrical forms or a structure of simple lines serving the general movement" beneath the "objective element" of the painting. He is writing, in 1911, primarily of Hodler's works formed by the repetition of figures or the lively postures of its characters, like *The Splendour of Lines* and *The Joyful Woman* featuring Godé-Darel, mentioned earlier. Vasily Kandinsky, "Über das Geistige in her Kunst," quoted in Ulf

Küster, "Ferdinand Hodler: Series and Variations," in *Ferdinand Hodler: View to Infinity*, ed. Jill Lloyd and Ulf Küster (Ostfildern: Hatje Cantz Verlag, 2012), 19.
11 Quoted in Lloyd, "Valentine Godé-Darel: Time and Eternity," 48.
12 Lloyd, 48.
13 Oskar Bätschmann warns with this example against the "fatality" of "sentimental findings based on assumptions about his probable state of mind that have not been checked against documentary evidence." Hodler painted two self-portraits in 1914 as Valentine is dying, which have been described as "related to paternity, on the one hand, and with the mortal illness of his lover, on the other." But "Hodler sent both these self-portraits to Gertrud Müller in Solothurn, at her request, so that she could choose one. The message of one of them—in which Hodler depicted himself with raised eyebrows, surrounded by red and white roses behind his shoulder—was a rather clear question to the woman whom he desired. This self-portrait was immediately refused by Müller, who retained the one with a more skeptically inquiring expression and rejected the message of love with roses." The "clear question" Bätschmann sees in the raised eyebrows and roses may be a matter of interpretation as well, though it is bolstered by letters suggesting Hodler's romantic interest in Müller, who became a close friend. Bätschmann, "Ferdinand Hodler: Late Work and Last Works," in *Ferdinand Hodler: View to Infinity*, ed. Jill Lloyd and Ulf Küster (Ostfildern: Hatje Cantz Verlag, 2012), 30.
14 Lloyd, "Valentine Godé-Darel: Time and Eternity," 42. Lloyd suggests from her reading of Hodler's letters that this absence was the result of relational conflict or withdrawal, not the demands of her treatment or demands on his schedule elsewhere.
15 Hodler's version of this technique, while named for the artist, is different in a few significant ways from Dürer's original technique. Dürer used a pane marked with a compositional grid—or even a pane made from string, making up a compositional grid—to view a person or object and see how it should be represented in perspective on a two-dimensional plane. Dürer did not draw on the pane itself, as Hodler did, but still placed the pane (or string grid) between him and the object to understand how to render it on a flat surface. The technique was developed as part of his experimentation with perspective, not as a way to trace from life, as Hodler's technique seemed to be. For Dürer's own discussion of his technique, see Albrecht Dürer, *The Painter's Manual*, trans. Walter Strauss (Norwalk, CT: Abaris Books, 1977). I'm grateful to Elizabeth Kassler-Taub for her tutorial on Dürer's technologies for drawing and perspective.
16 On Hodler's use of Dürer glass, see Bätschmann, "Ferdinand Hodler: Late Work and Last Works," 28–29.
17 Bätschmann, 29.
18 Elisabeth Bronfen, *Over Her Dead Body: Death, Femininity and the Aesthetic* (New York: Routledge, 1992).
19 Bronfen, 51.
20 Bronfen, 50.

21 Alexander Nehamas, *Only a Promise of Happiness* (Princeton, NJ: Princeton University Press, 2007), 7, and Adriana Cavarero, *Relating Narratives: Storytelling and Selfhood*, trans. Paul A. Kottman (London and New York: Routledge, 2000), 53. For a more detailed discussion of these points in Nehamas and Cavarero, see chap. 1, "Wanting Without Knowing."
22 Bronfen, *Over Her Dead Body*, 53.
23 Bronfen, 48.
24 Lloyd, "Valentine Godé-Darel: Time and Eternity," 51.
25 Bronfen, *Over Her Dead Body*, 47. Some were displayed publicly before then, having come into the possession of collectors and museums because of financial needs of the family or by unknown means during World War II. A favorite artist of many German Jewish collectors, Hodler's work was taken by Nazis from many Jewish homes and has been part of numerous art restitution cases, including to the family of famed collector Ernst Flersheim. Thirty-five works by Hodler remain in the German Lost Art database. Though none of the Godé-Darel pieces have clearly established ties to Nazi spoliation, many have gaps in known provenance that suggest the chaos of the war period and obscure their path out of private possession by Hodler's family and friends. See "Hodler" in the Lost Art Datenbank, https://www.lostart.de, last accessed March 18, 2023. For the records of art restitution to the Flersheim family, led by Ernst Flersheim's grandson, Walter Eberstadt, see Walter A. Eberstadt, *Walter Eberstadt Collection, 1945–1951, 1998–2007*, held at the Leo Baeck Institute Archives, New York, NY.
26 Bronfen, *Over Her Dead Body*, 47.
27 Bronfen, 47.
28 Bronfen, 47.
29 Harold Schweizer, *On Waiting* (New York: Routledge, 2008).
30 Schweizer, 101.
31 Schweizer, 90.
32 Simone Weil, *Waiting for God*, trans. Emma Crauford (New York: Perennial Classics, 2001), 64. Quoted also in Schweizer, *On Waiting*, 88.
33 Schweizer, 88.
34 Schweizer, 88.
35 Schweizer, 8.
36 Schweizer, 88. Emphasis added.
37 Schweizer, 89.
38 Schweizer, 101. Emphasis in original.
39 Schweizer, 90.
40 I direct this criticism at Schweizer's development of the idea of attention, not at Weil's. I think she is susceptible to a version of this critique as well, but the lines would need to be redrawn: her separation of the mechanistic world from the spiritual entangles the physical provisions of care with the mechanisms of suffering itself, so physical care, in her work, is sometimes an intentional act emerging from orientations of the soul, and sometimes mere mechanism as physical

beings. Her interest in the superiority of the spiritual world is often overstated in the interpretation of her ethics. Her view of emptying bedpans would require a consideration of texts beyond her spiritual writings, and is beyond the scope of my discussion here.

41 Care is also necessary after a person dies: care for their bodies, and for what and whom they leave behind. But in many cultural practices, care for the dead is a separate and distinct responsibility from care for the living, done by different people than those who cared for the person in life. Sometimes this corresponds to understandings of the dead body as unclean or otherwise not to be touched as one touches a living body; in other contexts it seems to recognize that the prior caregivers are now in mourning, and should not be expected to do the work required to care for the dead. For a breadth of examples of these and other practices, see *Death, Mourning, and Burial: A Cross-Cultural Reader*, ed. Antonius C. G. M. Robben (Oxford: Blackwell, 2004).

42 See Lloyd, "Valentine Godé-Darel: Time and Eternity," and Bätschmann, "Ferdinand Hodler: Late Work and Last Works."

43 Tony Kushner, *Angels in America* (New York: Theater Communications Group, 2013).

44 Kushner, 31. Ellipses original.

45 Kushner, 271.

46 Kushner, 57–58. Ellipses original.

47 Kushner, 45–46. Ellipses original.

48 Kushner, 85.

49 Kushner, 86. Ellipses original.

50 Kushner, 271.

51 See, for example, Alan Soble, *The Structure of Love* (New Haven, CT: Yale University Press, 1990), Nicholas Wolterstorff, *Justice in Love* (Grand Rapids, MI: Eerdmans, 2015), and William Frankena, *Ethics* (Englewood Cliffs, NJ: Prentice-Hall, Inc., 1973).

52 See, among other discussions of this distinction, Eva Feder Kittay, *Love's Labour* (New York: Routledge, 1999).

53 See, for example and for an overview of arguments of this kind, Erinn C. Gilson, *The Ethics of Vulnerability* (New York, Routeledge, 2014).

AFTERWORD

1 Carol Gilligan, *In a Different Voice* (Cambridge, MA: Harvard University Press, 1982).

Bibliography

Barth, Karl. *Church Dogmatics IV/2*. Edited by T. F. Torrance. Translated by G. W. Bromiley. London: T&T Clark, 1958.

Bätschmann, Oskar. "Ferdinand Hodler the Painter." Translated by Michael Johnson. In *Ferdinand Hodler, Views and Visions*, 26–65. Zurich: Swiss Institute for Art Research, 1994.

Bätschmann, Oskar. "Ferdinand Hodler: Late Work and Last Works." In *Ferdinand Hodler: View to Infinity*, edited by Jill Lloyd and Ulf Küster, 30. Ostfildern: Hatje Cantz Verlag, 2012.

Baum, Kelly, Andrea Bayer, and Sheena Wagstaff. *Unfinished: Thoughts Left Visible*. New York: Museum of Modern Art, 2016.

Brandom, Robert B. *Making It Explicit: Reasoning, Representing, and Discursive Commitment*. Cambridge, MA: Harvard University Press, 1994.

Bronfen, Elisabeth. *Over Her Dead Body: Death, Femininity and the Aesthetic*. Manchester: Manchester University Press, 1992.

Carson, Anne. *Eros the Bittersweet*. Princeton, NJ: Princeton University Press, 1986.

Cavarero, Adriana. *Inclinations: A Critique of Rectitude*. Translated by Adam Sitze and Amanda Minervini. Stanford, CA: Stanford University Press, 2016.

Cavarero, Adriana. *Relating Narratives: Storytelling and Selfhood*. Translated by Paul A. Kottman. London and New York: Routledge, 2000.

D'Arcy, Martin Cyril. *The Mind and Heart of Love: A Study in Eros and Agape*. New York: Meridian Books, 1956.

De Sousa, Ronald. *The Rationality of Emotion*. Cambridge, MA: MIT Press, 1987.

Dreifuss-Kattan, Esther. "Ferdinand Hodler: From the Vertical of Life to the Horizontal of Death." In *Art and Mourning: The Role of Creativity in Healing Trauma and Loss*, 81–100. New York: Routledge, 2016. https://doi.org/10.4324/9781315714479.

Dürer, Albrecht. *The Painter's Manual*. Translated by Walter L. Strauss. Norwalk, CT: Abaris Books, 1977.

Frankena, William K. *Ethics*. 2nd ed. Englewood Cliffs, NJ: Prentice-Hall, Inc, 1973.
Frankfurt, Harry G. *The Importance of What We Care About: Philosophical Essays*. Cambridge: Cambridge University Press, 1988.
Frankfurt, Harry G. *Necessity, Volition, and Love*. Cambridge: Cambridge University Press, 1998.
Frankfurt, Harry G. *The Reasons of Love*. Princeton, NJ: Princeton University Press, 2004.
Frankfurt, Harry G. *Taking Ourselves Seriously and Getting It Right*. Stanford, CA: Stanford University Press, 2006.
Gilligan, Carol. *In a Different Voice: Psychological Theory and Women's Development*. Cambridge, MA: Harvard University Press, 1982.
Gilson, Erinn C. *The Ethics of Vulnerability: A Feminist Analysis of Social Life and Practice*. New York: Routledge, 2014.
Han, Byung-Chul. *The Agony of Eros*. Translated by Erik Butler. Cambridge, MA: MIT Press, 2017.
Held, Shai. *Judaism Is About Love: Recovering the Heart of Jewish Life*. New York: Farrar, Straus, and Giroux, 2024.
Hodler, Ferdinand. *Ferdinand Hodler: Views and Visions*. Zurich and Washington, DC: Swiss Institute for Art Research, 1994.
Honig, Bonnie. *A Feminist Theory of Refusal*. Cambridge, MA, and London: Harvard University Press, 2021.
hooks, bell. *All About Love: New Visions*. New York: William Morrow and Company, 2000.
Jackson, Timothy P. *Love Disconsoled: Meditations on Christian Charity*. Cambridge: Cambridge University Press, 1999.
Jenkins, Carrie. *What Love Is: And What It Could Be*. New York: Basic Books, 2017.
Kierkegaard, Søren. *Fear and Trembling/Repetition*. Translated by Edna H. Hong and Howard V. Hong. Princeton, NJ: Princeton University Press, 1983.
Kierkegaard, Søren. *Works of Love*. Translated by Howard Hong and Edna Hong. New York: Harper Perennial Modern Thought, 2009.
Kierkegaard, Søren. *Works of Love*. Translated by Howard Hong and Edna Hong. Princeton, NJ: Princeton University Press, 1995.
Kierkegaard, Søren. *Concluding Unscientific Postscript*. Edited and translated by Howard V. Hong and Edna H. Hong. Princeton, NJ: Princeton University Press, 1992.
Kittay, Eva Feder. *Love's Labor: Essays on Women, Equality, and Dependency*. New York: Routledge, 1999.
Kushner, Tony. *Angels in America: A Gay Fantasia on National Themes; Revised and Complete Edition*. New York: Theatre Communications Group, 2013.
Küster, Ulf. "Ferdinand Hodler: Series and Variations." In *Ferdinand Hodler: View to Infinity*, edited by Jill Lloyd and Ulf Küster. Ostfildern: Hatje Cantz Verlag, 2012.

Lewis, C. S. *The Four Loves*. New York: Harcourt Brace, 1960.
Lloyd, Jill. "Valentine Godé-Darel: Time and Eternity." In *Ferdinand Hodler: View to Infinity*, edited by Jill Lloyd and Ulf Küster, 40–53. Ostfildern: Hatje Cantz Verlag, 2012.
Marin, Louis. *To Destroy Painting*. Translated by Mette Hjort. Chicago: The University of Chicago Press, 1995.
Nehamas, Alexander. *The Art of Living*. Berkeley: University of California Press, 1998.
Nehamas, Alexander. *On Friendship*. New York: Basic Books, 2016.
Nehamas, Alexander. *Only a Promise of Happiness: The Place of Beauty in a World of Art*. Princeton, NJ: Princeton University Press, 2007.
Niebuhr, Reinhold. *An Interpretation of Christian Ethics*. Louisville, KY: Westminster John Knox Press, 2013.
Nussbaum, Martha C. *The Fragility of Goodness: Luck and Ethics in Greek Tragedy and Philosophy*. Revised edition. Cambridge and New York: Cambridge University Press, 2001.
Nygren, Anders. *Agape and Eros*. Translated by Philip S. Watson. London: SPCK, 1982.
Outka, Gene. *Agape: An Ethical Analysis*. New Haven, CT: Yale University Press, 1972.
Pestalozzi, Bernhard C. "Looking at the Dying Patient: The Ferdinand Hodler Paintings of Valentine Godé-Darel." *Journal of Clinical Oncology* 20, no. 7 (2002): 1948–1950. ascopubs.org.
Pigliucci, Massimo. "Rationally Speaking: Love and Reason?" *Rationally Speaking* (blog), May 20, 2013. http://rationallyspeaking.blogspot.com/2013/05/love-and-reason.html.
Plato. "Euthyphro." Translated by Harold North Fowler and W. R. M. Lamb. In *Euthyphro, Apology, Crito, Phaedo (Loeb Classical Library)*. Cambridge, MA: Harvard University Press, 1995 [1914].
Plato. "Phaedrus." Translated by Chris Emlyn-Jones and William. In *Lysis, Symposium, Phaedrus (Loeb Classical Library)*. Cambridge, MA: Harvard University Press, 2022.
Plato. *Symposium*. Edited by Kenneth Dover. Cambridge: Cambridge University Press, 1980.
Rieff, Philip. "Eros Cross-Examined." Review of *Agape and Eros* by Anders Nygren, translated by Philip S. Watson. *Kenyon Review* 16, no. 4 (1954): 645–48, 650–52. http://www.jstor.org/stable/4333533.
Robben, Antonius C. G. M., ed. *Death, Mourning, and Burial: A Cross-Cultural Reader*. Oxford: Blackwell, 2004
Rorty, Richard. *Contingency, Irony, and Solidarity*. Cambridge and New York: Cambridge University Press, 1989.
Rorty, Richard. "Religion as a Conversation-Stopper." In *Philosophy and Social Hope*, 168–74. London: Penguin Books, 1999.

Rudd, Anthony, and John Davenport, eds. *Love, Reason, and Will: Kierkegaard After Frankfurt.* New York: Bloomsbury Academic, 2015.

Schweizer, Harold. *On Waiting.* London and New York: Routledge, 2008.

Simmons, Frederick V., and Brian Sorrells, eds. *Love and Christian Ethics: Tradition, Theory, and Society.* Washington, DC: Georgetown University Press, 2016.

Soble, Alan. *The Structure of Love.* New Haven, CT: Yale University Press, 1990.

Stout, Jeffrey. *Democracy and Tradition.* Princeton, NJ: Princeton University Press, 2004.

Streiker, Lowell D. "The Christian Understanding of Platonic Love: A Critique of Anders Nygren's 'Agape and Eros.'" *Christian Scholar* 47, no. 4 (1964): 331–40. http://www.jstor.org/stable/41177405.

Eleonore Stump, "Love, By All Accounts." *Proceedings and Addresses of the American Philosophical Association* 80, no. 2 (2006): 25–43. http://www.jstor.org/stable/27645191.

Tillich, Paul. *Systematic Theology.* Digswell Place: James Misbet and Company, 1968.

Weil, Simone. *Waiting for God.* Translated by Emma Crauford. New York: First Perennial Classics, 2001.

Wolf, Susan. "The True, the Good, and the Lovable: Frankfurt's Avoidance of Objectivity." In *The Contours of Agency*, edited by Sarah Buss and Lee Overton, 227-244. Cambridge, MA: MIT Press, 2002.

Wolterstorff, Nicholas. *Justice in Love.* Grand Rapids, MI: Eerdmans, 2015.

Index

abandonment: and agape, 76, 89; and care, 115, 138–44, 148–49, 152
Abraham and Isaac (biblical story), 52–53, 59, 165n31, 166nn34–36
agape: and abandonment, 76, 89; Augustinian, 80; and commitment, 97, 109; constancy and stability of, 97, 101, 103, 106, 111; creative nature of, 89, 93; definitions of, 77, 79, 90–93, 95, 98, 103, 105–6, 109–10, 168n9, 172n64; and desire, 84, 90–91; divine, 57, 95, 111; and divine perfectionism, 76–96; as equal regard, 103; and eros, 76–81, 83–85, 90–93, 100, 103, 105–6, 109–10, 164n11, 168n9, 171n53, 172n64; ethics of, 97–105, 110–11; and independence from worldly goods, 88–96; and justice, 108–10, 168n9; and love, 57, 73, 93, 98, 168n9; and motivation, 73–78, 83–87, 95–96, 110; as spontaneous and unmotivated, 84–90, 96; and value, 78, 89–90, 93, 105; and vulnerability of worldly goods, 70–112; and worthiness, 82, 84–86, 94, 100–101, 108. See also Christian love; eros; God's love
Agape and Eros (Nygren), 76–78
agapism: and love, 99; modern, 76–77, 81, 93–111, 168n9; and value, 102. See also agape

AIDS, 114, 137, 139–40
Alcibiades, 161n8
allegory, 115, 120, 127, 129–30, 133
alterity, 12–13, 18, 20
Anacreon, 2
analogy, 25, 44. See also metaphor
Angels in America (Kushner), 114, 136–50, 177n43
anticipation and expectations, of love, xv, 32, 37, 41, 73, 124, 147–50, 166n36. See also motivations
antisemitism, 169n18
Apology (Plato), 45–46
Arendt, Hannah, 23–24
Aristotle, 29–30, 163n41, 171n50
art, xiv, 20–21, 114–49, 155, 174n9, 176n25; and attention, 130–36; and evaluation, 25–30; and heroic artists, 126–29, 135–36; as objectification, 124–36, 146
Augustine, 80–81, 171n53

Barth, Karl, 100, 169n9
Bätschmann, Oskar, 125, 173n1, 175n13, 175n16
beauty: in art, 20–21, 119; and desire, 21–22; and goodness, 72; knowledge of, 22; and love, 22, 30; love for, 90; philosophy of, 21–22; pursuit of, 29–30
beloveds: alterity of, 13; change in,

beloveds (*continued*)
2–3, 6, 138, 141; evaluation of, 25–30; incommensurability of, 162n8; knowledge of, 20; and motivations, 103; narration of, 24–25, 120–21, 127–28; particularity of, 19–33, 104–5, 128; term usage, xv; value of, xiii–xiv, 5–16, 18–20, 22, 33, 38, 41–42, 46–49, 72–73, 76–77, 83–84, 86–90, 92, 96–97, 100–101, 103–10, 121, 164n11, 171n56, 172n64

Bialek, Max, 173n79

Body of the Dead Christ in the Tomb, The (Holbein painting), 114, 118, 173n1

Bronfen, Elisabeth, 126–30

Brüschweiler, Jura, 128

Caravaggio, 174n9

care: and abandonment, 125, 138–44, 148–49, 152; and attention, 125, 131–33; commitment to, 65–67, 113–50; constancy of, 111; and conversations, 138, 141–43; defined, 64; and desire, xiv, 64, 118, 137, 142–43, 146–49; for the dying, xiv, 113–53; ethics of, 113, 130, 146, 151–53, 177n41; expectations of, xiv, 124, 129, 136, 147–50; failures to, 136, 144, 149; feminist ethics of, 151–52; and imagination, 150; as indeterminate, 113–14, 121–22, 133–34, 138–39, 145–47; and love, 40, 50–51, 55–58, 64, 97, 124, 129, 134, 136–50, 159; motivations for, xiv, 131, 136–37; and objectification and attention, 125–36; and overdetermination, 132–33, 146–47; after person dies, 177n41; promises and obligations to, xiv, 113–53; reasons for, 55–56, 61; responsibility for, 147, 177n41; term usage, 165n26; and uncertainties, 113–14. *See also* caregiving; death; obligations

caregiving, 111, 114, 131–37, 142, 144–47, 149, 165n26, 167n46, 176–77nn40–41. *See also* care

Carson, Anne, 34–35, 38, 71

Cavarero, Adriana, 23–25, 29, 120–21, 128, 130–31, 174n9, 176n21

change: and beloveds, 2–3, 6, 138, 141; possibility of, 7, 37, 72, 89, 101; and vulnerabilities, 7, 95–96. *See also* uncertainties; vulnerabilities

Christian ethics, 73–76, 82, 97–99, 164n11, 168n9, 172n79

Christian love, xiv, 71–83, 98–103, 106, 164n11, 168n9; ethical theories of, 164n11. *See also* agape; God's love

Christian theology, 93, 171n50

Christian thought, 71, 77, 99–100, 172n64

Christianity: God of, 83, 94, 171n53; and history of Christian thought, 99–100; and "motif-research," 79; Protestant, xiv, 73, 97, 169n9; as religion of love, 170n28; religious nature of, 94; singular God of, 171n53; worldview of, 95

circularities, 36–37, 45, 48–50, 54, 60, 64, 68, 88, 164n13. *See also* tautologies

commitment: and agape, 97, 109; to care, 65–67, 113–50; and constancy, ix, x; and desire, 137; and evaluation, 25–30; to future, 26–27, 29, 148; and love, 37, 39, 65–67

constancy: of care, 111; and commitment, ix, x; and equality, 101; of excess, 110; and motivations, 106; promises of, 74, 111; and security, 74; and stability, 106; and vulnerabilities, 71, 103

consumerism, 10–19, 22–25, 132–33, 162n13

conversations, xiii–xiv, 1, 21, 29–30, 43–44, 46, 53, 61, 66–69, 76, 102, 168n9; and beloveds, 164n11; and care, 138, 141–43; circularities of, 164n13; political, 167n53; and vocabularies, 68–69

Dante Alighieri, 127

D'Arcy, Martin, 168n9

Index 185

De Sousa, Ronald, 163n8
death: care after, 177n41; care for the dying, xiv, 113–53; expectations of, 113, 129–30, 147–50; and love, xiv, 113–53; and love's failure and end, 136, 139–44; and unfinished love, 116–21; and waiting, 131–32. *See also* care
desire, 39–40; and agape, 84, 90–91; and beauty, 21–22; and care, xiv, 64, 118, 137, 142–43, 146–49; and commitment, 137; and concerns, 64; continuation of, 147; and description, 20–25; and discovery, 21; and dislike, 106; and evaluation, 25–30; and fear, 153; for future, 28, 33; and knowledge, 1–33; and market value, 10–16; and narration, 16–19, 23–24; and needs, 11, 39, 109; and passion, 21; and philosophy, 22–23; and pleasure, 21; and possible end(s), 172n79; and responsibility, xii–xiv; romantic, 59; and value, 10; and vulnerabilities, xiii–xiv, 37, 75
dialectics, x–xi, 23, 77
Diotima, 161n8
divine justice, 149–50
divine love, xiv, 57, 71, 74, 88–90, 94–96, 106, 109, 111. *See also* agape: divine; eternal love
divine perfectionism, 74, 76–96
Dupin, Augustine, 118–19, 174n8
Dürer, Albrecht, 125–26, 175nn15–16

Eberstadt, Walter A., 176n25
egocentric love, 77, 90–91
Enlightenment, 21
eros: as acquisitive love, 90–91; and agape, 76–81, 83–85, 90–93, 100, 103, 105–6, 109–10, 164n11, 168n9, 171n53, 172n64; appraising nature of, 90–91; and beauty, 22; definitions of, 77, 90–92, 105–6, 171n50, 172n64; as egocentric love, 77, 90–91; heavenly, 80–81, 109–10, 171n53; and justice, 76,

109; as man's way to the divine, 90, 99; negation of, 93–94; and *philia*, 98, 100; and value, 88–92, 172n64. *See also* agape
erotic love, 38, 72, 77, 80, 84–92, 101, 106, 164n11
eternal love, ix–x, 84, 106–7. *See also* divine love
ethics: of agape, 97–105, 110–11; of art viewing, 130–34; of care, 113, 130, 144, 146, 151–53, 177n41; Christian, 74–76, 82, 97–99, 164n11, 168n9, 172n79; and justice, 110; and knowledge, 33, 152–53; and love, ix, 29, 99; and obligations, 144, 146; and politics, 30, 98–99; social, 108, 110, 167n43; and time, 152; and uncertainties, xii; and vulnerabilities, 153. *See also* feminist ethics of care
Euthyphro, xiii, 39–48, 59, 95, 164n11, 164n13
expectations. *See* anticipation and expectations, of love

feminist ethics of care, 151–52
fidelity, 71
finitude, ix–xiv, 37, 39, 54, 73–75, 82–83, 92, 96, 99, 104, 111–12, 127; and finite lives, ix, xii, xiv, 71, 73–74, 83, 114; and particularity, 23; and unfinished love, 116–21; and vulnerabilities, x. *See also* temporality
Flersheim, Ernst, 176n25
Frankena, William K., 99
Frankfurt, Harry G., xiii, 45, 48–67, 86–89, 162n9, 165nn26–27, 165n30, 166n35
friendships: and erotic love, 72, 106; and love, 27–30, 71–72, 98, 101, 166n42, 172n64; and romantic love, 103; and virtues, 163n41
fundamental motifs, 78–84, 94–98. *See also* "motif-research"
future: and care, 113–14, 121–22, 134, 136, 138–39, 145–53; commitment to,

future (*continued*)
26–27, 29, 148; and endurance, 150; fears of, 153; indeterminate, 3, 18, 27–28, 31, 37, 113–14, 121–22, 138–39, 145; and love, 147, 150; possibility of, 139; uncertain, xiii–xiv, 4, 31, 111–13, 134, 152; unknown, x, 13, 20, 28, 37, 112, 151; and vulnerabilities, 153

German Lost Art database, 176n25
Gilligan, Carol, 151, 177n1
God: and agape, 83, 89–97; of Christianity, 83, 94, 171n53; perfection of, 82–83. *See also* God's love
Godé-Darel, Valentine, 114–36, 144–49, 173n1, 174n8, 174n10, 175n13, 176n25
God's love, xiv, 53, 60, 71–98, 101–3, 105–7, 164n11, 166n35, 168n9, 171n53. *See also* agape; Christian love

Han, Byung-Chul, 12–14, 16, 21, 26, 132
Hegel, Georg Wilhelm Friedrich, 23, 138
Hodler, Ferdinand, 114–31, 134–36, 144–45, 149, 155, 159, 173–74nn1–2, 174n10, 175nn13–16, 176n25
Holbein, Hans (the Younger), 114, 118, 121, 173n1
holiness and unholiness, 42–45, 48
homosexual love, 166n42
humility, 59

Illouz, Eva, 16–17
indeterminacy, 3, 18, 27–28, 31, 37, 113–14, 121–22, 133–34, 138, 145–47, 152
infatuation, 2, 39–40
Ironson, Louis, 136–50
Isaac and Abraham. *See* Abraham and Isaac (biblical story)

Jackson, Timothy P., 100, 109–11, 169n9
Johannes de Silentio. *See* Kierkegaard, Søren
Joyful Woman, The (Hodler painting), 115, 174n10

Judaism: antisemitic treatment of, 169n18; as religion of law, 79, 80–83, 169n18, 170nn28–29
justice: and agape, 108–10, 168n9; divine, 149–50; and eros, 76, 109; and ethics, 110; and judgment, 141; and love, 76, 108, 168n9

Kafka, Franz, 34, 38, 41
Kandinsky, Vasily, 174n10
Kant, Immanuel, 21, 167n43
Kierkegaard, Søren, xiv, 71–74, 89–90, 98, 100–101, 106–7, 164n11, 166n35, 169n9, 172n79
knowledge: articulated, 43; of beauty, 22; of beloveds, 20; completeness of, 3, 4; and definitions, 42, 45–46; and description, 29–30, 33; and desire, 1–33; desire for, 4–19, 22, 28, 33; and ethical theory, 33, 152–53; and evaluation, 25–30; exact, 42–43, 45–46; failures of, 20; lack of, 75, 87; and love, xi, 3, 20, 33; and narration, 16–25; and philosophy, 23, 28–29, 33; possibility of, 23; pursuit of, 29; of truth, 45; and uncertainties, 30, 75; and worthiness, 5, 8, 10–11, 20–21, 26–27, 29–30
Kushner, Tony, 114, 177n43

Levinas, Emmanuel, 130–31, 144
linguistics, 18–19, 68
Lloyd, Jill, 120, 123–24, 173n2, 175n14
Lost Art database, 176n25
love: accounting for, 7–8, 20–22, 30, 33–69, 70, 77, 87, 138, 141, 146, 149, 164n11, 165nn26–27, 165n30, 166nn35–36, 166n42, 167nn46–47; acquisitive, 90–91; bad, xvi; for the beautiful and the good, 90; beginnings of, ix; claims to, 67, 109; definitions of, x–xi, xiii–xvi, 36–37, 44, 47, 64, 84, 106, 145, 165n27; and duty, 106–7; end and failure of, ix, 1–6, 20, 33, 106, 136, 139–44, 148–50; exam-

Index 187

ples of, xvi; and finding ourselves, 46–54; forms of, xv, 31, 37, 40, 72–73, 76–77, 86, 91, 93, 97–100, 105–6, 110, 161n1, 164n11, 168n9, 172n64; good, xvi; joy of, 24, 149; justification for and entitlement to, 65–69; ladder, 161n8; limits of, xiv, 114; multiplicity of, xv; paradigmatic, 108, 123, 149; proper, 59; reasons for and reasoning about, xiii, 38–69; spontaneous and unmotivated, 84–90, 96; and surprise, 53–54; taboos, 59, 166n42; term usage, xv–xvi, 165n27; understanding, x, 35, 41, 70, 106, 152, 162n9; unfinished, 116–21; and vagaries of life, xi, 72, 107. *See also* agape; agapism; Christian love; desire; divine love; egocentric love; erotic love; eternal love; God's love; homosexual love; parental love; romantic love; unconditional love; worldly love

lovers, term usage, xv, 3–4. *See also* beloveds

Lysias, xiii, 1–6, 8, 13–16, 19, 22, 24, 30, 38, 162n8

Marin, Louis, 174n9
metaphor, 16, 35, 80, 172n79. *See also* analogy
Miller, Oskar, 173n2
misrecognition, 58, 109
moral reasoning, in psychological development, 151
"motif-research," 78–84, 94–98, 171n50. *See also* fundamental motifs
motivations: and agape, 73–78, 83–87, 95–96, 110; and beloveds, 103; for care, xiv, 131, 136–37; and constancy, 106; in definitions of agape and eros, 105; for love, 29–30, 37, 73, 76, 85, 104–7, 122; worldly, 77, 95. *See also* anticipation and expectations, of love
Mühlstein, Hans, 120

narratives: of beloveds and lovers, 24–25, 120–21, 127–28; and care, 146; and depiction, 128; and desire, 16–19, 23–25; and exposure, reciprocal, 25; and information, 16–19; and knowledge, 16–25; and love, ix, 24; and philosophy, 23
Nehamas, Alexander, 20–22, 25–30, 121–22, 127, 159, 163n41, 164n13, 176n21
Neoplatonism, 171n50
Niebuhr, Reinhold, 76–77, 108–9, 169n9
nomos, 79
Nussbaum, Martha C., 39, 162n8, 164n14
Nygren, Anders, xiv, 73–111, 164n11, 168n9, 169n18, 170n29, 171n50, 171n53, 171n56, 172n79

objectification: art as, 124–36, 146; and fictionalization, 128–29; and subjectivity, 127; and sympathy, 133
obligations: to care for the dying, xiv, 113–53; and caregiving, 167n46; and description, 131; endless, 131; ethical, 144, 146; and ordering of loves, 40–41. *See also* care; promises
Olsen, Regine, 172n79
On Friendship (Nehamas), 26
Only a Promise of Happiness (Nehamas), 20–21, 26, 28, 122
otherness, 12–14
Outka, Gene, 100–103, 105, 109, 168n9

pan-rationalism, 50, 65–67
parental love, xv, 32, 50–52, 61–65, 103, 114, 167nn46–47
passion: and desire, 21; and love, 51–52
perfectionism, divine, 74, 76–96
Petrarch, 127
Phaedrus (Plato), xiii, 1–2, 16, 161n1, 162n8
philia, 77; defined, 172n64; and eros, 98, 100

philosophy: of the aesthetic, 22; of beauty, 21–22; and contemplation, 23; and desire, 22–23; and dialectics, 23; and knowledge, 23, 28–29, 33; and love, 36, 41–42, 45, 49; and narratives, 23; and religion, ix, xiii–xv, 79, 171n53; seduced, 23
Piggliucci, Massimo, 41–42, 164n11
Plato, xiii, 4, 16, 19, 21–23, 29, 91, 164n11, 164n13, 171n50. *See also* Neoplatonism
politics, 30, 98–99
promises: and care, xiv, 113–53; of constancy, 74, 111; and duties, ix; of happiness, 20–21, 26–28, 30, 122–23; indeterminate, 27, 145–46; and love, 137, 139, 147; poetic, 72; of unhappiness, 121–24. *See also* obligations
psychological development, moral reasoning in, 151

Ramsey, Paul, 169n9
Rauschenbusch, Walter, 77, 108
regret, 3, 8, 38, 53
religion: and faith-claims, 66–67; internal coherence of, 78–79; and philosophy, ix, xiii–xv; and politics, 167n53; and reasoning, 66–67. *See also* fundamental motifs; theology; *and specific religions*
reproductive options, 162n23
rhetoric, 2–3
romantic love, x, xv, 1, 31–32, 59, 73, 98–100, 103, 119, 123–24, 126, 166n42, 175n13
Rorty, Richard, 66–69

Sappho, 2
Schweizer, Harold, 130–34, 176n40
seduction, 23, 172n79
self-achievement, 26, 111
self-alienation, 55, 58
self-assertion, 77, 89, 91; egoistic, 75, 97, 126
self-consciousness, x–xi

self-defeat, 35, 143
self-definition, 95
self-deprecation, 1
self-distinction, 42
self-division, 68
self-fulfillment or achievement, 111
self-giving, 40–41
selfishness, 26, 40, 77, 133
self-protection, 3–4, 15
self-sabotage, 143
Soble, Alan, 163n8, 177n51
social ethics, 108, 110, 167n43
social norms, xvi, 37, 59–60, 63, 149, 166n36, 167n42
Socrates, xiii, 1–2, 19, 39–46, 59, 161n8, 164n13
Splendour of Lines, The (Hodler painting), 115, 174n10
Stout, Jeffrey, 66–69, 167n50
susceptibility, and danger, xi–xii
Symposium (Plato), 161n8

taboos, 59, 166n42
tautologies, xiii, 165n27. *See also* circularities
temporality, ix–x, xii–xiii, 2, 4, 74–75, 84, 86, 119, 124, 134, 174n9. *See also* finitude
theology, x–xi, 78; Christian, 93, 171n50; of divine constancy and divine perfection, 74. *See also* religion
Tillich, Paul, 168n9
time: abandonment of, 152; definition of, 131–32; and ethics, 152; learning from, 153; and love, 8, 29, 35–36, 139, 153, 156; love in, x, xii–xv, 33, 37, 139, 152; outside of, 17, 75, 84; together, x, xii, 4, 7, 13, 21, 27, 30–33, 113–14, 118–27, 137–39, 142–45

uncertainties: and agape, 111–12; and care, 113–14; desire for, xii–xiii, 4; and ethics, xii; of finite and temporal lives, xii–xiii, 75; of future, xiii–xiv,

4, 31, 111–13, 134, 152; and knowledge, 30, 75; and love, xi–xiii, 4, 33, 70–71, 152; and risk, xii–xiii, 30; and vulnerabilities, 70–71, 74–75, 78. *See also* change; vulnerabilities
unconditional love, 97, 99–100
uniqueness, 5, 20, 23–25, 29, 93–94, 99, 127

Valentine Godé-Darel on Her Deathbed (Hodler painting), 116–17
value: aesthetic, 21, 25; and agape, 78, 89–90, 93, 105; and agapism, 102; and desire, 10; and eros, 88–92, 172n64; and grace, 101; of humans, inherent, 94; indeterminate, 3; and love, 6–16, 41–42, 73, 84, 87, 89–92, 102–4, 106, 141, 146, 162n9, 164n11, 171n56; and regard, 104–5; term usage, 102; and worthiness, 54, 56–57. *See also* beloveds: evaluation of; worthiness
vulnerabilities: and agape, 70–112; and constancy, 71, 103; and desire, xiii–xiv, 37, 75; and ethics, 153; and fearlessness, 151–53; and finitude, x; and future, 153; and humility, 59; and love, xiii–xv, 6, 37, 59, 72, 74, 84, 92–93, 96–112, 181n79; of love and life, 71, 110–11; mitigated, 4, 25; multiplicity of, 6; and needs, 129; and pain, xiv, 133, 144; as particular, 130–31; and responsibility, xiv; and suffering, 135; of temporal life, xii; and uncertainties, 70–71, 74–75, 78; of worldly goods, 70–112, 172n79. *See also* change; uncertainties

Walter, Prior, 136–50
wanting, without knowing, 1–33, 161–62nn8–9, 162n13, 162n23, 163n41. *See also* desire; knowledge
Weil, Simone, 131–32, 176n40
Wolf, Susan, 10–11, 57–58
Wolterstorff, Nicholas, 100, 103, 109, 168n9
Works of Love (Kierkegaard), 71, 172n79
worldly love, 71, 107, 110–11
worthiness: and agape, 82, 84–86, 94, 100–101, 106; and care, 56–58, 142–43, 146, 153; and knowledge, 5, 8, 10–11, 20–21, 26–27, 29–30; and love, xi, 4–5, 8, 10–11, 13, 26–27, 38–41, 47, 49, 54–58, 71, 88–90, 146; and value, 54, 56–57. *See also* value

www.ingramcontent.com/pod-product-compliance
Lightning Source LLC
Chambersburg PA
CBHW032337300426
44109CB00041B/1131